United Nations

CW00735316

# Flags at the United Nations

## The First Avenue Flag Row: 1945–2023

by Eliot Sela

© 2023 Eliot Sela, all rights reserved.

Published by Eliot Sela in New York City with the cooperation of the United Nations.
ISBN: 978-0-578-38021-6.

# Table of contents

## Preface

As a New Yorker given to walking past United Nations headquarters, I came to admire and consider the row of flags representing the international organization's member states. Over the years, as empires dissolve, nations merge or split and colonies break free, the flags on First Avenue change accordingly. This book seeks to recreate the yearly alterations so far.

As US President Woodrow Wilson noted, a flag is "more than a piece of cloth." A flag is "the embodiment not of sentiment but of history."

Photo: AdobeStock by Allen G. All other photos in this book have been taken by the author.

## Acknowledgment

My personal thanks to all those who helped me in my historical research.

Christopher David Ramos, publishing
Caroline Beaumont, editing and proofreading
Carol Wilson, editing

### The North American Vexillological Association (NAVA)

NAVA

Ted Kaye, secretary
Peter Ansoff, president
Zachary Harden, member
Anna Jankowski, member

www.nava.org

### United Nations (UN)

UN

The employees of the Dag Hammarskjöld Library

www.un.org

### Centro Italiano Studi Vessillologici (CISV)

CISV

Pier Paolo Lugli, president

www.cisv.it

### La Fédération Internationale des Associations Vexillologiques (FIAV)

FIAV

Željko Heimer, president

www.fiav.org

### Croatia's National Vexillological Association (HGZD)

HGZD

Željko Heimer, president

www.hgzd.hr

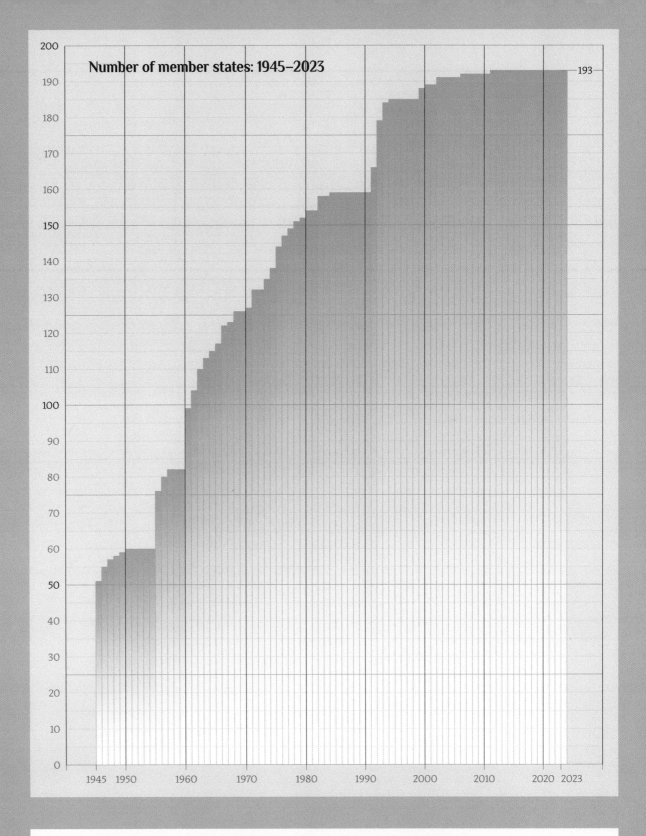

Number of member states: 1945–2023

193

## Growth of the United Nations' First Avenue Flag Row

*From the initial 51 member states, of whom four were not yet independent nations, the UN has grown to 193 sovereign state members. Their flags on First Avenue have borne colorful witness to the changes of the past 78 years.*

# UN members flag display along First Avenue, as of 2023: Photos

## Group A: Northern Park

Between East 48th and East 47th Streets.
13 Flags: Afghanistan to Bahrain.

## Group E: South of Main Entrance

South of East 43rd Street.
13 Flags: Togo to United States of America.

## Group B: The Long Walk

From East 47th to South of East 46th Streets.
58 Flags: Bangladesh to Guinea.

## Group D: The Oval

Between East 45th and East 43rd Streets.
84 Flags: Kenya to Timor-Leste.

## Group F: Southern Wall

North of East 42nd Street.
8 Flags: Uruguay to Zimbabwe.

## Group G: Observers

By East 42nd Street.
2 Flags: Observer States.

## Group C: By Main Exit

North of East 45th Street.
17 Flags: Guinea-Bissau to Kazakhstan.

The Oval was the original location of all member's
flags before more space was needed.

# UN members flag display along First Avenue, as of 2023: Map

## Group A: 13 flags

Afghanistan
Albania
Algeria
Andorra
Angola
Antigua and Barbuda
Argentina
Armenia
Australia
Austria
Azerbaijan
Bahamas
Bahrain

## Group C: 17 flags

Guinea-Bissau
Guyana
Haiti
Honduras
Hungary
Iceland
India
Indonesia
Iran (Islamic Republic of)
Iraq
Ireland
Israel
Italy
Jamaica
Japan
Jordan
Kazakhstan

## Group E: 13 flags

Togo
Tonga
Trinidad and Tobago
Tunisia
Türkiye
Turkmenistan
Tuvalu
Uganda
Ukraine
United Arab Emirates
United Kingdom of
    Great Britain and
    Northern Ireland
United Republic
    of Tanzania
United States of America

## Group F: 8 flags

Uruguay
Uzbekistan
Vanuatu
Venezuela (Bolivarian Rep. of)
Viet Nam
Yemen
Zambia
Zimbabwe

## Group G: 2 flags

Holy See, Observer State
State of Palestine, Observer State

## Group B: 58 flags

Bangladesh
Barbados
Belarus
Belgium
Belize
Benin
Bhutan
Bolivia (Plurinational State of)
Bosnia and Herzegovina
Botswana
Brazil
Brunei Darussalam
Bulgaria
Burkina Faso
Burundi
Cabo Verde
Cambodia
Cameroon
Canada
Central African Republic
Chad
Chile
China
Colombia
Comoros
Congo
Costa Rica
Côte d'Ivoire
Croatia
Cuba
Cyprus

Czechia
Democratic People's Republic
    of Korea
Democratic Republic
    of the Congo
Denmark
Djibouti
Dominica
Dominican Republic
Ecuador
Egypt
El Salvador
Equatorial Guinea
Eritrea
Estonia
Eswatini
Ethiopia
Fiji
Finland
France
Gabon
Gambia (Republic of The)
Georgia
Germany
Ghana
Greece
Grenada
Guatemala
Guinea

## Group D: 84 flags

Kenya
Kiribati
Kuwait
Kyrgyzstan
Lao People's
    Democratic
    Republic
Latvia
Lebanon
Lesotho
Liberia
Libya
Liechtenstein
Lithuania
Luxembourg
Madagascar
Malawi
Malaysia
Maldives
Mali
Malta
Marshall Islands
Mauritania
Mauritius
Mexico
Micronesia
    (Federated
    States of)
Monaco
Mongolia
Montenegro
Morocco
Mozambique
Myanmar
Namibia
Nauru
Nepal
Netherlands
New Zealand

Nicaragua
Niger
Nigeria
North Macedonia
Norway
Oman
Pakistan
Palau
Panama
Papua New Guinea
Paraguay
Peru
Philippines
Poland
Portugal
Qatar
Republic of Korea
Republic of Moldova
Romania
Russian Federation
Rwanda
Saint Kitts
    and Nevis
Saint Lucia
Saint Vincent
    and the Grenadines
Samoa
San Marino
Sao Tome
    and Principe
Saudi Arabia
Senegal
Serbia
Seychelles
Sierra Leone
Singapore
Slovakia
Slovenia
Solomon Islands

Somalia
South Africa
South Sudan
Spain
Sri Lanka
Sudan
Suriname
Sweden
Switzerland
Syrian Arab Republic
Tajikistan
Mauritania
Timor-Leste

Flags are displayed in the alphabetical order of members' names
in English according to the UN Official Terminology Code. An
exception is made when a member asks to be listed differently.

East 48th Street

East 47th Street

A

East 46th Street

B

## United Nations Compound

UN Flag

C

East 45th Street

FIRST AVENUE

EAST RIVER

East 44th Street

D

UN Flag

East 43rd Street

E

F

G

East 42nd Street

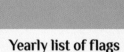

## Yearly list of flags

In the above area, on each yearly spread, member states' flags are shown alphabetically, according to the official English UN list for each specific year. As the years progress, this list widens.

## Color standardization

In recent years, many member states announced color standardization for their national flags. These announcements are not mentioned here since no actual changes took place.

## Timeline

On the following pages, each spread represents a year in which changes were made to the UN members list or to any of the members' national flags. The timeline below indicates the progression in years and in the number of member states.

## Flag proportions

Since 1945, all member flags, regardless of their official specifications, are flown by the UN in proportions of 2:3.

The exceptions are:

Nepal: 1:1.21901033.

Switzerland: 1:1.

Holy See, Observer State: 1:1.
But sometimes flown at 2:3

Proportions of a 2:3 flag

| Year | United Nations | # |
| --- | --- | --- |
| Year | United Nations | Member states |

Member states flags with non-standard proportions

Nepal
*Pre 1962 flag*

Nepal
*Post 1962 flag*

Switzerland

Holy See
*Observer State*

## Non-independent members

Philippine Republic, a US Territory, which gained independence in 1946, had already been granted UN membership in 1945.

India, part of the British Empire, which gained independence in 1947, had already been granted UN membership in 1945.

Belarus and Ukraine, parts of the USSR, which gained independence in 1991, had already been granted UN membership in 1945.

## Non-independent member states

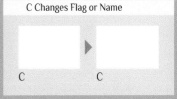

**Byelorussian** Soviet Socialist Republic | **India** (United Kingdom) | **Philippine** Republic (United States) | **Ukrainian** Soviet Socialist Republic

## Windows reflecting changes

 An additional member.
B gained independence from A.

No additional member.
C changed name or flag.

### B Splits from A

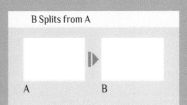

A          B

### C Changes Flag or Name

C          C

Argentina  Australia  Belgium  Bolivia  Brazil  Byelorussian
Soviet Socialist Republic  Canada  Chile  China

Colombia  Costa Rica  Cuba  Czechoslovakia  Denmark  Dominican
Republic  Ecuador  Egypt  El Salvador

Ethiopia  France  Greece  Guatemala  Haiti  Honduras  India
(United Kingdom)  Iran  Iraq

## The organization's birth

The United Nations Charter was signed
in San Francisco on June 26, 1945.
Its 51 founding members were admitted
later that year.

1945
Year

United Nations

51
Member states

Lebanon

Liberia

Luxembourg

Mexico

Netherlands

New Zealand

Nicaragua

Norway

Panama

Paraguay

Peru

Philippine
Republic (*United States*)

Poland

Saudi Arabia

Syria

Turkey

Ukrainian
Soviet Socialist Republic

Union of
South Africa

USSR
Soviet Union

United Kingdom

United States

Uruguay

Venezuela

Yugoslavia

## Fifty-one new members

Argentina

Australia

Belgium

Bolivia

Brazil

Byelorussian
Soviet Socialist Republic

Canada

Chile

China

Colombia

Costa Rica

Cuba

Czechoslovakia

Denmark

Dominican
Republic

Ecuador

Egypt

El Salvador

Ethiopia

France

Greece

Guatemala

Haiti

Honduras

India
(*United Kingdom*)

Iran

Iraq

Lebanon

Liberia

Luxembourg

Mexico

Netherlands

New Zealand

Nicaragua

Norway

Panama

Paraguay

Peru

Philippine
Republic (*United States*)

Poland

Saudi Arabia

Syria

Turkey

Ukrainian
Soviet Socialist Republic

Union of
South Africa

USSR
Soviet Union

United Kingdom

United States

Uruguay

Venezuela

Yugoslavia

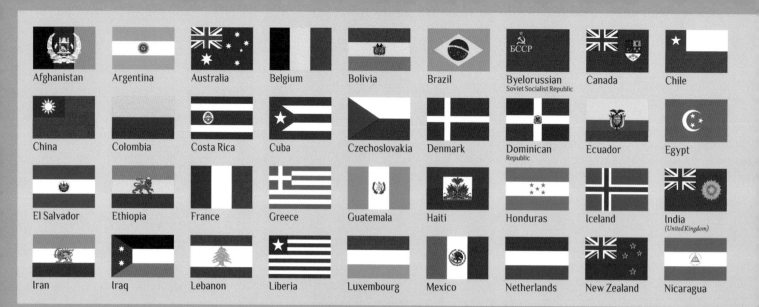

Afghanistan · Argentina · Australia · Belgium · Bolivia · Brazil · Byelorussian Soviet Socialist Republic · Canada · Chile

China · Colombia · Costa Rica · Cuba · Czechoslovakia · Denmark · Dominican Republic · Ecuador · Egypt

El Salvador · Ethiopia · France · Greece · Guatemala · Haiti · Honduras · Iceland · India (United Kingdom)

Iran · Iraq · Lebanon · Liberia · Luxembourg · Mexico · Netherlands · New Zealand · Nicaragua

1946 — Year · United Nations · 55 — Member states

Flag change

United Nations ▸ United Nations

Norway

Panama

Paraguay

Peru

Philippine
Republic

Poland

Saudi Arabia

Siam

Sweden

Syria

Turkey

Ukrainian
Soviet Socialist Republic

Union of
South Africa

USSR
Soviet Union

United Kingdom

United States

Uruguay

Venezuela

Yugoslavia

Four new members

Afghanistan

Iceland

Siam

Sweden

Independence from

United States

Philippine
Republic

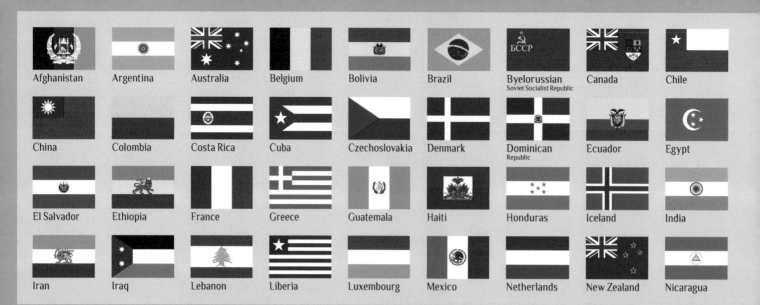

Afghanistan • Argentina • Australia • Belgium • Bolivia • Brazil • Byelorussian Soviet Socialist Republic • Canada • Chile

China • Colombia • Costa Rica • Cuba • Czechoslovakia • Denmark • Dominican Republic • Ecuador • Egypt

El Salvador • Ethiopia • France • Greece • Guatemala • Haiti • Honduras • Iceland • India

Iran • Iraq • Lebanon • Liberia • Luxembourg • Mexico • Netherlands • New Zealand • Nicaragua

1947
Year

United Nations

57
Member states

Norway

Pakistan

Panama

Paraguay

Peru

Philippines

Poland

Saudi Arabia

Siam

Sweden

Syria

Turkey

Ukrainian
Soviet Socialist Republic

Union of
South Africa

USSR
Soviet Union

United Kingdom

United States

Uruguay

Venezuela

Yemen

Yugoslavia

New member

Yemen

Independence from

United Kingdom    India

New member — separation from

India    Pakistan

Flag change

India    India

Name change

Philippine
Republic    Philippines

Afghanistan
Argentina
Australia
Belgium
Bolivia
Brazil
Burma
Byelorussian
Soviet Socialist Republic
Canada

Chile
China
Colombia
Costa Rica
Cuba
Czechoslovakia
Denmark
Dominican
Republic
Ecuador

Egypt
El Salvador
Ethiopia
France
Greece
Guatemala
Haiti
Honduras
Iceland

India
Iran
Iraq
Lebanon
Liberia
Luxembourg
Mexico
Netherlands
New Zealand

Timeline                          page 18

| 1948 | | 58 |
|---|---|---|
| Year | United Nations | Member states |

Nicaragua
 Norway
 Pakistan
 Panama
Paraguay
 Peru
Philippines
Poland
 Saudi Arabia

 Siam
 Sweden
 Syria
 Turkey
 Ukrainian
Soviet Socialist Republic
 Union of
South Africa
USSR
Soviet Union
 United Kingdom
 United States

 Uruguay
 Venezuela
 Yemen
Yugoslavia

New member — independence from

United Kingdom ▷ Burma

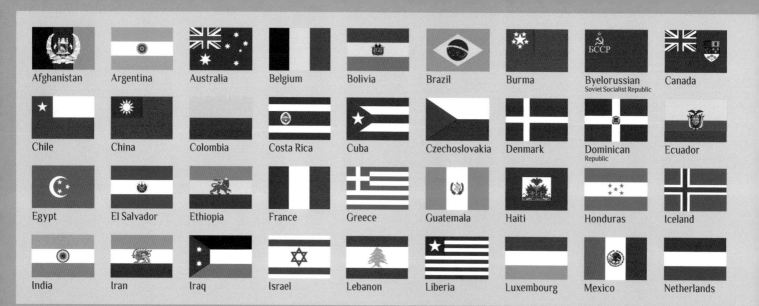

Afghanistan | Argentina | Australia | Belgium | Bolivia | Brazil | Burma | Byelorussian Soviet Socialist Republic | Canada

Chile | China | Colombia | Costa Rica | Cuba | Czechoslovakia | Denmark | Dominican Republic | Ecuador

Egypt | El Salvador | Ethiopia | France | Greece | Guatemala | Haiti | Honduras | Iceland

India | Iran | Iraq | Israel | Lebanon | Liberia | Luxembourg | Mexico | Netherlands

1949
Year

United Nations

59
Member states

New Zealand

Nicaragua

Norway

Pakistan

Panama

Paraguay

Peru

Philippines

Poland

Saudi Arabia

Sweden

Syria

Thailand

Turkey

Ukrainian
Soviet Socialist Republic

Union of
South Africa

USSR
Soviet Union

United Kingdom

United States

Uruguay

Venezuela

Yemen

Yugoslavia

New member — independence from

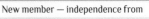

United Kingdom

Israel

Name change

Siam     Thailand

Flag change

Ukrainian
Soviet Socialist Republic

Ukrainian
Soviet Socialist Republic

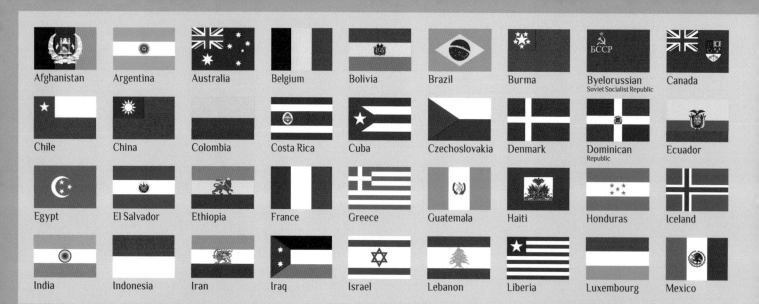

Afghanistan
Argentina
Australia
Belgium
Bolivia
Brazil
Burma
Byelorussian
Soviet Socialist Republic
Canada

Chile
China
Colombia
Costa Rica
Cuba
Czechoslovakia
Denmark
Dominican
Republic
Ecuador

Egypt
El Salvador
Ethiopia
France
Greece
Guatemala
Haiti
Honduras
Iceland

India
Indonesia
Iran
Iraq
Israel
Lebanon
Liberia
Luxembourg
Mexico

1950
Year

United Nations

60
Member states

Netherlands

 New Zealand

 Nicaragua

 Norway

 Pakistan

 Panama

 Paraguay

 Peru

 Philippines

 Poland

 Saudi Arabia

Sweden

 Syria

 Thailand

 Turkey

 Ukrainian
Soviet Socialist Republic

Union of
South Africa

USSR
Soviet Union

 United Kingdom

 United States

 Uruguay

 Venezuela

 Yemen

 Yugoslavia

New member — independence from

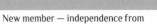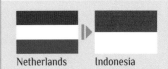

Netherlands          Indonesia

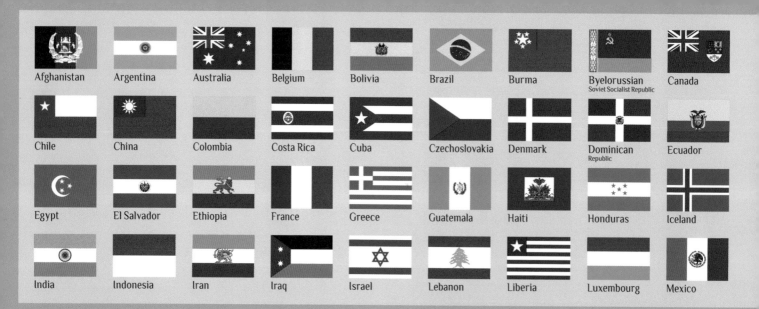

Afghanistan Argentina Australia Belgium Bolivia Brazil Burma Byelorussian Soviet Socialist Republic Canada

Chile China Colombia Costa Rica Cuba Czechoslovakia Denmark Dominican Republic Ecuador

Egypt El Salvador Ethiopia France Greece Guatemala Haiti Honduras Iceland

India Indonesia Iran Iraq Israel Lebanon Liberia Luxembourg Mexico

| 1951 | United Nations | 60 |
|------|----------------|-----|
| Year | United Nations | Member states |

Netherlands | New Zealand | Nicaragua | Norway | Pakistan | Panama | Paraguay | Peru | Philippines

Poland | Saudi Arabia | Sweden | Syria | Thailand | Turkey | Ukrainian Soviet Socialist Republic | Union of South Africa | USSR Soviet Union

United Kingdom | United States | Uruguay | Venezuela | Yemen | Yugoslavia

Flag change

Byelorussian
Soviet Socialist Republic

Byelorussian
Soviet Socialist Republic

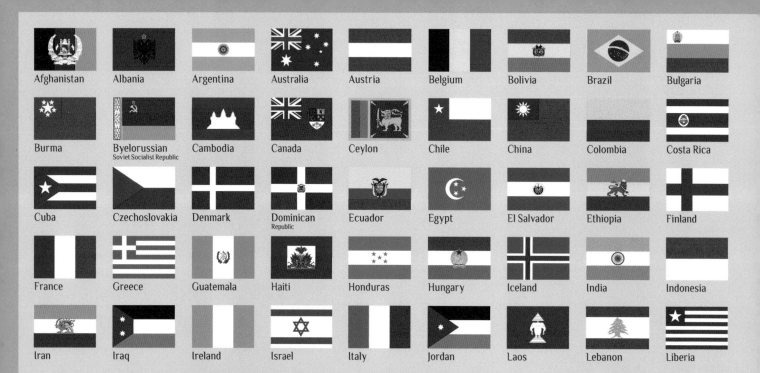

Afghanistan · Albania · Argentina · Australia · Austria · Belgium · Bolivia · Brazil · Bulgaria

Burma · Byelorussian Soviet Socialist Republic · Cambodia · Canada · Ceylon · Chile · China · Colombia · Costa Rica

Cuba · Czechoslovakia · Denmark · Dominican Republic · Ecuador · Egypt · El Salvador · Ethiopia · Finland

France · Greece · Guatemala · Haiti · Honduras · Hungary · Iceland · India · Indonesia

Iran · Iraq · Ireland · Israel · Italy · Jordan · Laos · Lebanon · Liberia

No changes in 1952, 1953 and 1954

Timeline                              page 26

| 1955 | | 76 |
|------|---|----|
| Year | United Nations | Member states |

Libya | Luxembourg | Mexico | Nepal | Netherlands | New Zealand | Nicaragua | Norway | Pakistan

  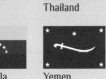        

Panama | Paraguay | Peru | Philippines | Poland | Portugal | Romania | Saudi Arabia | Spain

Sweden | Syria | Thailand | Turkey | Ukrainian Soviet Socialist Republic | Union of South Africa | USSR Soviet Union | United Kingdom | United States

Uruguay | Venezuela | Yemen | Yugoslavia

## Twelve new members

Albania | Austria | Bulgaria | Finland | Hungary | Ireland

Italy | Jordan | Nepal | Portugal | Romania | Spain

## Two new members — independence from

France ▸ Cambodia | Laos

## New member — independence from

Italy ▸ France + United Kingdom ▸ Libya

## New member — independence from

United Kingdom ▸ Ceylon

## Flag change

USSR Soviet Union ▸ USSR Soviet Union

Afghanistan Albania Argentina Australia Austria Belgium Bolivia Brazil Bulgaria

Burma Byelorussian Soviet Socialist Republic Cambodia Canada Ceylon Chile China Colombia Costa Rica

Cuba Czechoslovakia Denmark Dominican Republic Ecuador Egypt El Salvador Ethiopia Finland

France Greece Guatemala Haiti Honduras Hungary Iceland India Indonesia

Iran Iraq Ireland Israel Italy Japan Jordan Laos Lebanon

| 1956 | | 80 |
|------|--|----|
| Year | United Nations | Member states |

| | | | |
|---|---|---|---|
| Liberia | Libya | Luxembourg | Mexico |
| Morocco | Nepal | Netherlands | New Zealand |
| Nicaragua | Norway | Pakistan | Panama |
| Paraguay | Peru | Philippines | Poland |
| Portugal | Romania | Saudi Arabia | Spain |
| Sudan | Sweden | Syria | Thailand |
| Tunisia | Turkey | Ukrainian Soviet Socialist Republic | Union of South Africa |
| USSR Soviet Union | United Kingdom | United States | Uruguay |
| Venezuela | Yemen | Yugoslavia | |

**New member**

Japan

**New member — independence from**

Egypt + United Kingdom ▷ Sudan

**New member — independence from**

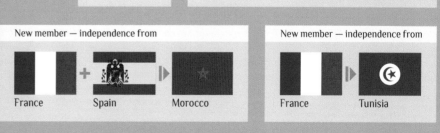

France + Spain ▷ Morocco

**New member — independence from**

France ▷ Tunisia

**Flag change**

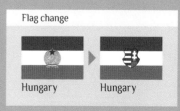

Hungary ▷ Hungary

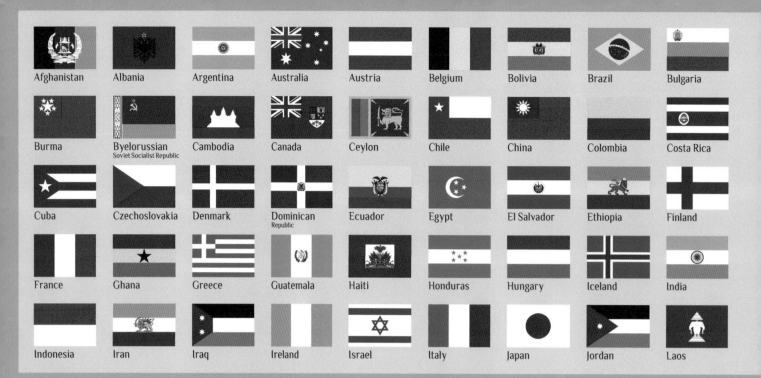

| | | | |
|---|---|---|---|
| Afghanistan | Albania | Argentina | Australia |
| Austria | Belgium | Bolivia | Brazil |
| Bulgaria | Burma | Byelorussian Soviet Socialist Republic | Cambodia |
| Canada | Ceylon | Chile | China |
| Colombia | Costa Rica | Cuba | Czechoslovakia |
| Denmark | Dominican Republic | Ecuador | Egypt |
| El Salvador | Ethiopia | Finland | France |
| Ghana | Greece | Guatemala | Haiti |
| Honduras | Hungary | Iceland | India |
| Indonesia | Iran | Iraq | Ireland |
| Israel | Italy | Japan | Jordan |
| Laos | | | |

| 1957 | | 82 |
|---|---|---|
| Year | United Nations | Member states |

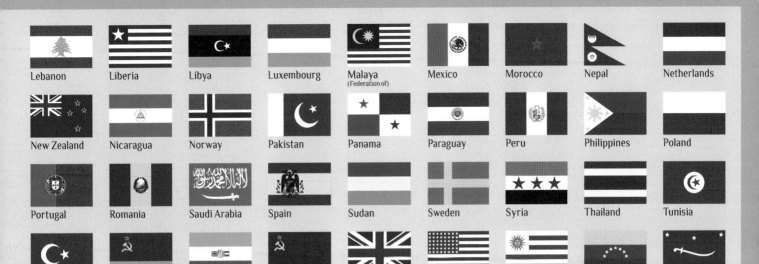

Lebanon | Liberia | Libya | Luxembourg | Malaya (Federation of) | Mexico | Morocco | Nepal | Netherlands

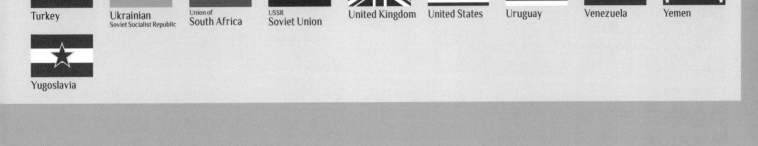

New Zealand | Nicaragua | Norway | Pakistan | Panama | Paraguay | Peru | Philippines | Poland

Portugal | Romania | Saudi Arabia | Spain | Sudan | Sweden | Syria | Thailand | Tunisia

Turkey | Ukrainian Soviet Socialist Republic | Union of South Africa | USSR Soviet Union | United Kingdom | United States | Uruguay | Venezuela | Yemen

Yugoslavia

Two new members — independence from

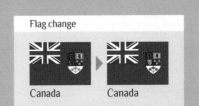

United Kingdom | Ghana | Malaya (Federation of)

Flag change

Canada | Canada

Flag change

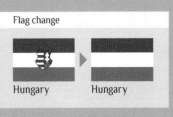

Hungary | Hungary

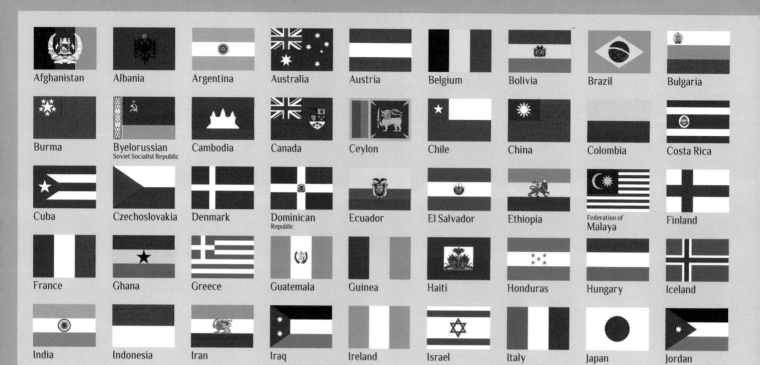

Afghanistan Albania Argentina Australia Austria Belgium Bolivia Brazil Bulgaria

Burma Byelorussian Soviet Socialist Republic Cambodia Canada Ceylon Chile China Colombia Costa Rica

Cuba Czechoslovakia Denmark Dominican Republic Ecuador El Salvador Ethiopia Federation of Malaya Finland

France Ghana Greece Guatemala Guinea Haiti Honduras Hungary Iceland

India Indonesia Iran Iraq Ireland Israel Italy Japan Jordan

1958
Year

United Nations

82
Member states

Laos

Lebanon

Liberia

Libya

Luxembourg

Mexico

Morocco

Nepal

Netherlands

New Zealand

Nicaragua

Norway

Pakistan

Panama

Paraguay

Peru

Philippines

Poland

Portugal

Romania

Saudi Arabia

Spain

Sudan

Sweden

Thailand

Tunisia

Turkey

Ukrainian
Soviet Socialist Republic

Union of
South Africa

USSR
Soviet Union

United Arab Rep.
*(Egypt & Syria)*

United Kingdom

United States

Uruguay

Venezuela

Yemen

Yugoslavia

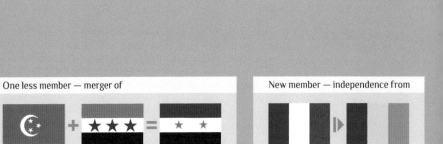

One less member — merger of

Egypt $+$ Syria $=$ United Arab Rep.
*(Egypt & Syria)*

New member — independence from

France ▶ Guinea

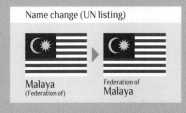

Name change (UN listing)

Malaya
(Federation of)

Federation of
Malaya

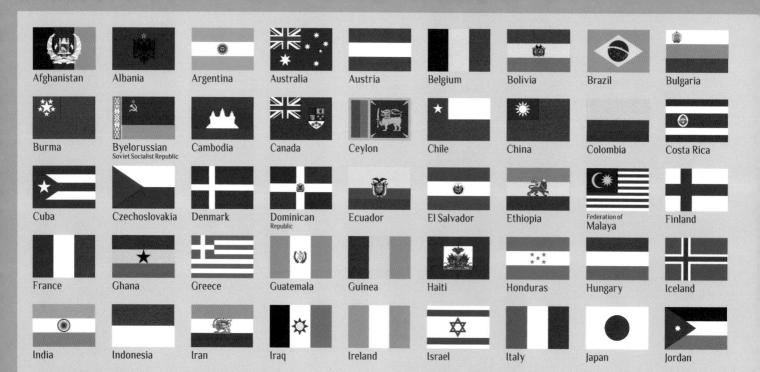

| Afghanistan | Albania | Argentina | Australia | Austria | Belgium | Bolivia | Brazil | Bulgaria |
| Burma | Byelorussian Soviet Socialist Republic | Cambodia | Canada | Ceylon | Chile | China | Colombia | Costa Rica |
| Cuba | Czechoslovakia | Denmark | Dominican Republic | Ecuador | El Salvador | Ethiopia | Federation of Malaya | Finland |
| France | Ghana | Greece | Guatemala | Guinea | Haiti | Honduras | Hungary | Iceland |
| India | Indonesia | Iran | Iraq | Ireland | Israel | Italy | Japan | Jordan |

| 1959 | | 82 |
| Year | United Nations | Member states |

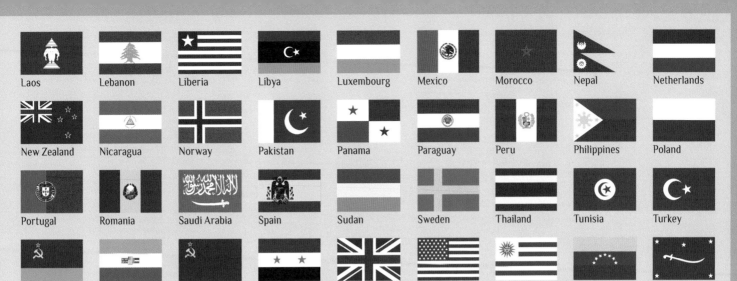

| | | |
|---|---|---|
| Laos | Lebanon | Liberia |
| Libya | Luxembourg | Mexico |
| Morocco | Nepal | Netherlands |

| | | |
|---|---|---|
| New Zealand | Nicaragua | Norway |
| Pakistan | Panama | Paraguay |
| Peru | Philippines | Poland |

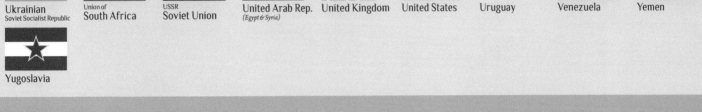

| | | |
|---|---|---|
| Portugal | Romania | Saudi Arabia |
| Spain | Sudan | Sweden |
| Thailand | Tunisia | Turkey |

| | | |
|---|---|---|
| Ukrainian Soviet Socialist Republic | Union of South Africa | USSR Soviet Union |
| United Arab Rep. (Egypt & Syria) | United Kingdom | United States |
| Uruguay | Venezuela | Yemen |

Yugoslavia

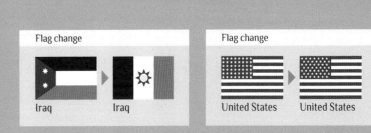

Flag change

Iraq → Iraq

Flag change

United States → United States

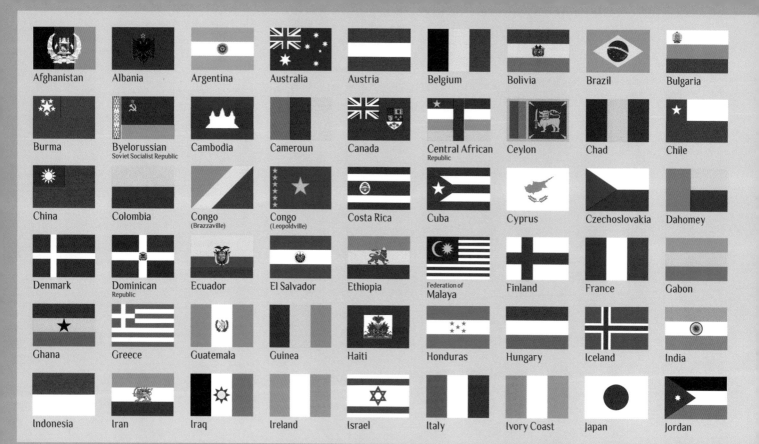

Afghanistan   Albania   Argentina   Australia   Austria   Belgium   Bolivia   Brazil   Bulgaria

Burma   Byelorussian
Soviet Socialist Republic   Cambodia   Cameroun   Canada   Central African
Republic   Ceylon   Chad   Chile

China   Colombia   Congo
(Brazzaville)   Congo
(Leopoldville)   Costa Rica   Cuba   Cyprus   Czechoslovakia   Dahomey

Denmark   Dominican
Republic   Ecuador   El Salvador   Ethiopia   Federation of
Malaya   Finland   France   Gabon

Ghana   Greece   Guatemala   Guinea   Haiti   Honduras   Hungary   Iceland   India

Indonesia   Iran   Iraq   Ireland   Israel   Italy   Ivory Coast   Japan   Jordan

| 1960 | United Nations | 99 |
|------|----------------|-----|
| Year | | Member states |

| | | | | | | | | |
|---|---|---|---|---|---|---|---|---|
| Laos | Lebanon | Liberia | Libya | Luxembourg | Malagasy Republic | Mali | Mexico | Morocco |
| Nepal | Netherlands | New Zealand | Nicaragua | Niger | Nigeria | Norway | Pakistan | Panama |
| Paraguay | Peru | Philippines | Poland | Portugal | Romania | Saudi Arabia | Senegal | Somalia |
| Spain | Sudan | Sweden | Thailand | Togo | Tunisia | Turkey | Ukrainian Soviet Socialist Republic | Union of South Africa |
| USSR Soviet Union | United Arab Rep. (Egypt & Syria) | United Kingdom | United States | Upper Volta | Uruguay | Venezuela | Yemen | Yugoslavia |

**Thirteen new members — independence from**

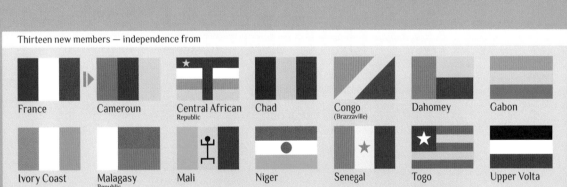

| | | | | | | |
|---|---|---|---|---|---|---|
| France ▷ Cameroun | Central African Republic | Chad | Congo (Brazzaville) | Dahomey | Gabon |
| Ivory Coast | Malagasy Republic | Mali | Niger | Senegal | Togo | Upper Volta |

**Two new members — independence from**

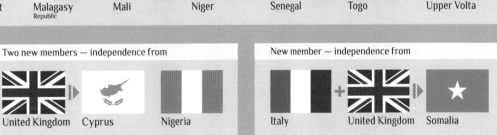

United Kingdom ▷ Cyprus    Nigeria

**New member — independence from**

Italy + United Kingdom ▷ Somalia

**New member — independence from**

Belgium    Congo (Leopoldville)

**Flag change**

United States ▷ United States

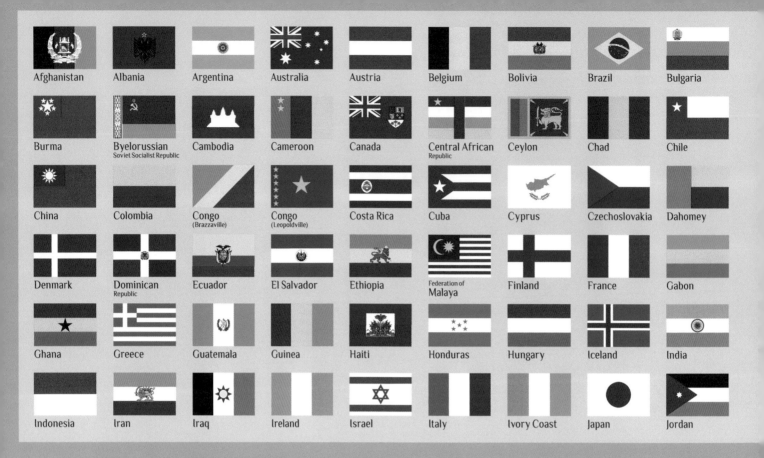

Afghanistan | Albania | Argentina | Australia | Austria | Belgium | Bolivia | Brazil | Bulgaria

Burma | Byelorussian
Soviet Socialist Republic | Cambodia | Cameroon | Canada | Central African
Republic | Ceylon | Chad | Chile

China | Colombia | Congo
(Brazzaville) | Congo
(Leopoldville) | Costa Rica | Cuba | Cyprus | Czechoslovakia | Dahomey

Denmark | Dominican
Republic | Ecuador | El Salvador | Ethiopia | Federation of
Malaya | Finland | France | Gabon

Ghana | Greece | Guatemala | Guinea | Haiti | Honduras | Hungary | Iceland | India

Indonesia | Iran | Iraq | Ireland | Israel | Italy | Ivory Coast | Japan | Jordan

1961
Year

United Nations

104
Member states

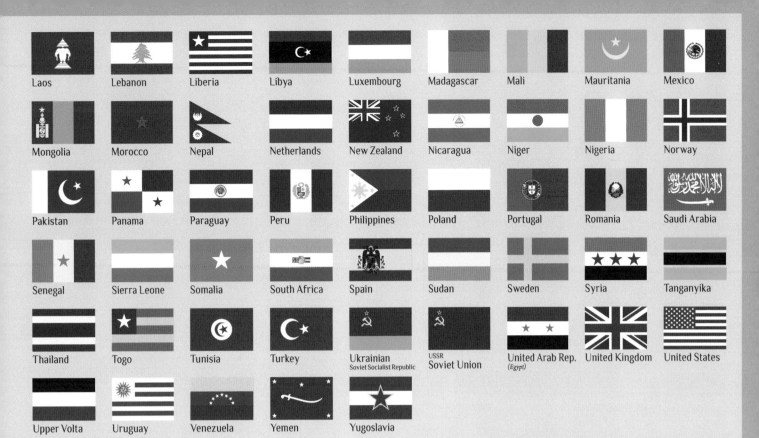

Laos · Lebanon · Liberia · Libya · Luxembourg · Madagascar · Mali · Mauritania · Mexico

Mongolia · Morocco · Nepal · Netherlands · New Zealand · Nicaragua · Niger · Nigeria · Norway

Pakistan · Panama · Paraguay · Peru · Philippines · Poland · Portugal · Romania · Saudi Arabia

Senegal · Sierra Leone · Somalia · South Africa · Spain · Sudan · Sweden · Syria · Tanganyika

Thailand · Togo · Tunisia · Turkey · Ukrainian Soviet Socialist Republic · USSR Soviet Union · United Arab Rep. (Egypt) · United Kingdom · United States

Upper Volta · Uruguay · Venezuela · Yemen · Yugoslavia

**Two new members — independence from**

United Kingdom · Sierra Leone · Tanganyika

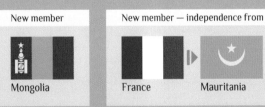

**New member**

Mongolia

**New member — independence from**

France · Mauritania

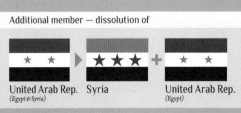

**Additional member — dissolution of**

United Arab Rep. (Egypt & Syria) · Syria · United Arab Rep. (Egypt)

**Flag and name change**

Cameroun · Cameroon

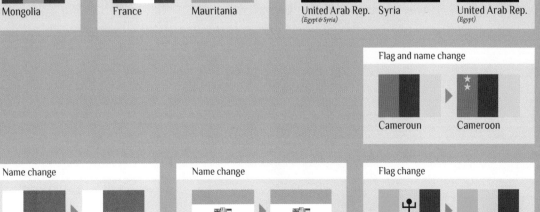

**Name change**

Malagasy Republic · Madagascar

**Name change**

Union of South Africa · South Africa

**Flag change**

Mali · Mali

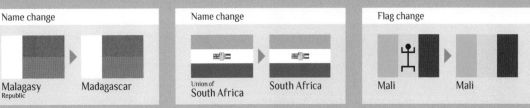

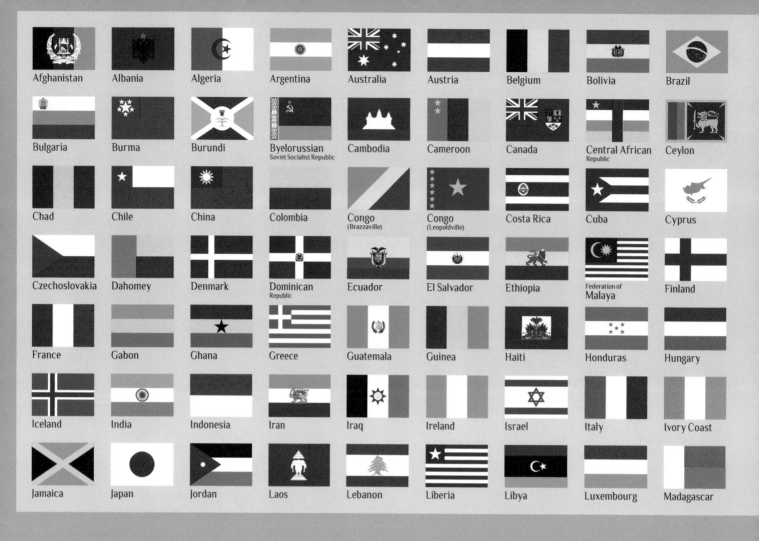

| | | | | | | | | |
|---|---|---|---|---|---|---|---|---|
| Afghanistan | Albania | Algeria | Argentina | Australia | Austria | Belgium | Bolivia | Brazil |
| Bulgaria | Burma | Burundi | Byelorussian Soviet Socialist Republic | Cambodia | Cameroon | Canada | Central African Republic | Ceylon |
| Chad | Chile | China | Colombia | Congo (Brazzaville) | Congo (Leopoldville) | Costa Rica | Cuba | Cyprus |
| Czechoslovakia | Dahomey | Denmark | Dominican Republic | Ecuador | El Salvador | Ethiopia | Federation of Malaya | Finland |
| France | Gabon | Ghana | Greece | Guatemala | Guinea | Haiti | Honduras | Hungary |
| Iceland | India | Indonesia | Iran | Iraq | Ireland | Israel | Italy | Ivory Coast |
| Jamaica | Japan | Jordan | Laos | Lebanon | Liberia | Libya | Luxembourg | Madagascar |

| 1962 | | 110 |
|---|---|---|
| Year | United Nations | Member states |

Mali    Mauritania    Mexico    Mongolia    Morocco    Nepal    Netherlands    New Zealand    Nicaragua

Niger    Nigeria    Norway    Pakistan    Panama    Paraguay    Peru    Philippines    Poland

Portugal    Romania    Rwanda    Saudi Arabia    Senegal    Sierra Leone    Somalia    South Africa    Spain

Sudan    Sweden    Syria    Tanganyika    Thailand    Togo    Trinidad and Tobago    Tunisia    Turkey

Uganda    Ukrainian Soviet Socialist Republic    USSR Soviet Union    United Arab Rep. (Egypt)    United Kingdom    United States    Upper Volta    Uruguay    Venezuela

Yemen    Yugoslavia

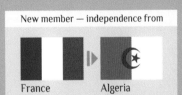

New member — independence from

France ▶ Algeria

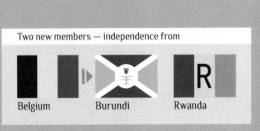

Two new members — independence from

Belgium ▶ Burundi    Rwanda

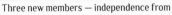

Three new members — independence from

United Kingdom ▶ Jamaica    Trinidad and Tobago    Uganda

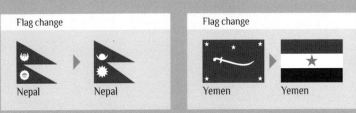

Flag change

Nepal ▶ Nepal

Flag change

Yemen ▶ Yemen

| | | | | | | | | |
|---|---|---|---|---|---|---|---|---|
| Afghanistan | Albania | Algeria | Argentina | Australia | Austria | Belgium | Bolivia | Brazil |
| Bulgaria | Burma | Burundi | Byelorussian Soviet Socialist Republic | Cambodia | Cameroon | Canada | Central African Republic | Ceylon |
| Chad | Chile | China | Colombia | Congo (Brazzaville) | Congo (Leopoldville) | Costa Rica | Cuba | Cyprus |
| Czechoslovakia | Dahomey | Denmark | Dominican Republic | Ecuador | El Salvador | Ethiopia | Finland | France |
| Gabon | Ghana | Greece | Guatemala | Guinea | Haiti | Honduras | Hungary | Iceland |
| India | Indonesia | Iran | Iraq | Ireland | Israel | Italy | Ivory Coast | Jamaica |
| Japan | Jordan | Kenya | Kuwait | Laos | Lebanon | Liberia | Libya | Luxembourg |

1963
Year

United Nations

113
Member states

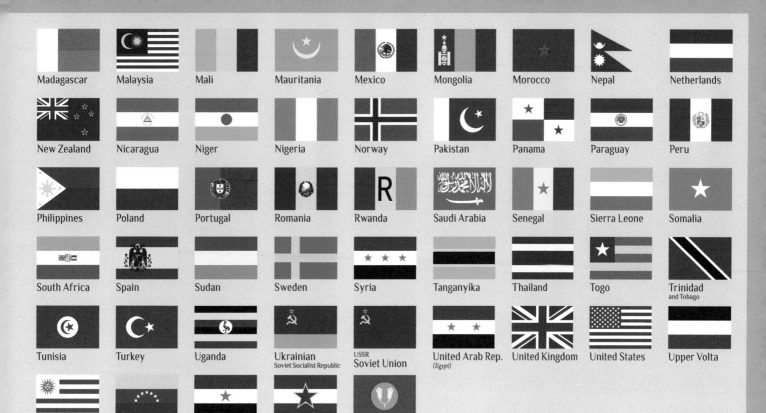

| Madagascar | Malaysia | Mali | Mauritania | Mexico | Mongolia | Morocco | Nepal | Netherlands |
| New Zealand | Nicaragua | Niger | Nigeria | Norway | Pakistan | Panama | Paraguay | Peru |
| Philippines | Poland | Portugal | Romania | Rwanda | Saudi Arabia | Senegal | Sierra Leone | Somalia |
| South Africa | Spain | Sudan | Sweden | Syria | Tanganyika | Thailand | Togo | Trinidad and Tobago |
| Tunisia | Turkey | Uganda | Ukrainian Soviet Socialist Republic | USSR Soviet Union | United Arab Rep. (Egypt) | United Kingdom | United States | Upper Volta |
| Uruguay | Venezuela | Yemen | Yugoslavia | Zanzibar | | | | |

**Three new members — independence from**

United Kingdom → Kenya — Kuwait — Zanzibar

**Flag and name change**

Federation of Malaya → Malaysia

**Flag change**

Congo (Leopoldville) → Congo (Leopoldville)

**Flag change**

Iraq → Iraq

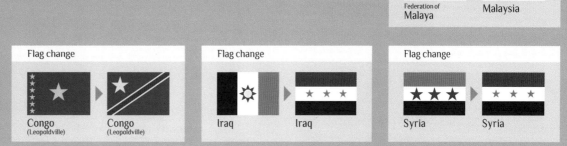

**Flag change**

Syria → Syria

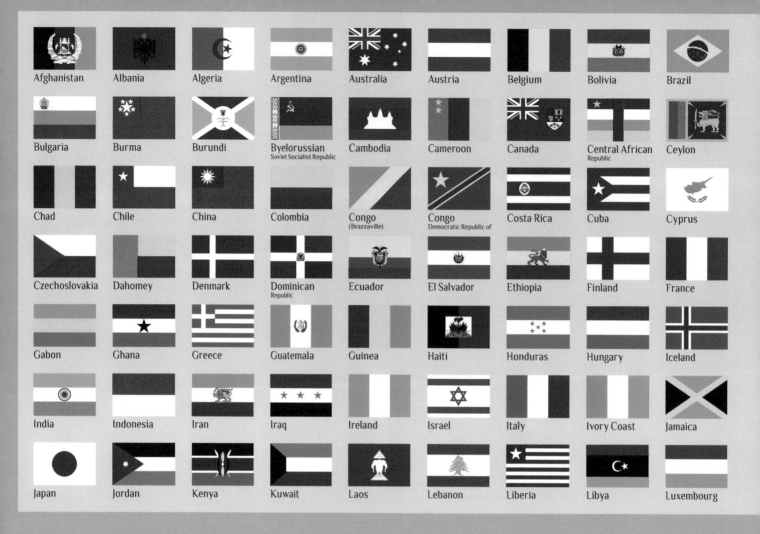

Afghanistan
Albania
Algeria
Argentina
Australia
Austria
Belgium
Bolivia
Brazil

Bulgaria
Burma
Burundi
Byelorussian
Soviet Socialist Republic
Cambodia
Cameroon
Canada
Central African
Republic
Ceylon

Chad
Chile
China
Colombia
Congo
(Brazzaville)
Congo
Democratic Republic of
Costa Rica
Cuba
Cyprus

Czechoslovakia
Dahomey
Denmark
Dominican
Republic
Ecuador
El Salvador
Ethiopia
Finland
France

Gabon
Ghana
Greece
Guatemala
Guinea
Haiti
Honduras
Hungary
Iceland

India
Indonesia
Iran
Iraq
Ireland
Israel
Italy
Ivory Coast
Jamaica

Japan
Jordan
Kenya
Kuwait
Laos
Lebanon
Liberia
Libya
Luxembourg

1964
Year

United Nations

115
Member states

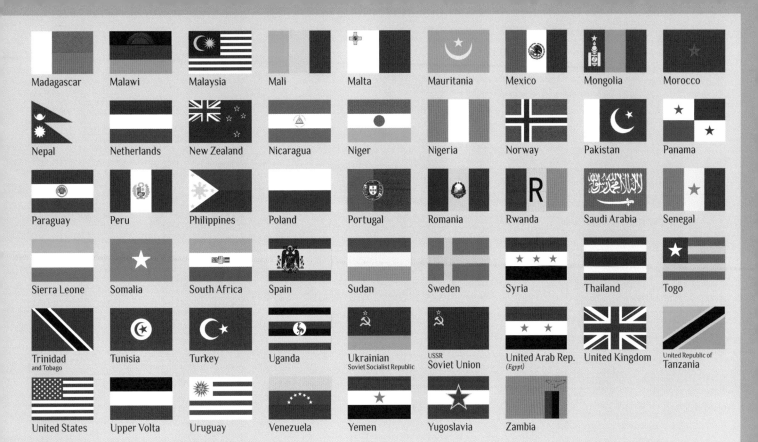

Madagascar | Malawi | Malaysia | Mali | Malta | Mauritania | Mexico | Mongolia | Morocco

Nepal | Netherlands | New Zealand | Nicaragua | Niger | Nigeria | Norway | Pakistan | Panama

Paraguay | Peru | Philippines | Poland | Portugal | Romania | Rwanda | Saudi Arabia | Senegal

Sierra Leone | Somalia | South Africa | Spain | Sudan | Sweden | Syria | Thailand | Togo

Trinidad and Tobago | Tunisia | Turkey | Uganda | Ukrainian Soviet Socialist Republic | USSR Soviet Union | United Arab Rep. (Egypt) | United Kingdom | United Republic of Tanzania

United States | Upper Volta | Uruguay | Venezuela | Yemen | Yugoslavia | Zambia

Three new members — independence from

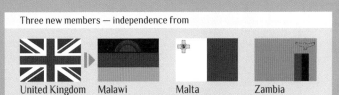

United Kingdom | Malawi | Malta | Zambia

Flag change

Zanzibar | Zanzibar

One less member — merger of

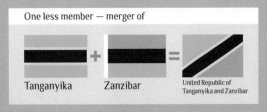

Tanganyika + Zanzibar = United Republic of Tanganyika and Zanzibar

Name change

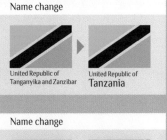

United Republic of Tanganyika and Zanzibar | United Republic of Tanzania

Name change

Congo (Leopoldville) | Congo Democratic Republic of

Flag change

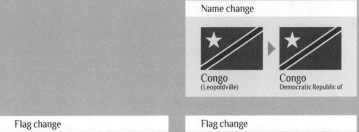

Ghana | Ghana

Flag change

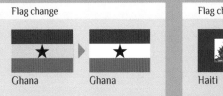

Haiti | Haiti

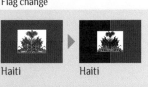

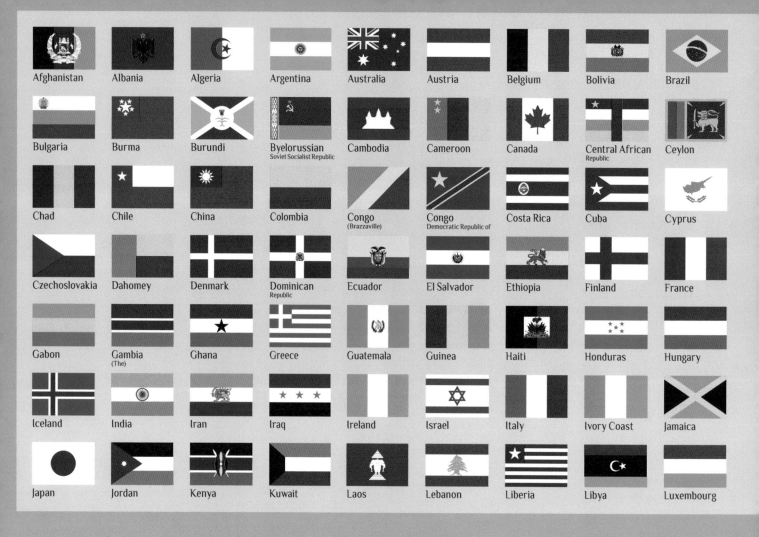

Afghanistan · Albania · Algeria · Argentina · Australia · Austria · Belgium · Bolivia · Brazil

Bulgaria · Burma · Burundi · Byelorussian Soviet Socialist Republic · Cambodia · Cameroon · Canada · Central African Republic · Ceylon

Chad · Chile · China · Colombia · Congo (Brazzaville) · Congo Democratic Republic of · Costa Rica · Cuba · Cyprus

Czechoslovakia · Dahomey · Denmark · Dominican Republic · Ecuador · El Salvador · Ethiopia · Finland · France

Gabon · Gambia (The) · Ghana · Greece · Guatemala · Guinea · Haiti · Honduras · Hungary

Iceland · India · Iran · Iraq · Ireland · Israel · Italy · Ivory Coast · Jamaica

Japan · Jordan · Kenya · Kuwait · Laos · Lebanon · Liberia · Libya · Luxembourg

1965
Year

United Nations

117
Member states

| | | | | | | | | |
|---|---|---|---|---|---|---|---|---|
| Madagascar | Malawi | Malaysia | Maldive Islands | Mali | Malta | Mauritania | Mexico | Mongolia |
| Morocco | Nepal | Netherlands | New Zealand | Nicaragua | Niger | Nigeria | Norway | Pakistan |
| Panama | Paraguay | Peru | Philippines | Poland | Portugal | Romania | Rwanda | Saudi Arabia |
| Senegal | Sierra Leone | Singapore | Somalia | South Africa | Spain | Sudan | Sweden | Syria |
| Thailand | Togo | Trinidad and Tobago | Tunisia | Turkey | Uganda | Ukrainian Soviet Socialist Republic | USSR Soviet Union | United Arab Rep. (Egypt) |
| United Kingdom | United Republic of Tanzania | United States | Upper Volta | Uruguay | Venezuela | Yemen | Yugoslavia | Zambia |

| Member withdraws | Three new members — independence from | | |
|---|---|---|---|
| Indonesia | United Kingdom ▶ Gambia (The) | Maldive Islands | Singapore |

| Flag change |
|---|
| Romania ▶ Romania |

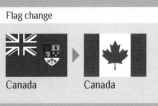

| Flag change |
|---|
| Canada ▶ Canada |

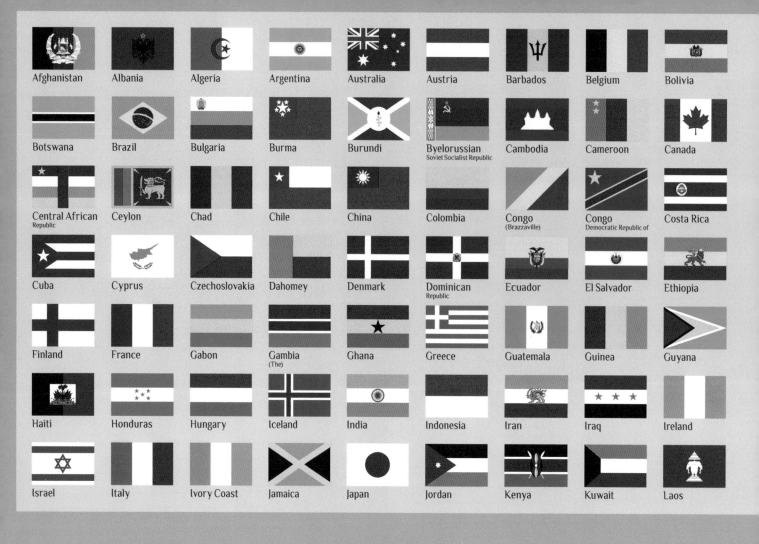

Afghanistan · Albania · Algeria · Argentina · Australia · Austria · Barbados · Belgium · Bolivia

Botswana · Brazil · Bulgaria · Burma · Burundi · Byelorussian Soviet Socialist Republic · Cambodia · Cameroon · Canada

Central African Republic · Ceylon · Chad · Chile · China · Colombia · Congo (Brazzaville) · Congo Democratic Republic of · Costa Rica

Cuba · Cyprus · Czechoslovakia · Dahomey · Denmark · Dominican Republic · Ecuador · El Salvador · Ethiopia

Finland · France · Gabon · Gambia (The) · Ghana · Greece · Guatemala · Guinea · Guyana

Haiti · Honduras · Hungary · Iceland · India · Indonesia · Iran · Iraq · Ireland

Israel · Italy · Ivory Coast · Jamaica · Japan · Jordan · Kenya · Kuwait · Laos

1966
Year

United Nations

122
Member states

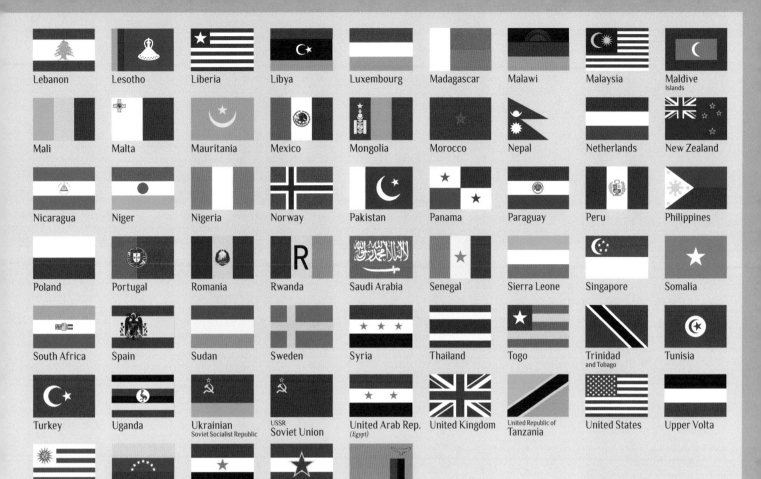

| | | | | | | | | |
|---|---|---|---|---|---|---|---|---|
| Lebanon | Lesotho | Liberia | Libya | Luxembourg | Madagascar | Malawi | Malaysia | Maldive Islands |
| Mali | Malta | Mauritania | Mexico | Mongolia | Morocco | Nepal | Netherlands | New Zealand |
| Nicaragua | Niger | Nigeria | Norway | Pakistan | Panama | Paraguay | Peru | Philippines |
| Poland | Portugal | Romania | Rwanda | Saudi Arabia | Senegal | Sierra Leone | Singapore | Somalia |
| South Africa | Spain | Sudan | Sweden | Syria | Thailand | Togo | Trinidad and Tobago | Tunisia |
| Turkey | Uganda | Ukrainian Soviet Socialist Republic | USSR Soviet Union | United Arab Rep. (Egypt) | United Kingdom | United Republic of Tanzania | United States | Upper Volta |
| Uruguay | Venezuela | Yemen | Yugoslavia | Zambia | | | | |

**Member rejoins**

Indonesia

**Four new members — independence from**

United Kingdom ▷ Barbados  Botswana  Guyana  Lesotho

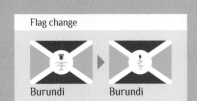

**Flag change**

Burundi ▷ Burundi

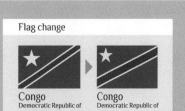

**Flag change**

Congo
Democratic Republic of ▷ Congo
Democratic Republic of

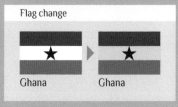

**Flag change**

Ghana ▷ Ghana

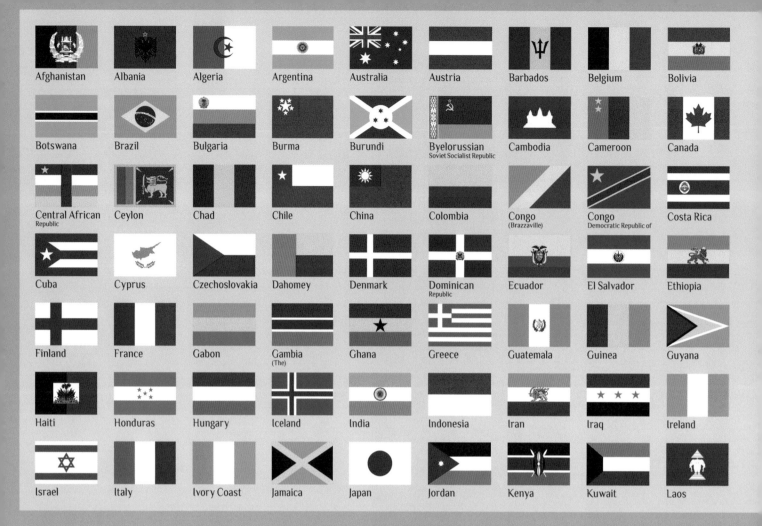

Afghanistan · Albania · Algeria · Argentina · Australia · Austria · Barbados · Belgium · Bolivia

Botswana · Brazil · Bulgaria · Burma · Burundi · Byelorussian Soviet Socialist Republic · Cambodia · Cameroon · Canada

Central African Republic · Ceylon · Chad · Chile · China · Colombia · Congo (Brazzaville) · Congo Democratic Republic of · Costa Rica

Cuba · Cyprus · Czechoslovakia · Dahomey · Denmark · Dominican Republic · Ecuador · El Salvador · Ethiopia

Finland · France · Gabon · Gambia (The) · Ghana · Greece · Guatemala · Guinea · Guyana

Haiti · Honduras · Hungary · Iceland · India · Indonesia · Iran · Iraq · Ireland

Israel · Italy · Ivory Coast · Jamaica · Japan · Jordan · Kenya · Kuwait · Laos

1967
Year

United Nations

123
Member states

Lebanon | Lesotho | Liberia | Libya | Luxembourg | Madagascar | Malawi | Malaysia | Maldive Islands

Mali | Malta | Mauritania | Mexico | Mongolia | Morocco | Nepal | Netherlands | New Zealand

Nicaragua | Niger | Nigeria | Norway | Pakistan | Panama | Paraguay | Peru | Philippines

Poland | Portugal | Romania | Rwanda | Saudi Arabia | Senegal | Sierra Leone | Singapore | Somalia

South Africa | Southern Yemen | Spain | Sudan | Sweden | Syria | Thailand | Togo | Trinidad and Tobago

Tunisia | Turkey | Uganda | Ukrainian Soviet Socialist Republic | USSR Soviet Union | United Arab Rep. (Egypt) | United Kingdom | United Republic of Tanzania | United States

Upper Volta | Uruguay | Venezuela | Yemen | Yugoslavia | Zambia

New member — independence from

United Kingdom ▷ Southern Yemen

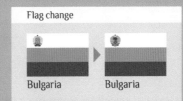

Flag change

Bulgaria ▷ Bulgaria

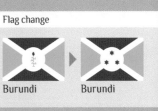

Flag change

Burundi ▷ Burundi

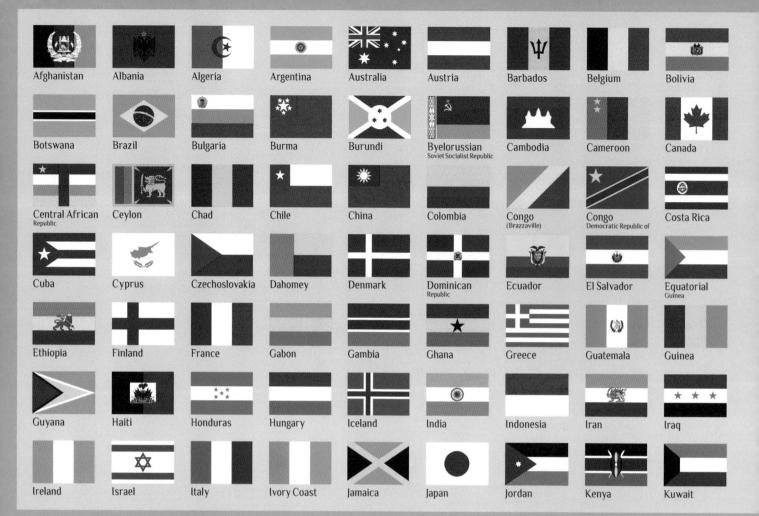

Afghanistan Albania Algeria Argentina Australia Austria Barbados Belgium Bolivia

Botswana Brazil Bulgaria Burma Burundi Byelorussian Soviet Socialist Republic Cambodia Cameroon Canada

Central African Republic Ceylon Chad Chile China Colombia Congo (Brazzaville) Congo Democratic Republic of Costa Rica

Cuba Cyprus Czechoslovakia Dahomey Denmark Dominican Republic Ecuador El Salvador Equatorial Guinea

Ethiopia Finland France Gabon Gambia Ghana Greece Guatemala Guinea

Guyana Haiti Honduras Hungary Iceland India Indonesia Iran Iraq

Ireland Israel Italy Ivory Coast Jamaica Japan Jordan Kenya Kuwait

1968
Year

United Nations

126
Member states

| | | | |
|---|---|---|---|
| Laos | Lebanon | Lesotho | Liberia |
| Libya | Luxembourg | Madagascar | Malawi |
| Malaysia | Maldive Islands | Mali | Malta |
| Mauritania | Mauritius | Mexico | Mongolia |
| Morocco | Nepal | Netherlands | New Zealand |
| Nicaragua | Niger | Nigeria | Norway |
| Pakistan | Panama | Paraguay | Peru |
| Philippines | Poland | Portugal | Romania |
| Rwanda | Saudi Arabia | Senegal | Sierra Leone |
| Singapore | Somalia | South Africa | Southern Yemen |
| Spain | Sudan | Swaziland | Sweden |
| Syria | Thailand | Togo | Trinidad and Tobago |
| Tunisia | Turkey | Uganda | Ukrainian Soviet Socialist Republic |
| USSR Soviet Union | United Arab Rep. (Egypt) | United Kingdom | United Republic of Tanzania |
| United States | Upper Volta | Uruguay | Venezuela |
| Yemen | Yugoslavia | Zambia | |

New member — independence from

Spain ▶ Equatorial Guinea

Two new members — independence from

United Kingdom ▶ Mauritius    Swaziland

Name change (UN listing)

Gambia (The) ▶ Gambia

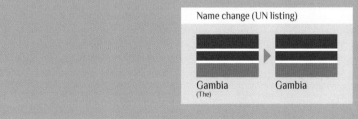

Flag change

Brazil ▶ Brazil

Flag change

Mexico ▶ Mexico

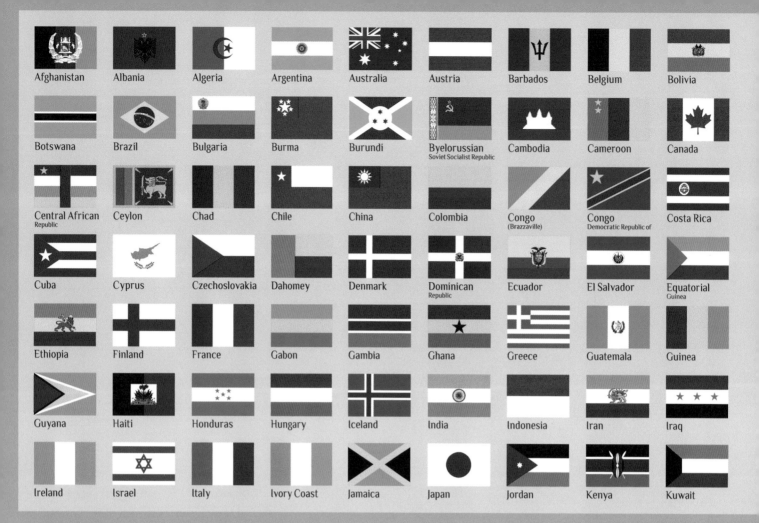

Afghanistan
Albania
Algeria
Argentina
Australia
Austria
Barbados
Belgium
Bolivia

Botswana
Brazil
Bulgaria
Burma
Burundi
Byelorussian
Soviet Socialist Republic
Cambodia
Cameroon
Canada

Central African
Republic
Ceylon
Chad
Chile
China
Colombia
Congo
(Brazzaville)
Congo
Democratic Republic of
Costa Rica

Cuba
Cyprus
Czechoslovakia
Dahomey
Denmark
Dominican
Republic
Ecuador
El Salvador
Equatorial
Guinea

Ethiopia
Finland
France
Gabon
Gambia
Ghana
Greece
Guatemala
Guinea

Guyana
Haiti
Honduras
Hungary
Iceland
India
Indonesia
Iran
Iraq

Ireland
Israel
Italy
Ivory Coast
Jamaica
Japan
Jordan
Kenya
Kuwait

1969
Year

United Nations

126
Member states

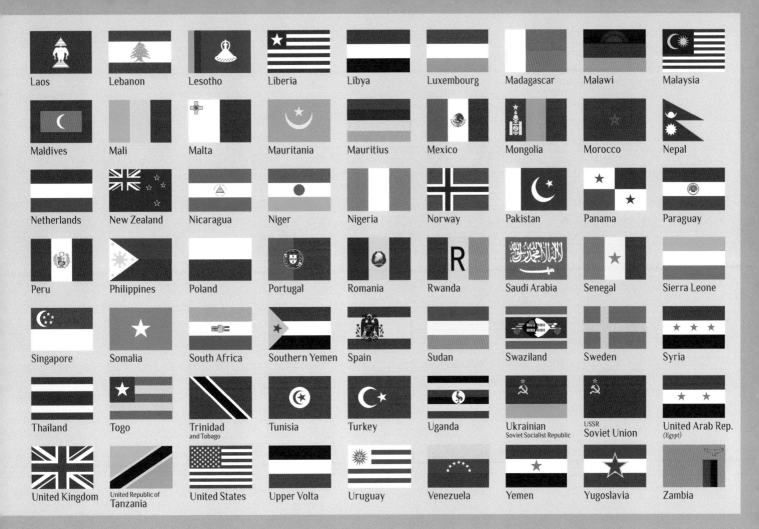

Laos

Lebanon

Lesotho

Liberia

Libya

Luxembourg

Madagascar

Malawi

Malaysia

Maldives

Mali

Malta

Mauritania

Mauritius

Mexico

Mongolia

Morocco

Nepal

Netherlands

New Zealand

Nicaragua

Niger

Nigeria

Norway

Pakistan

Panama

Paraguay

Peru

Philippines

Poland

Portugal

Romania

Rwanda

Saudi Arabia

Senegal

Sierra Leone

Singapore

Somalia

South Africa

Southern Yemen

Spain

Sudan

Swaziland

Sweden

Syria

Thailand

Togo

Trinidad
and Tobago

Tunisia

Turkey

Uganda

Ukrainian
Soviet Socialist Republic

USSR
Soviet Union

United Arab Rep.
(Egypt)

United Kingdom

United Republic of
Tanzania

United States

Upper Volta

Uruguay

Venezuela

Yemen

Yugoslavia

Zambia

Name change

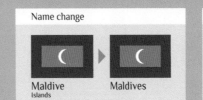

Maldive
Islands

Maldives

Flag change

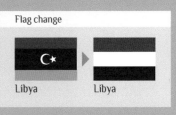

Libya

Libya

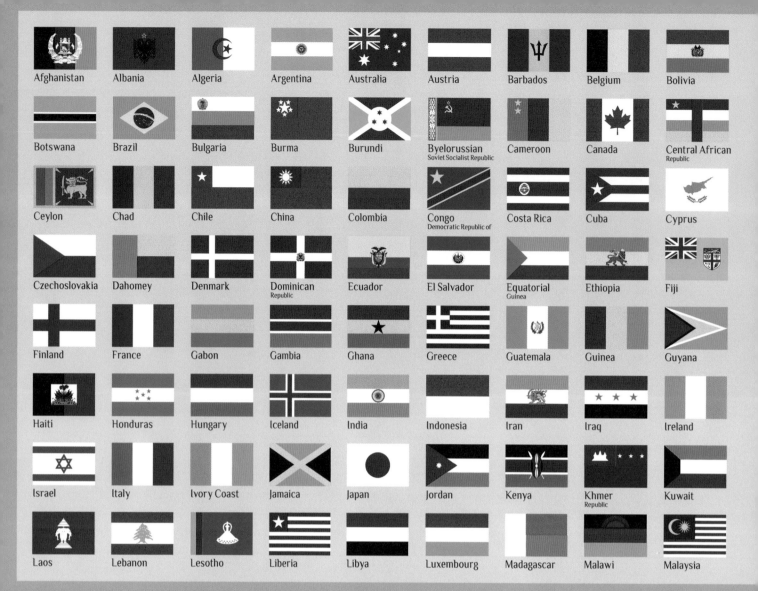

Afghanistan · Albania · Algeria · Argentina · Australia · Austria · Barbados · Belgium · Bolivia

Botswana · Brazil · Bulgaria · Burma · Burundi · Byelorussian Soviet Socialist Republic · Cameroon · Canada · Central African Republic

Ceylon · Chad · Chile · China · Colombia · Congo Democratic Republic of · Costa Rica · Cuba · Cyprus

Czechoslovakia · Dahomey · Denmark · Dominican Republic · Ecuador · El Salvador · Equatorial Guinea · Ethiopia · Fiji

Finland · France · Gabon · Gambia · Ghana · Greece · Guatemala · Guinea · Guyana

Haiti · Honduras · Hungary · Iceland · India · Indonesia · Iran · Iraq · Ireland

Israel · Italy · Ivory Coast · Jamaica · Japan · Jordan · Kenya · Khmer Republic · Kuwait

Laos · Lebanon · Lesotho · Liberia · Libya · Luxembourg · Madagascar · Malawi · Malaysia

Timeline                                   page 56

1970
Year

United Nations

127
Member states

Maldives · Mali · Malta · Mauritania · Mauritius · Mexico · Mongolia · Morocco · Nepal

Netherlands · New Zealand · Nicaragua · Niger · Nigeria · Norway · Pakistan · Panama · Paraguay

People's Dem. Rep. of **Yemen** · People's Rep. of the **Congo** · Peru · Philippines · Poland · Portugal · Romania · Rwanda · Saudi Arabia

Senegal · Sierra Leone · Singapore · Somalia · South Africa · Spain · Sudan · Swaziland · Sweden

Syria · Thailand · Togo · Trinidad and Tobago · Tunisia · Turkey · Uganda · Ukrainian Soviet Socialist Republic · USSR Soviet Union

United Arab Rep. (Egypt) · United Kingdom · United Republic of Tanzania · United States · Upper Volta · Uruguay · Venezuela · Yemen · Yugoslavia

Zambia

New member — independence from

United Kingdom    Fiji

Flag and name change

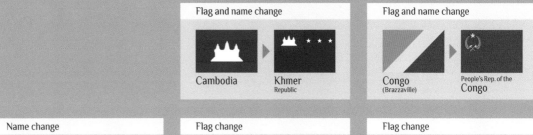

Cambodia    Khmer Republic

Flag and name change

Congo (Brazzaville)    People's Dem. Rep. of Congo

Name change

Southern Yemen    People's Dem. Rep. of Yemen

Flag change

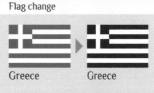

Greece    Greece

Flag change

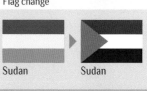

Sudan    Sudan

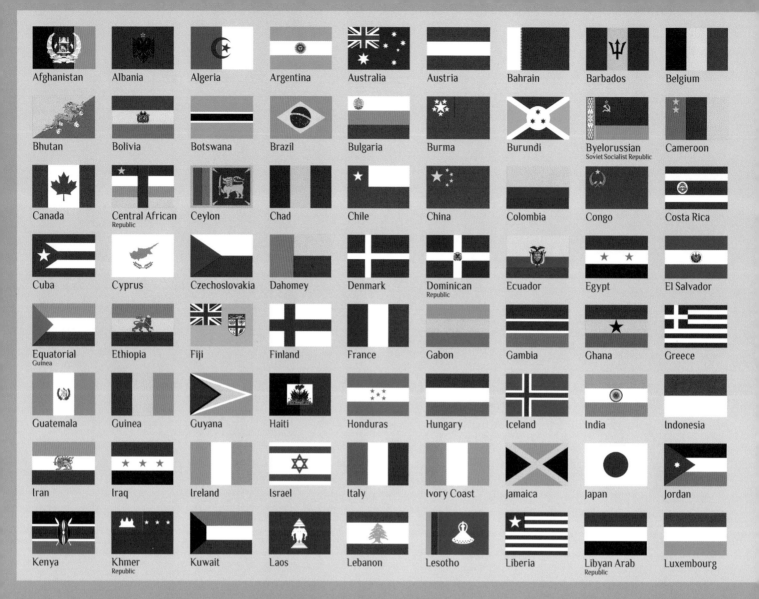

Afghanistan, Albania, Algeria, Argentina, Australia, Austria, Bahrain, Barbados, Belgium

Bhutan, Bolivia, Botswana, Brazil, Bulgaria, Burma, Burundi, Byelorussian Soviet Socialist Republic, Cameroon

Canada, Central African Republic, Ceylon, Chad, Chile, China, Colombia, Congo, Costa Rica

Cuba, Cyprus, Czechoslovakia, Dahomey, Denmark, Dominican Republic, Ecuador, Egypt, El Salvador

Equatorial Guinea, Ethiopia, Fiji, Finland, France, Gabon, Gambia, Ghana, Greece

Guatemala, Guinea, Guyana, Haiti, Honduras, Hungary, Iceland, India, Indonesia

Iran, Iraq, Ireland, Israel, Italy, Ivory Coast, Jamaica, Japan, Jordan

Kenya, Khmer Republic, Kuwait, Laos, Lebanon, Lesotho, Liberia, Libyan Arab Republic, Luxembourg

## China's membership switch

China's membership switched from
the Republic of China *(Taiwan)* to the
People's Republic of China *(Mainland)* on
15 November 1971. The UN listing's name
remained China.

1971
Year

United Nations

132
Member states

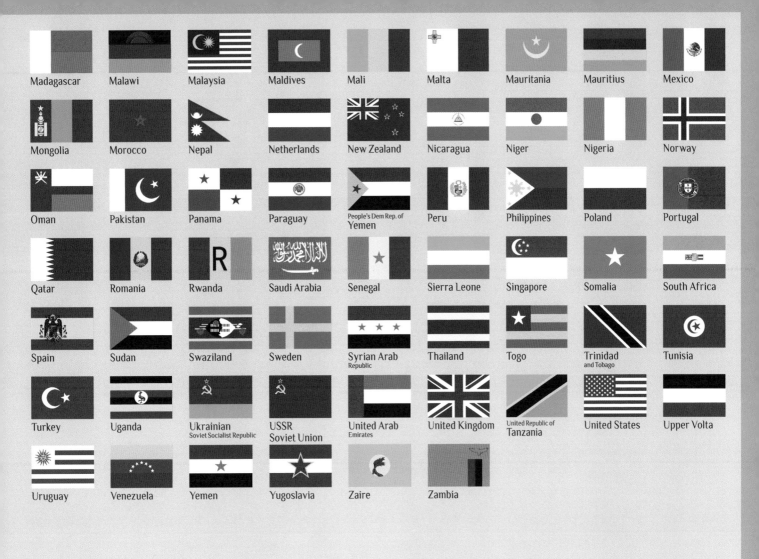

Madagascar · Malawi · Malaysia · Maldives · Mali · Malta · Mauritania · Mauritius · Mexico

Mongolia · Morocco · Nepal · Netherlands · New Zealand · Nicaragua · Niger · Nigeria · Norway

Oman · Pakistan · Panama · Paraguay · People's Dem Rep. of Yemen · Peru · Philippines · Poland · Portugal

Qatar · Romania · Rwanda · Saudi Arabia · Senegal · Sierra Leone · Singapore · Somalia · South Africa

Spain · Sudan · Swaziland · Sweden · Syrian Arab Republic · Thailand · Togo · Trinidad and Tobago · Tunisia

Turkey · Uganda · Ukrainian Soviet Socialist Republic · USSR Soviet Union · United Arab Emirates · United Kingdom · United Republic of Tanzania · United States · Upper Volta

Uruguay · Venezuela · Yemen · Yugoslavia · Zaire · Zambia

**Switched membership**

China (Republic of) ▶ China (People's Republic of)

**New member**

Bhutan

**Four new members — independence from**

United Kingdom ▶ Bahrain · Oman · Qatar · United Arab Emirates

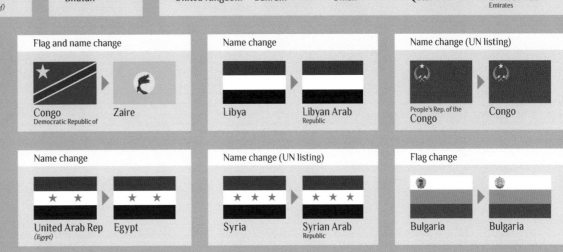

**Flag and name change**

Congo Democratic Republic of ▶ Zaire

**Name change**

Libya ▶ Libyan Arab Republic

**Name change (UN listing)**

People's Rep. of the Congo ▶ Congo

**Name change**

United Arab Rep (Egypt) ▶ Egypt

**Name change (UN listing)**

Syria ▶ Syrian Arab Republic

**Flag change**

Bulgaria ▶ Bulgaria

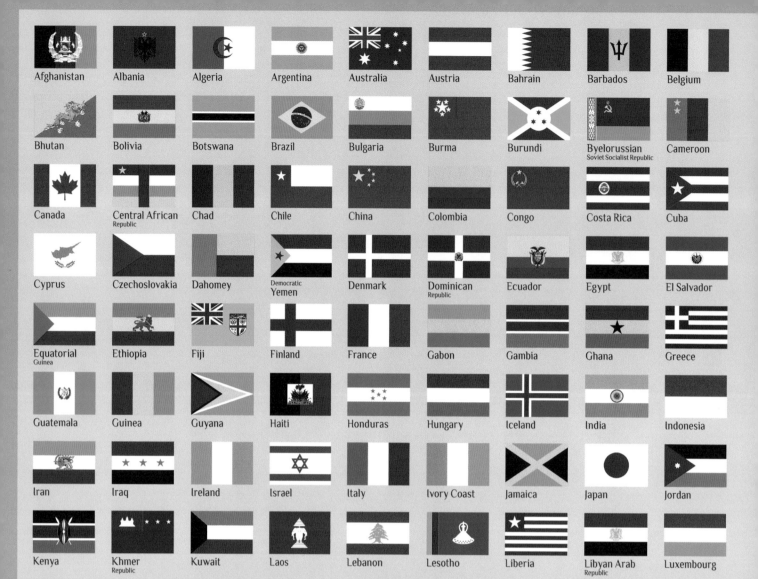

Afghanistan · Albania · Algeria · Argentina · Australia · Austria · Bahrain · Barbados · Belgium

Bhutan · Bolivia · Botswana · Brazil · Bulgaria · Burma · Burundi · Byelorussian Soviet Socialist Republic · Cameroon

Canada · Central African Republic · Chad · Chile · China · Colombia · Congo · Costa Rica · Cuba

Cyprus · Czechoslovakia · Dahomey · Democratic Yemen · Denmark · Dominican Republic · Ecuador · Egypt · El Salvador

Equatorial Guinea · Ethiopia · Fiji · Finland · France · Gabon · Gambia · Ghana · Greece

Guatemala · Guinea · Guyana · Haiti · Honduras · Hungary · Iceland · India · Indonesia

Iran · Iraq · Ireland · Israel · Italy · Ivory Coast · Jamaica · Japan · Jordan

Kenya · Khmer Republic · Kuwait · Laos · Lebanon · Lesotho · Liberia · Libyan Arab Republic · Luxembourg

1972
Year

United Nations

132
Member states

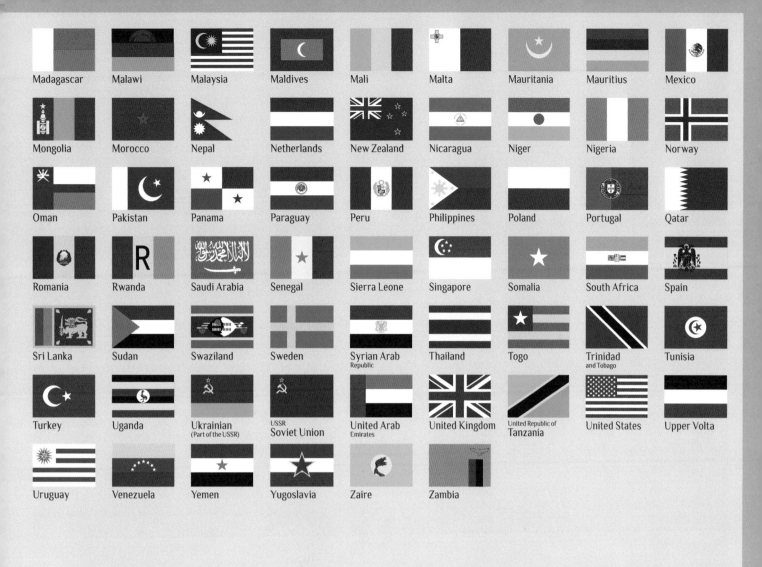

Madagascar · Malawi · Malaysia · Maldives · Mali · Malta · Mauritania · Mauritius · Mexico

Mongolia · Morocco · Nepal · Netherlands · New Zealand · Nicaragua · Niger · Nigeria · Norway

Oman · Pakistan · Panama · Paraguay · Peru · Philippines · Poland · Portugal · Qatar

Romania · Rwanda · Saudi Arabia · Senegal · Sierra Leone · Singapore · Somalia · South Africa · Spain

Sri Lanka · Sudan · Swaziland · Sweden · Syrian Arab Republic · Thailand · Togo · Trinidad and Tobago · Tunisia

Turkey · Uganda · Ukrainian (Part of the USSR) · USSR Soviet Union · United Arab Emirates · United Kingdom · United Republic of Tanzania · United States · Upper Volta

Uruguay · Venezuela · Yemen · Yugoslavia · Zaire · Zambia

---

**Flag and name change**

Ceylon ▸ Sri Lanka

---

**Name change**

People's Dem. Rep. of Yemen ▸ Democratic Yemen

**Flag change**

Bahrain ▸ Bahrain

---

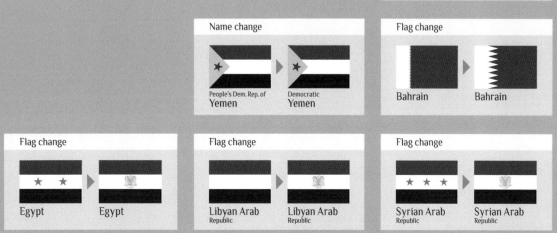

**Flag change**

Egypt ▸ Egypt

**Flag change**

Libyan Arab Republic ▸ Libyan Arab Republic

**Flag change**

Syrian Arab Republic ▸ Syrian Arab Republic

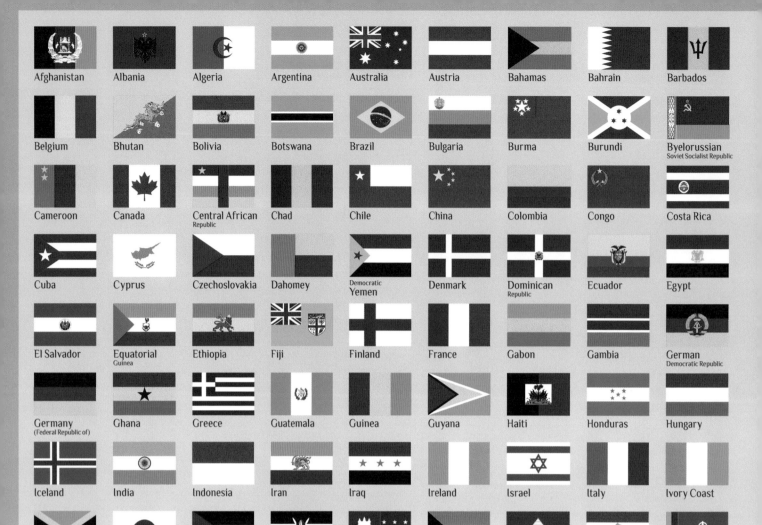

Afghanistan · Albania · Algeria · Argentina · Australia · Austria · Bahamas · Bahrain · Barbados

Belgium · Bhutan · Bolivia · Botswana · Brazil · Bulgaria · Burma · Burundi · Byelorussian Soviet Socialist Republic

Cameroon · Canada · Central African Republic · Chad · Chile · China · Colombia · Congo · Costa Rica

Cuba · Cyprus · Czechoslovakia · Dahomey · Democratic Yemen · Denmark · Dominican Republic · Ecuador · Egypt

El Salvador · Equatorial Guinea · Ethiopia · Fiji · Finland · France · Gabon · Gambia · German Democratic Republic

Germany (Federal Republic of) · Ghana · Greece · Guatemala · Guinea · Guyana · Haiti · Honduras · Hungary

Iceland · India · Indonesia · Iran · Iraq · Ireland · Israel · Italy · Ivory Coast

Jamaica · Japan · Jordan · Kenya · Khmer Republic · Kuwait · Laos · Lebanon · Lesotho

1973 — Year

United Nations

135 — Member states

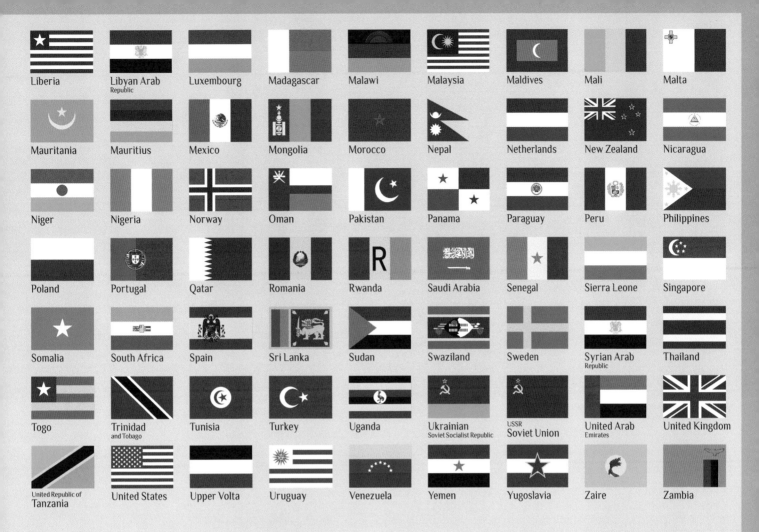

Liberia | Libyan Arab Republic | Luxembourg | Madagascar | Malawi | Malaysia | Maldives | Mali | Malta

Mauritania | Mauritius | Mexico | Mongolia | Morocco | Nepal | Netherlands | New Zealand | Nicaragua

Niger | Nigeria | Norway | Oman | Pakistan | Panama | Paraguay | Peru | Philippines

Poland | Portugal | Qatar | Romania | Rwanda | Saudi Arabia | Senegal | Sierra Leone | Singapore

Somalia | South Africa | Spain | Sri Lanka | Sudan | Swaziland | Sweden | Syrian Arab Republic | Thailand

Togo | Trinidad and Tobago | Tunisia | Turkey | Uganda | Ukrainian Soviet Socialist Republic | USSR Soviet Union | United Arab Emirates | United Kingdom

United Republic of Tanzania | United States | Upper Volta | Uruguay | Venezuela | Yemen | Yugoslavia | Zaire | Zambia

Two new members

German Democratic Republic | Germany (Federal Republic of)

New member — independence from

United Kingdom ▸ Bahamas

Flag change

Afghanistan ▸ Afghanistan

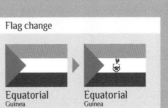

Flag change

Equatorial Guinea ▸ Equatorial Guinea

Flag change

Saudi Arabia ▸ Saudi Arabia

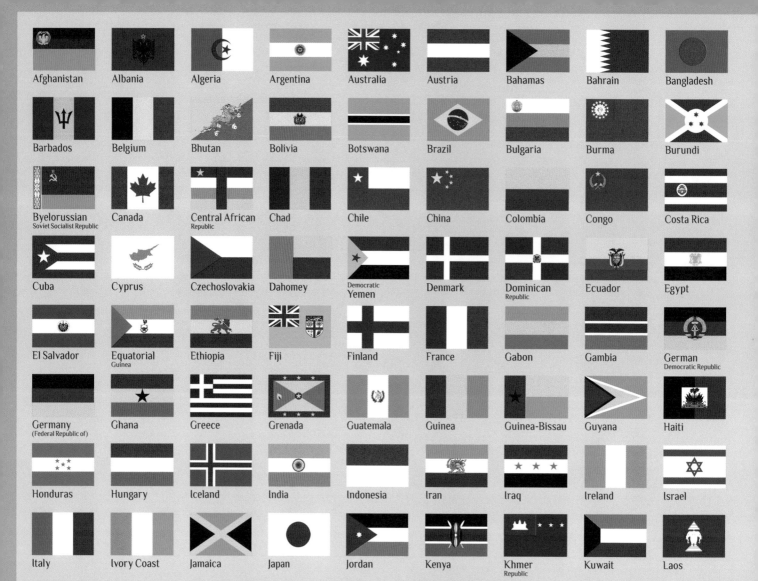

Afghanistan | Albania | Algeria | Argentina | Australia | Austria | Bahamas | Bahrain | Bangladesh

Barbados | Belgium | Bhutan | Bolivia | Botswana | Brazil | Bulgaria | Burma | Burundi

Byelorussian Soviet Socialist Republic | Canada | Central African Republic | Chad | Chile | China | Colombia | Congo | Costa Rica

Cuba | Cyprus | Czechoslovakia | Dahomey | Democratic Yemen | Denmark | Dominican Republic | Ecuador | Egypt

El Salvador | Equatorial Guinea | Ethiopia | Fiji | Finland | France | Gabon | Gambia | German Democratic Republic

Germany (Federal Republic of) | Ghana | Greece | Grenada | Guatemala | Guinea | Guinea-Bissau | Guyana | Haiti

Honduras | Hungary | Iceland | India | Indonesia | Iran | Iraq | Ireland | Israel

Italy | Ivory Coast | Jamaica | Japan | Jordan | Kenya | Khmer Republic | Kuwait | Laos

1974
Year

United Nations

138
Member states

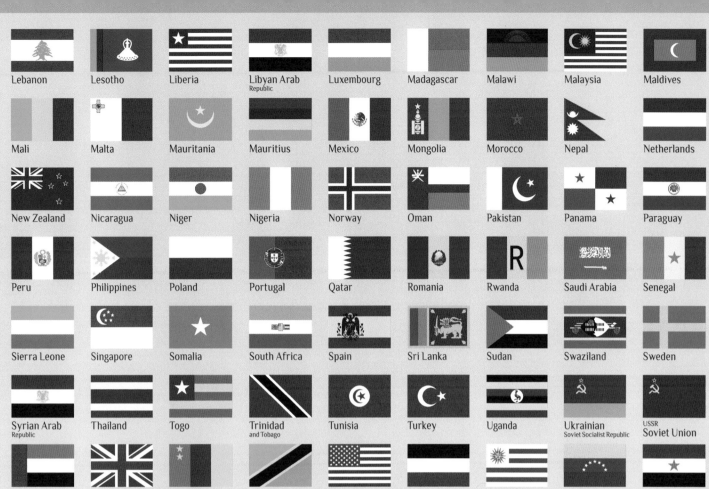

Lebanon · Lesotho · Liberia · Libyan Arab Republic · Luxembourg · Madagascar · Malawi · Malaysia · Maldives

Mali · Malta · Mauritania · Mauritius · Mexico · Mongolia · Morocco · Nepal · Netherlands

New Zealand · Nicaragua · Niger · Nigeria · Norway · Oman · Pakistan · Panama · Paraguay

Peru · Philippines · Poland · Portugal · Qatar · Romania · Rwanda · Saudi Arabia · Senegal

Sierra Leone · Singapore · Somalia · South Africa · Spain · Sri Lanka · Sudan · Swaziland · Sweden

Syrian Arab Republic · Thailand · Togo · Trinidad and Tobago · Tunisia · Turkey · Uganda · Ukrainian Soviet Socialist Republic · USSR Soviet Union

United Arab Emirates · United Kingdom · United Republic of Cameroon · United Republic of Tanzania · United States · Upper Volta · Uruguay · Venezuela · Yemen

Yugoslavia · Zaire · Zambia

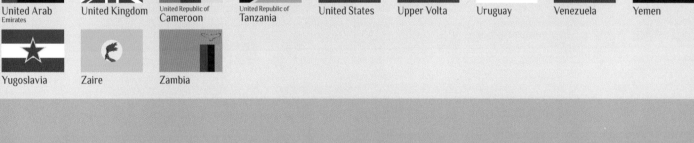

New member — separation from
Pakistan ▶ Bangladesh

New member — independence from
United Kingdom ▶ Grenada

New member — independence from
Portugal ▶ Guinea-Bissau

Name change
Cameroon ▶ United Republic of Cameroon

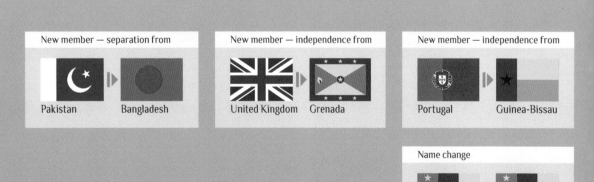

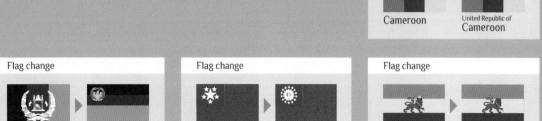

Flag change
Afghanistan ▶ Afghanistan

Flag change
Burma ▶ Burma

Flag change
Ethiopia ▶ Ethiopia

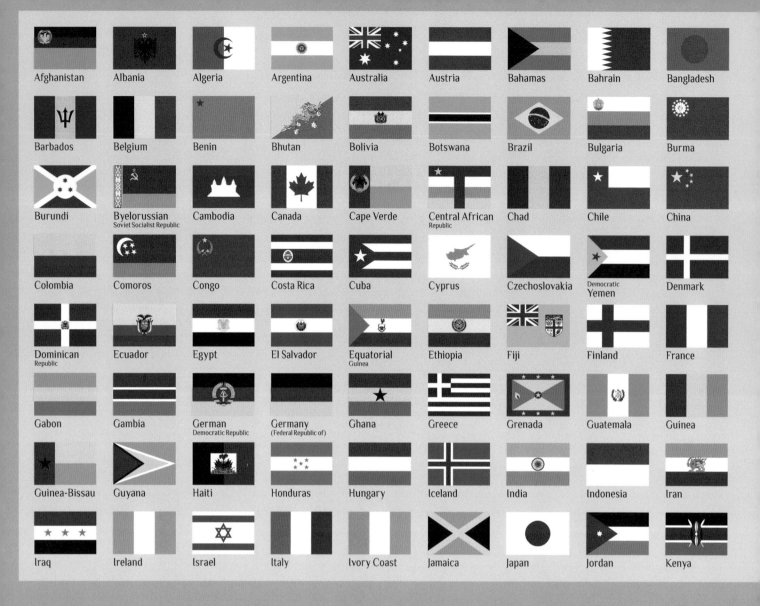

Afghanistan Albania Algeria Argentina Australia Austria Bahamas Bahrain Bangladesh

Barbados Belgium Benin Bhutan Bolivia Botswana Brazil Bulgaria Burma

Burundi Byelorussian Soviet Socialist Republic Cambodia Canada Cape Verde Central African Republic Chad Chile China

Colombia Comoros Congo Costa Rica Cuba Cyprus Czechoslovakia Democratic Yemen Denmark

Dominican Republic Ecuador Egypt El Salvador Equatorial Guinea Ethiopia Fiji Finland France

Gabon Gambia German Democratic Republic Germany (Federal Republic of) Ghana Greece Grenada Guatemala Guinea

Guinea-Bissau Guyana Haiti Honduras Hungary Iceland India Indonesia Iran

Iraq Ireland Israel Italy Ivory Coast Jamaica Japan Jordan Kenya

Timeline                     page 66

1975
Year

United Nations

144
Member states

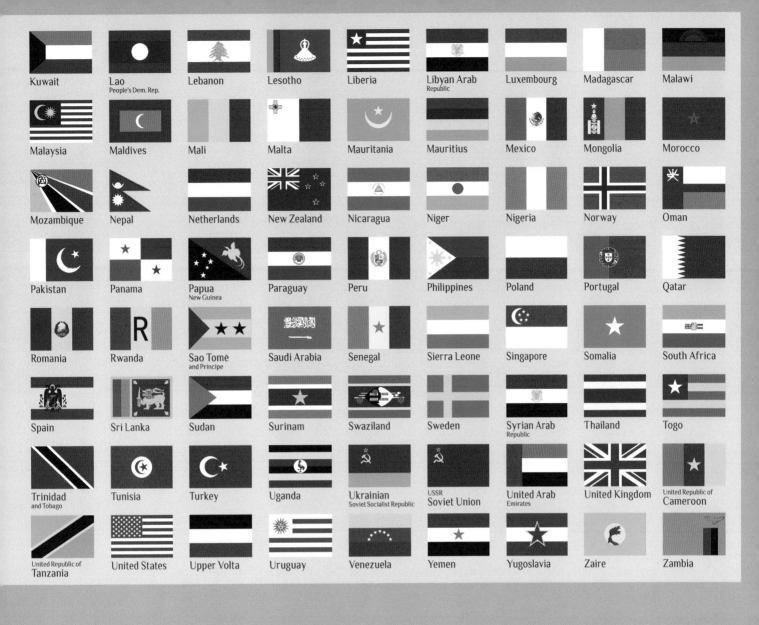

Kuwait

Lao
People's Dem. Rep.

Lebanon

Lesotho

Liberia

Libyan Arab
Republic

Luxembourg

Madagascar

Malawi

Malaysia

Maldives

Mali

Malta

Mauritania

Mauritius

Mexico

Mongolia

Morocco

Mozambique

Nepal

Netherlands

New Zealand

Nicaragua

Niger

Nigeria

Norway

Oman

Pakistan

Panama

Papua
New Guinea

Paraguay

Peru

Philippines

Poland

Portugal

Qatar

Romania

Rwanda

Sao Tomé
and Principe

Saudi Arabia

Senegal

Sierra Leone

Singapore

Somalia

South Africa

Spain

Sri Lanka

Sudan

Surinam

Swaziland

Sweden

Syrian Arab
Republic

Thailand

Togo

Trinidad
and Tobago

Tunisia

Turkey

Uganda

Ukrainian
Soviet Socialist Republic

USSR
Soviet Union

United Arab
Emirates

United Kingdom

United Republic of
Cameroon

United Republic of
Tanzania

United States

Upper Volta

Uruguay

Venezuela

Yemen

Yugoslavia

Zaire

Zambia

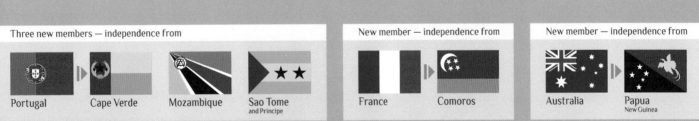

Three new members — independence from

Portugal ▶ Cape Verde

Mozambique

Sao Tome
and Principe

New member — independence from

France ▶ Comoros

New member — independence from

Australia ▶ Papua
New Guinea

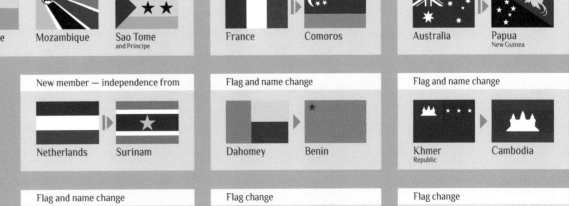

New member — independence from

Netherlands ▶ Surinam

Flag and name change

Dahomey ▶ Benin

Flag and name change

Khmer
Republic ▶ Cambodia

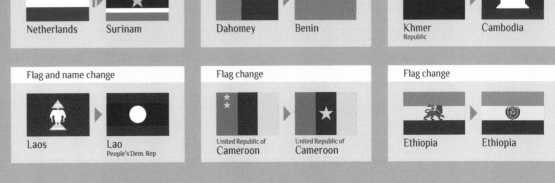

Flag and name change

Laos ▶ Lao
People's Dem. Rep

Flag change

United Republic of
Cameroon ▶ United Republic of
Cameroon

Flag change

Ethiopia ▶ Ethiopia

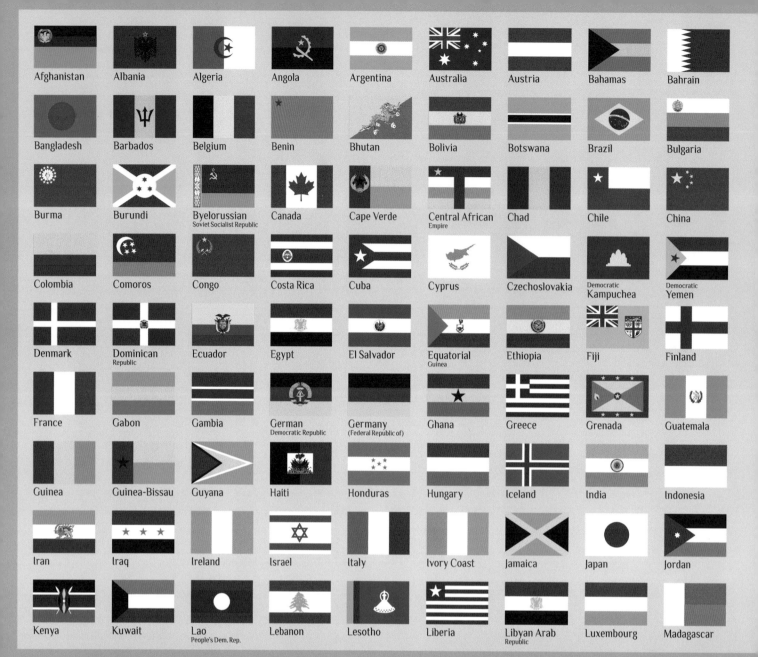

Afghanistan  Albania  Algeria  Angola  Argentina  Australia  Austria  Bahamas  Bahrain

Bangladesh  Barbados  Belgium  Benin  Bhutan  Bolivia  Botswana  Brazil  Bulgaria

Burma  Burundi  Byelorussian Soviet Socialist Republic  Canada  Cape Verde  Central African Empire  Chad  Chile  China

Colombia  Comoros  Congo  Costa Rica  Cuba  Cyprus  Czechoslovakia  Democratic Kampuchea  Democratic Yemen

Denmark  Dominican Republic  Ecuador  Egypt  El Salvador  Equatorial Guinea  Ethiopia  Fiji  Finland

France  Gabon  Gambia  German Democratic Republic  Germany (Federal Republic of)  Ghana  Greece  Grenada  Guatemala

Guinea  Guinea-Bissau  Guyana  Haiti  Honduras  Hungary  Iceland  India  Indonesia

Iran  Iraq  Ireland  Israel  Italy  Ivory Coast  Jamaica  Japan  Jordan

Kenya  Kuwait  Lao People's Dem. Rep.  Lebanon  Lesotho  Liberia  Libyan Arab Republic  Luxembourg  Madagascar

1976
Year

United Nations

147
Member states

Malawi  Malaysia  Maldives  Mali  Malta  Mauritania  Mauritius  Mexico  Mongolia

Morocco  Mozambique  Nepal  Netherlands  New Zealand  Nicaragua  Niger  Nigeria  Norway

Oman  Pakistan  Panama  Papua New Guinea  Paraguay  Peru  Philippines  Poland  Portugal

Qatar  Romania  Rwanda  Samoa  Sao Tome and Principe  Saudi Arabia  Senegal  Seychelles  Sierra Leone

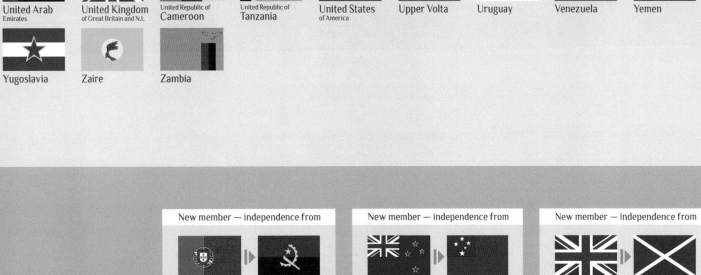

Singapore  Somalia  South Africa  Spain  Sri Lanka  Sudan  Surinam  Swaziland  Sweden

Syrian Arab Republic  Thailand  Togo  Trinidad and Tobago  Tunisia  Turkey  Uganda  Ukrainian Soviet Socialist Republic  USSR Soviet Union

United Arab Emirates  United Kingdom of Great Britain and N.I.  United Republic of Cameroon  United Republic of Tanzania  United States of America  Upper Volta  Uruguay  Venezuela  Yemen

Yugoslavia  Zaire  Zambia

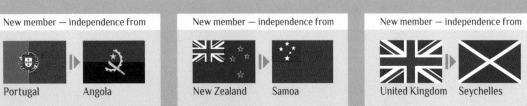

New member — independence from

Portugal  ▷  Angola

New member — independence from

New Zealand  ▷  Samoa

New member — independence from

United Kingdom  ▷  Seychelles

Flag and name change

Cambodia  ▷  Democratic Kampuchea

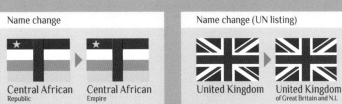

Name change

Central African Republic  ▷  Central African Empire

Name change (UN listing)

United Kingdom  ▷  United Kingdom of Great Britain and N.I.

Name change (UN listing)

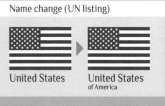

United States  ▷  United States of America

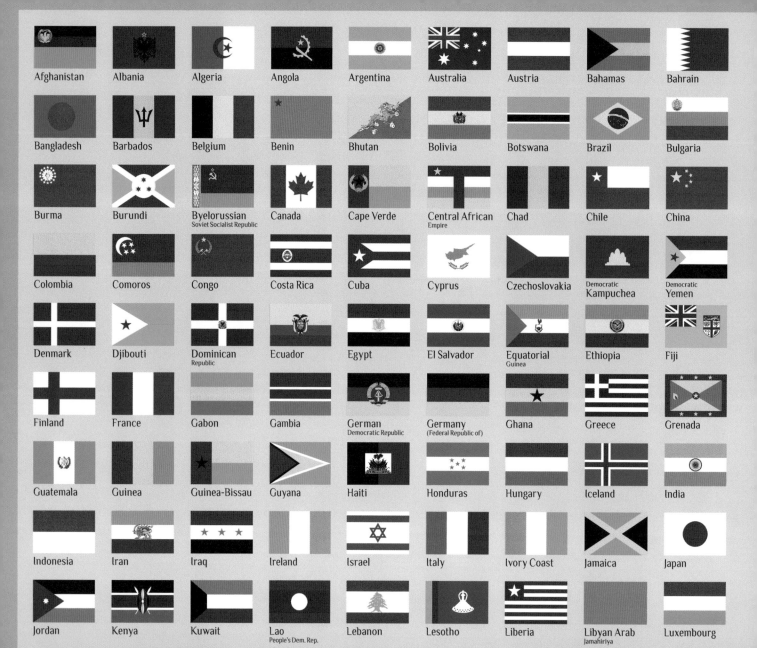

Afghanistan
Albania
Algeria
Angola
Argentina
Australia
Austria
Bahamas
Bahrain

Bangladesh
Barbados
Belgium
Benin
Bhutan
Bolivia
Botswana
Brazil
Bulgaria

Burma
Burundi
Byelorussian
Soviet Socialist Republic
Canada
Cape Verde
Central African
Empire
Chad
Chile
China

Colombia
Comoros
Congo
Costa Rica
Cuba
Cyprus
Czechoslovakia
Democratic
Kampuchea
Democratic
Yemen

Denmark
Djibouti
Dominican
Republic
Ecuador
Egypt
El Salvador
Equatorial
Guinea
Ethiopia
Fiji

Finland
France
Gabon
Gambia
German
Democratic Republic
Germany
(Federal Republic of)
Ghana
Greece
Grenada

Guatemala
Guinea
Guinea-Bissau
Guyana
Haiti
Honduras
Hungary
Iceland
India

Indonesia
Iran
Iraq
Ireland
Israel
Italy
Ivory Coast
Jamaica
Japan

Jordan
Kenya
Kuwait
Lao
People's Dem. Rep.
Lebanon
Lesotho
Liberia
Libyan Arab
Jamahiriya
Luxembourg

1977
Year

United Nations

149
Member states

Madagascar · Malawi · Malaysia · Maldives · Mali · Malta · Mauritania · Mauritius · Mexico

Mongolia · Morocco · Mozambique · Nepal · Netherlands · New Zealand · Nicaragua · Niger · Nigeria

Norway · Oman · Pakistan · Panama · Papua New Guinea · Paraguay · Peru · Philippines · Poland

Portugal · Qatar · Romania · Rwanda · Samoa · Sao Tome and Principe · Saudi Arabia · Senegal · Seychelles

Sierra Leone · Singapore · Somalia · South Africa · Spain · Sri Lanka · Sudan · Surinam · Swaziland

Sweden · Syrian Arab Republic · Thailand · Togo · Trinidad and Tobago · Tunisia · Turkey · Uganda · Ukrainian Soviet Socialist Republic

USSR Soviet Union · United Arab Emirates · United Kingdom of Great Britain and N.I. · United Republic of Cameroon · United Republic of Tanzania · United States of America · Upper Volta · Uruguay · Venezuela

Viet Nam · Yemen · Yugoslavia · Zaire · Zambia

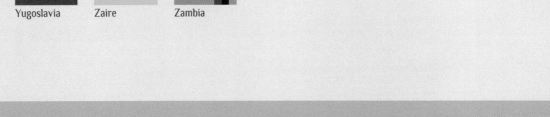

New member
Viet Nam

New member — independence from
France ▷ Djibouti

Flag and name change
Libyan Arab Republic ▷ Libyan Arab Jamahiriya

Flag change
Seychelles ▷ Seychelles

Flag change
Spain ▷ Spain

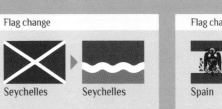

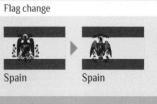

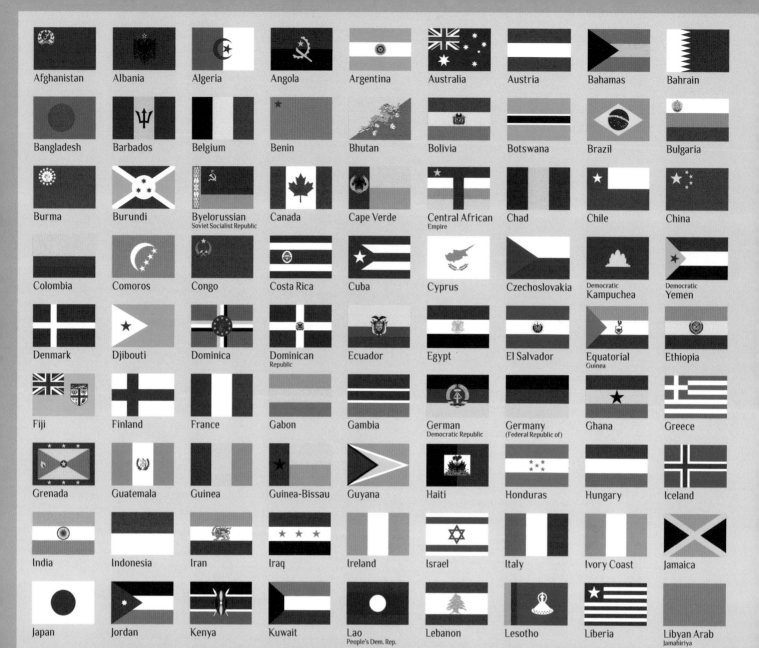

Afghanistan | Albania | Algeria | Angola | Argentina | Australia | Austria | Bahamas | Bahrain

Bangladesh | Barbados | Belgium | Benin | Bhutan | Bolivia | Botswana | Brazil | Bulgaria

Burma | Burundi | Byelorussian Soviet Socialist Republic | Canada | Cape Verde | Central African Empire | Chad | Chile | China

Colombia | Comoros | Congo | Costa Rica | Cuba | Cyprus | Czechoslovakia | Democratic Kampuchea | Democratic Yemen

Denmark | Djibouti | Dominica | Dominican Republic | Ecuador | Egypt | El Salvador | Equatorial Guinea | Ethiopia

Fiji | Finland | France | Gabon | Gambia | German Democratic Republic | Germany (Federal Republic of) | Ghana | Greece

Grenada | Guatemala | Guinea | Guinea-Bissau | Guyana | Haiti | Honduras | Hungary | Iceland

India | Indonesia | Iran | Iraq | Ireland | Israel | Italy | Ivory Coast | Jamaica

Japan | Jordan | Kenya | Kuwait | Lao People's Dem. Rep. | Lebanon | Lesotho | Liberia | Libyan Arab Jamahiriya

1978
Year

United Nations

151
Member states

Luxembourg | Madagascar | Malawi | Malaysia | Maldives | Mali | Malta | Mauritania | Mauritius

Mexico | Mongolia | Morocco | Mozambique | Nepal | Netherlands | New Zealand | Nicaragua | Niger

Nigeria | Norway | Oman | Pakistan | Panama | Papua New Guinea | Paraguay | Peru | Philippines

Poland | Portugal | Qatar | Romania | Rwanda | Samoa | Sao Tome and Principe | Saudi Arabia | Senegal

Seychelles | Sierra Leone | Singapore | Solomon Islands | Somalia | South Africa | Spain | Sri Lanka | Sudan

Suriname | Swaziland | Sweden | Syrian Arab Republic | Thailand | Togo | Trinidad and Tobago | Tunisia | Turkey

Uganda | Ukrainian Soviet Socialist Republic | USSR Soviet Union | United Arab Emirates | United Kingdom of Great Britain and N.I. | United Republic of Cameroon | United Republic of Tanzania | United States of America | Upper Volta

Uruguay | Venezuela | Viet Nam | Yemen | Yugoslavia | Zaire | Zambia

Two new members — independence from

United Kingdom of Great Britain and N.I. | Dominica | Solomon Islands

Name change

Surinam | Suriname

Two flag changes

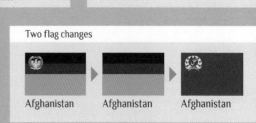

Afghanistan | Afghanistan | Afghanistan

Flag change

Comoros | Comoros

Flag change

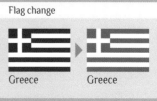

Greece | Greece

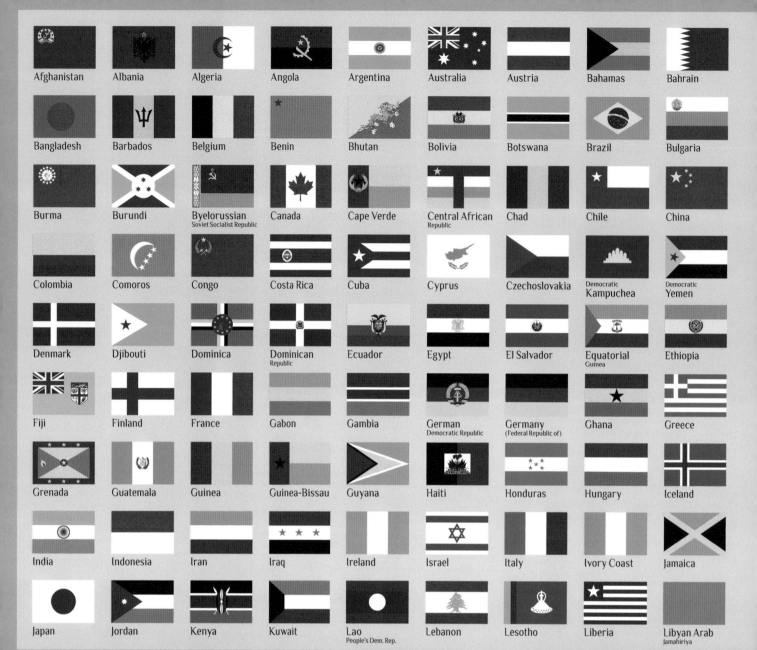

Afghanistan · Albania · Algeria · Angola · Argentina · Australia · Austria · Bahamas · Bahrain

Bangladesh · Barbados · Belgium · Benin · Bhutan · Bolivia · Botswana · Brazil · Bulgaria

Burma · Burundi · Byelorussian Soviet Socialist Republic · Canada · Cape Verde · Central African Republic · Chad · Chile · China

Colombia · Comoros · Congo · Costa Rica · Cuba · Cyprus · Czechoslovakia · Democratic Kampuchea · Democratic Yemen

Denmark · Djibouti · Dominica · Dominican Republic · Ecuador · Egypt · El Salvador · Equatorial Guinea · Ethiopia

Fiji · Finland · France · Gabon · Gambia · German Democratic Republic · Germany (Federal Republic of) · Ghana · Greece

Grenada · Guatemala · Guinea · Guinea-Bissau · Guyana · Haiti · Honduras · Hungary · Iceland

India · Indonesia · Iran · Iraq · Ireland · Israel · Italy · Ivory Coast · Jamaica

Japan · Jordan · Kenya · Kuwait · Lao People's Dem. Rep. · Lebanon · Lesotho · Liberia · Libyan Arab Jamahiriya

1979
Year

United Nations

152
Member states

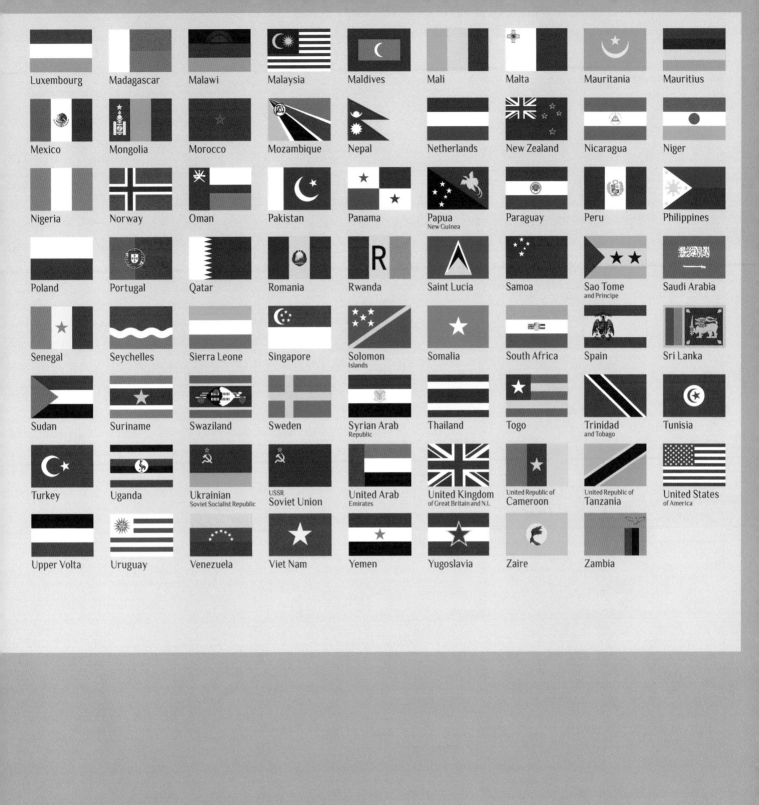

Luxembourg    Madagascar    Malawi    Malaysia    Maldives    Mali    Malta    Mauritania    Mauritius

Mexico    Mongolia    Morocco    Mozambique    Nepal    Netherlands    New Zealand    Nicaragua    Niger

Nigeria    Norway    Oman    Pakistan    Panama    Papua New Guinea    Paraguay    Peru    Philippines

Poland    Portugal    Qatar    Romania    Rwanda    Saint Lucia    Samoa    Sao Tome and Principe    Saudi Arabia

Senegal    Seychelles    Sierra Leone    Singapore    Solomon Islands    Somalia    South Africa    Spain    Sri Lanka

Sudan    Suriname    Swaziland    Sweden    Syrian Arab Republic    Thailand    Togo    Trinidad and Tobago    Tunisia

Turkey    Uganda    Ukrainian Soviet Socialist Republic    USSR Soviet Union    United Arab Emirates    United Kingdom of Great Britain and N.I.    United Republic of Cameroon    United Republic of Tanzania    United States of America

Upper Volta    Uruguay    Venezuela    Viet Nam    Yemen    Yugoslavia    Zaire    Zambia

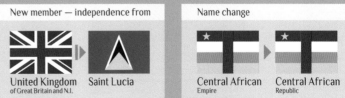

New member — independence from

United Kingdom of Great Britain and N.I. ▶ Saint Lucia

Name change

Central African Empire ▶ Central African Republic

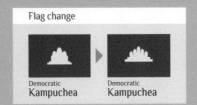

Flag change

Democratic Kampuchea ▶ Democratic Kampuchea

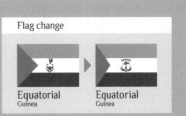

Flag change

Equatorial Guinea ▶ Equatorial Guinea

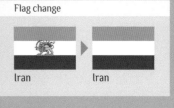

Flag change

Iran ▶ Iran

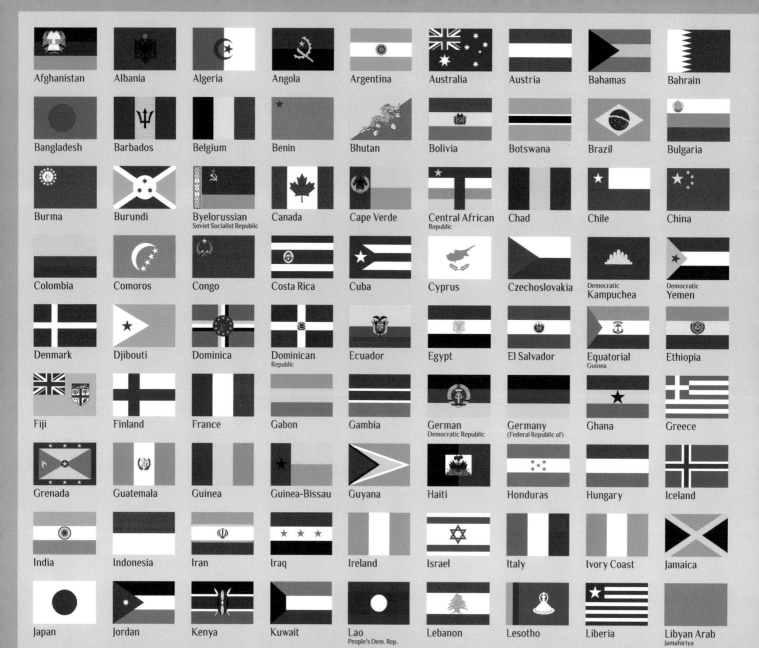

Afghanistan · Albania · Algeria · Angola · Argentina · Australia · Austria · Bahamas · Bahrain

Bangladesh · Barbados · Belgium · Benin · Bhutan · Bolivia · Botswana · Brazil · Bulgaria

Burma · Burundi · Byelorussian Soviet Socialist Republic · Canada · Cape Verde · Central African Republic · Chad · Chile · China

Colombia · Comoros · Congo · Costa Rica · Cuba · Cyprus · Czechoslovakia · Democratic Kampuchea · Democratic Yemen

Denmark · Djibouti · Dominica · Dominican Republic · Ecuador · Egypt · El Salvador · Equatorial Guinea · Ethiopia

Fiji · Finland · France · Gabon · Gambia · German Democratic Republic · Germany (Federal Republic of) · Ghana · Greece

Grenada · Guatemala · Guinea · Guinea-Bissau · Guyana · Haiti · Honduras · Hungary · Iceland

India · Indonesia · Iran · Iraq · Ireland · Israel · Italy · Ivory Coast · Jamaica

Japan · Jordan · Kenya · Kuwait · Lao People's Dem. Rep. · Lebanon · Lesotho · Liberia · Libyan Arab Jamahiriya

1980
Year

United Nations

154
Member states

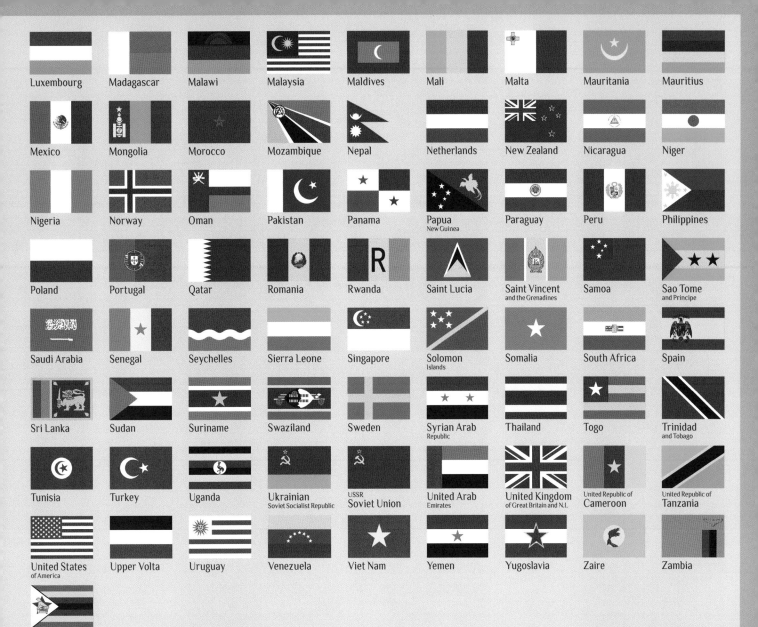

Luxembourg | Madagascar | Malawi | Malaysia | Maldives | Mali | Malta | Mauritania | Mauritius

Mexico | Mongolia | Morocco | Mozambique | Nepal | Netherlands | New Zealand | Nicaragua | Niger

Nigeria | Norway | Oman | Pakistan | Panama | Papua New Guinea | Paraguay | Peru | Philippines

Poland | Portugal | Qatar | Romania | Rwanda | Saint Lucia | Saint Vincent and the Grenadines | Samoa | Sao Tome and Principe

Saudi Arabia | Senegal | Seychelles | Sierra Leone | Singapore | Solomon Islands | Somalia | South Africa | Spain

Sri Lanka | Sudan | Suriname | Swaziland | Sweden | Syrian Arab Republic | Thailand | Togo | Trinidad and Tobago

Tunisia | Turkey | Uganda | Ukrainian Soviet Socialist Republic | USSR Soviet Union | United Arab Emirates | United Kingdom of Great Britain and N.I. | United Republic of Cameroon | United Republic of Tanzania

United States of America | Upper Volta | Uruguay | Venezuela | Viet Nam | Yemen | Yugoslavia | Zaire | Zambia

Zimbabwe

New member — independence from

France ▷ United Kingdom of Great Britain and N.I. ▷ Saint Vincent and the Grenadines

New member — evolution from

United Kingdom of Great Britain and N.I. ▷ Rhodesia ▷ Zimbabwe

Flag change

Afghanistan ▷ Afghanistan

Flag change

Iran ▷ Iran

Flag change

Syrian Arab Republic ▷ Syrian Arab Republic

Flag change

USSR Soviet Union ▷ USSR Soviet Union

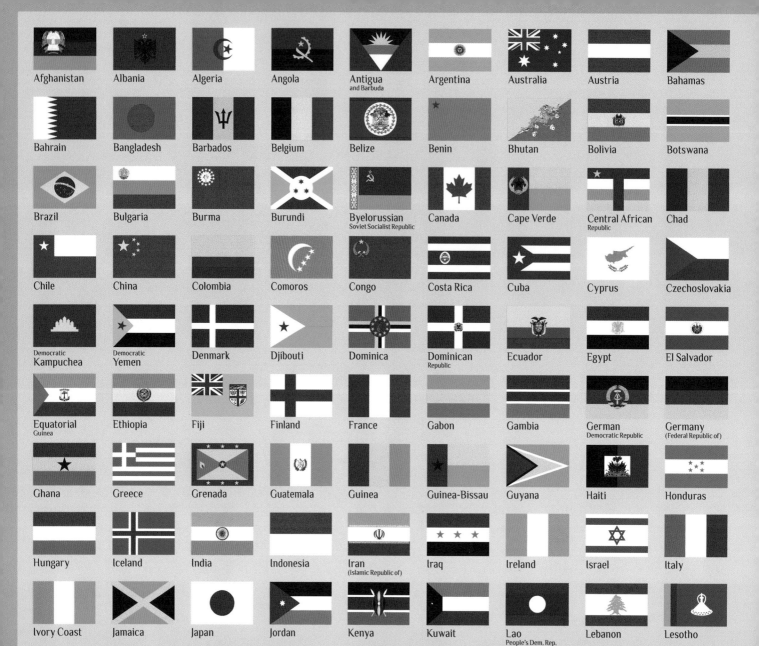

Afghanistan
Albania
Algeria
Angola
Antigua and Barbuda
Argentina
Australia
Austria
Bahamas

Bahrain
Bangladesh
Barbados
Belgium
Belize
Benin
Bhutan
Bolivia
Botswana

Brazil
Bulgaria
Burma
Burundi
Byelorussian Soviet Socialist Republic
Canada
Cape Verde
Central African Republic
Chad

Chile
China
Colombia
Comoros
Congo
Costa Rica
Cuba
Cyprus
Czechoslovakia

Democratic Kampuchea
Democratic Yemen
Denmark
Djibouti
Dominica
Dominican Republic
Ecuador
Egypt
El Salvador

Equatorial Guinea
Ethiopia
Fiji
Finland
France
Gabon
Gambia
German Democratic Republic
Germany (Federal Republic of)

Ghana
Greece
Grenada
Guatemala
Guinea
Guinea-Bissau
Guyana
Haiti
Honduras

Hungary
Iceland
India
Indonesia
Iran (Islamic Republic of)
Iraq
Ireland
Israel
Italy

Ivory Coast
Jamaica
Japan
Jordan
Kenya
Kuwait
Lao People's Dem. Rep.
Lebanon
Lesotho

1981
Year

United Nations

157
Member states

| | | | | | | | | |
|---|---|---|---|---|---|---|---|---|
| Liberia | Libyan Arab Jamahiriya | Luxembourg | Madagascar | Malawi | Malaysia | Maldives | Mali | Malta |
| Mauritania | Mauritius | Mexico | Mongolia | Morocco | Mozambique | Nepal | Netherlands | New Zealand |
| Nicaragua | Niger | Nigeria | Norway | Oman | Pakistan | Panama | Papua New Guinea | Paraguay |
| Peru | Philippines | Poland | Portugal | Qatar | Romania | Rwanda | Saint Lucia | Saint Vincent and the Grenadines |
| Samoa | Sao Tome and Principe | Saudi Arabia | Senegal | Seychelles | Sierra Leone | Singapore | Solomon Islands | Somalia |
| South Africa | Spain | Sri Lanka | Sudan | Suriname | Swaziland | Sweden | Syrian Arab Republic | Thailand |
| Togo | Trinidad and Tobago | Tunisia | Turkey | Uganda | Ukrainian Soviet Socialist Republic | USSR Soviet Union | United Arab Emirates | United Kingdom of Great Britain and N.I. |
| United Republic of Cameroon | United Republic of Tanzania | United States of America | Upper Volta | Uruguay | Vanuatu | Venezuela | Viet Nam | Yemen |
| Yugoslavia | Zaire | Zambia | Zimbabwe | | | | | |

Three new members — independence from

United Kingdom of Great Britain and N.I.

Antigua and Barbuda

Belize

Vanuatu

Name change

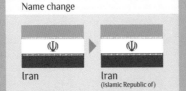

Iran → Iran (Islamic Republic of)

Flag change

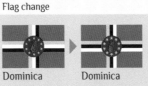

Dominica → Dominica

Flag change

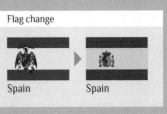

Spain → Spain

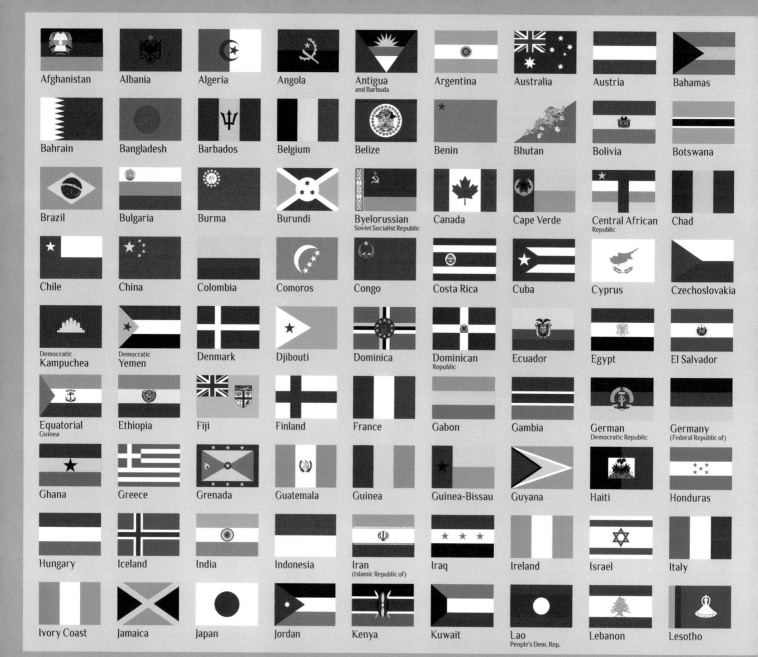

Afghanistan · Albania · Algeria · Angola · Antigua and Barbuda · Argentina · Australia · Austria · Bahamas

Bahrain · Bangladesh · Barbados · Belgium · Belize · Benin · Bhutan · Bolivia · Botswana

Brazil · Bulgaria · Burma · Burundi · Byelorussian Soviet Socialist Republic · Canada · Cape Verde · Central African Republic · Chad

Chile · China · Colombia · Comoros · Congo · Costa Rica · Cuba · Cyprus · Czechoslovakia

Democratic Kampuchea · Democratic Yemen · Denmark · Djibouti · Dominica · Dominican Republic · Ecuador · Egypt · El Salvador

Equatorial Guinea · Ethiopia · Fiji · Finland · France · Gabon · Gambia · German Democratic Republic · Germany (Federal Republic of)

Ghana · Greece · Grenada · Guatemala · Guinea · Guinea-Bissau · Guyana · Haiti · Honduras

Hungary · Iceland · India · Indonesia · Iran (Islamic Republic of) · Iraq · Ireland · Israel · Italy

Ivory Coast · Jamaica · Japan · Jordan · Kenya · Kuwait · Lao People's Dem. Rep. · Lebanon · Lesotho

## No changes in 1982

Timeline                    page 80

**1983**
Year

United Nations

**158**
Member states

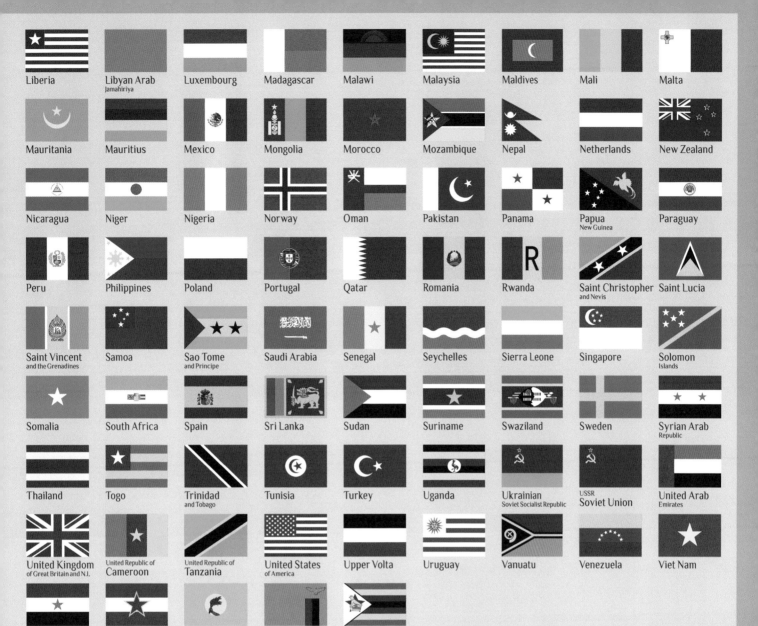

| | | | | | | | | |
|---|---|---|---|---|---|---|---|---|
| Liberia | Libyan Arab Jamahiriya | Luxembourg | Madagascar | Malawi | Malaysia | Maldives | Mali | Malta |
| Mauritania | Mauritius | Mexico | Mongolia | Morocco | Mozambique | Nepal | Netherlands | New Zealand |
| Nicaragua | Niger | Nigeria | Norway | Oman | Pakistan | Panama | Papua New Guinea | Paraguay |
| Peru | Philippines | Poland | Portugal | Qatar | Romania | Rwanda | Saint Christopher and Nevis | Saint Lucia |
| Saint Vincent and the Grenadines | Samoa | Sao Tome and Principe | Saudi Arabia | Senegal | Seychelles | Sierra Leone | Singapore | Solomon Islands |
| Somalia | South Africa | Spain | Sri Lanka | Sudan | Suriname | Swaziland | Sweden | Syrian Arab Republic |
| Thailand | Togo | Trinidad and Tobago | Tunisia | Turkey | Uganda | Ukrainian Soviet Socialist Republic | USSR Soviet Union | United Arab Emirates |
| United Kingdom of Great Britain and N.I. | United Republic of Cameroon | United Republic of Tanzania | United States of America | Upper Volta | Uruguay | Vanuatu | Venezuela | Viet Nam |
| Yemen | Yugoslavia | Zaire | Zambia | Zimbabwe | | | | |

New member — independence from

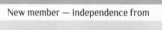

United Kingdom of Great Britain and N.I.

Saint Christopher and Nevis

Flag change

Mozambique

Mozambique

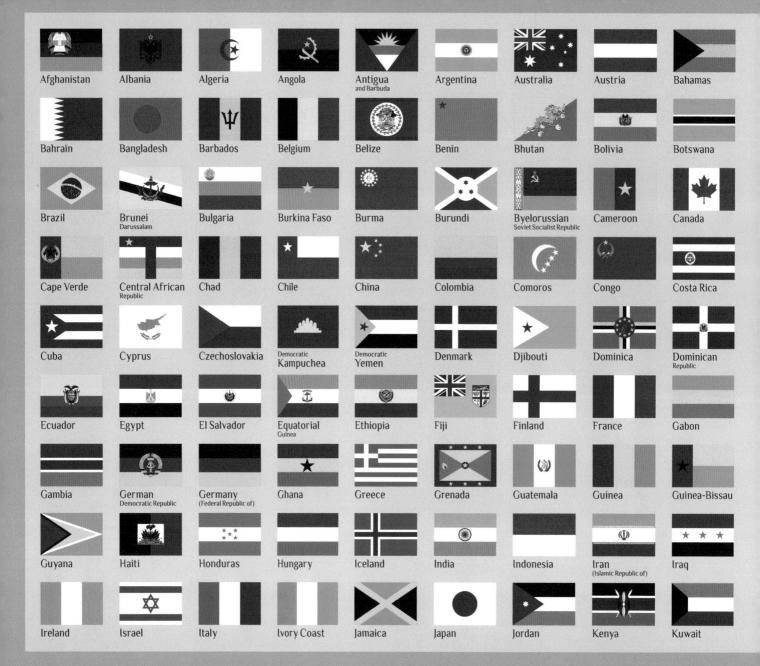

Afghanistan
Albania
Algeria
Angola
Antigua and Barbuda
Argentina
Australia
Austria
Bahamas

Bahrain
Bangladesh
Barbados
Belgium
Belize
Benin
Bhutan
Bolivia
Botswana

Brazil
Brunei Darussalam
Bulgaria
Burkina Faso
Burma
Burundi
Byelorussian Soviet Socialist Republic
Cameroon
Canada

Cape Verde
Central African Republic
Chad
Chile
China
Colombia
Comoros
Congo
Costa Rica

Cuba
Cyprus
Czechoslovakia
Democratic Kampuchea
Democratic Yemen
Denmark
Djibouti
Dominica
Dominican Republic

Ecuador
Egypt
El Salvador
Equatorial Guinea
Ethiopia
Fiji
Finland
France
Gabon

Gambia
German Democratic Republic
Germany (Federal Republic of)
Ghana
Greece
Grenada
Guatemala
Guinea
Guinea-Bissau

Guyana
Haiti
Honduras
Hungary
Iceland
India
Indonesia
Iran (Islamic Republic of)
Iraq

Ireland
Israel
Italy
Ivory Coast
Jamaica
Japan
Jordan
Kenya
Kuwait

1984
Year

United Nations

159
Member states

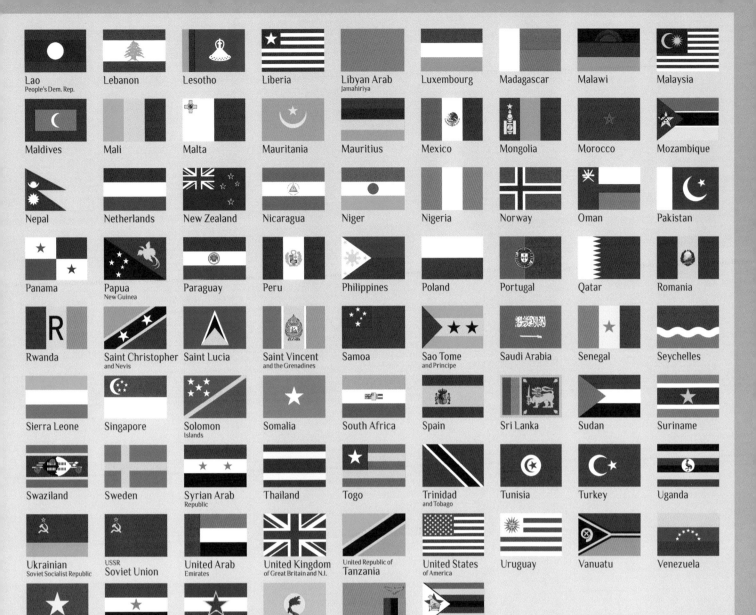

Lao People's Dem. Rep. | Lebanon | Lesotho | Liberia | Libyan Arab Jamahiriya | Luxembourg | Madagascar | Malawi | Malaysia

Maldives | Mali | Malta | Mauritania | Mauritius | Mexico | Mongolia | Morocco | Mozambique

Nepal | Netherlands | New Zealand | Nicaragua | Niger | Nigeria | Norway | Oman | Pakistan

Panama | Papua New Guinea | Paraguay | Peru | Philippines | Poland | Portugal | Qatar | Romania

Rwanda | Saint Christopher and Nevis | Saint Lucia | Saint Vincent and the Grenadines | Samoa | Sao Tome and Principe | Saudi Arabia | Senegal | Seychelles

Sierra Leone | Singapore | Solomon Islands | Somalia | South Africa | Spain | Sri Lanka | Sudan | Suriname

Swaziland | Sweden | Syrian Arab Republic | Thailand | Togo | Trinidad and Tobago | Tunisia | Turkey | Uganda

Ukrainian Soviet Socialist Republic | USSR Soviet Union | United Arab Emirates | United Kingdom of Great Britain and N.I. | United Republic of Tanzania | United States of America | Uruguay | Vanuatu | Venezuela

Viet Nam | Yemen | Yugoslavia | Zaire | Zambia | Zimbabwe

New member — independence from

United Kingdom of Great Britain and N.I. ▸ Brunei Darussalam

Flag and name change

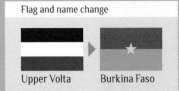

Upper Volta ▸ Burkina Faso

Name change

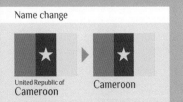

United Republic of Cameroon ▸ Cameroon

Flag change

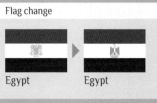

Egypt ▸ Egypt

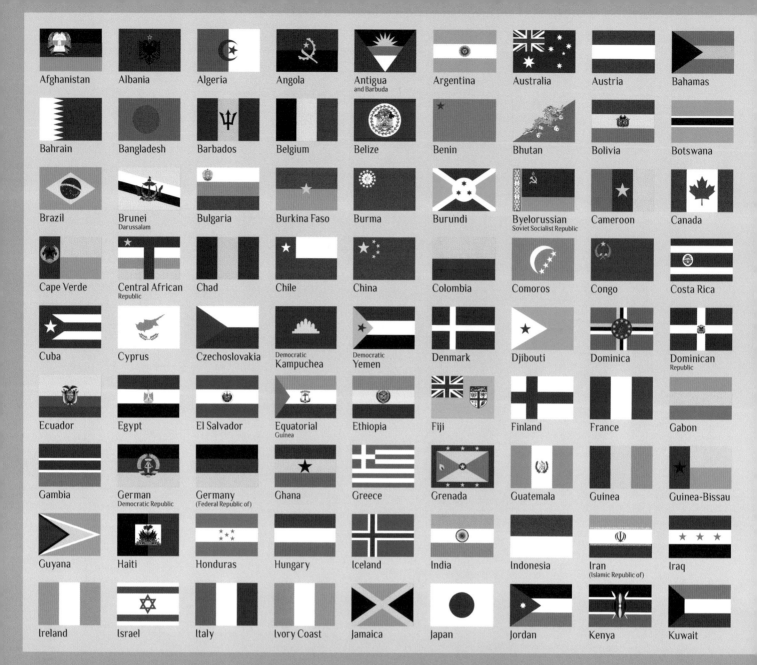

Afghanistan · Albania · Algeria · Angola · Antigua and Barbuda · Argentina · Australia · Austria · Bahamas

Bahrain · Bangladesh · Barbados · Belgium · Belize · Benin · Bhutan · Bolivia · Botswana

Brazil · Brunei Darussalam · Bulgaria · Burkina Faso · Burma · Burundi · Byelorussian Soviet Socialist Republic · Cameroon · Canada

Cape Verde · Central African Republic · Chad · Chile · China · Colombia · Comoros · Congo · Costa Rica

Cuba · Cyprus · Czechoslovakia · Democratic Kampuchea · Democratic Yemen · Denmark · Djibouti · Dominica · Dominican Republic

Ecuador · Egypt · El Salvador · Equatorial Guinea · Ethiopia · Fiji · Finland · France · Gabon

Gambia · German Democratic Republic · Germany (Federal Republic of) · Ghana · Greece · Grenada · Guatemala · Guinea · Guinea-Bissau

Guyana · Haiti · Honduras · Hungary · Iceland · India · Indonesia · Iran (Islamic Republic of) · Iraq

Ireland · Israel · Italy · Ivory Coast · Jamaica · Japan · Jordan · Kenya · Kuwait

Timeline                    page 84

1985
Year

United Nations

159
Member states

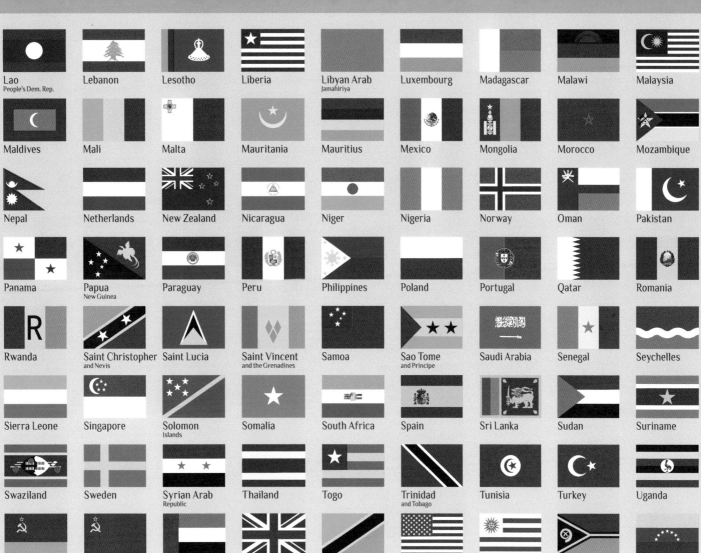

Lao
People's Dem. Rep.

Lebanon

Lesotho

Liberia

Libyan Arab
Jamahiriya

Luxembourg

Madagascar

Malawi

Malaysia

Maldives

Mali

Malta

Mauritania

Mauritius

Mexico

Mongolia

Morocco

Mozambique

Nepal

Netherlands

New Zealand

Nicaragua

Niger

Nigeria

Norway

Oman

Pakistan

Panama

Papua
New Guinea

Paraguay

Peru

Philippines

Poland

Portugal

Qatar

Romania

Rwanda

Saint Christopher
and Nevis

Saint Lucia

Saint Vincent
and the Grenadines

Samoa

Sao Tome
and Principe

Saudi Arabia

Senegal

Seychelles

Sierra Leone

Singapore

Solomon
Islands

Somalia

South Africa

Spain

Sri Lanka

Sudan

Suriname

Swaziland

Sweden

Syrian Arab
Republic

Thailand

Togo

Trinidad
and Tobago

Tunisia

Turkey

Uganda

Ukrainian
Soviet Socialist Republic

USSR
Soviet Union

United Arab
Emirates

United Kingdom
of Great Britain and N.I.

United Republic of
Tanzania

United States
of America

Uruguay

Vanuatu

Venezuela

Viet Nam

Yemen

Yugoslavia

Zaire

Zambia

Zimbabwe

Two flag changes

Saint Vincent
and the Grenadines

Saint Vincent
and the Grenadines

Saint Vincent
and the Grenadines

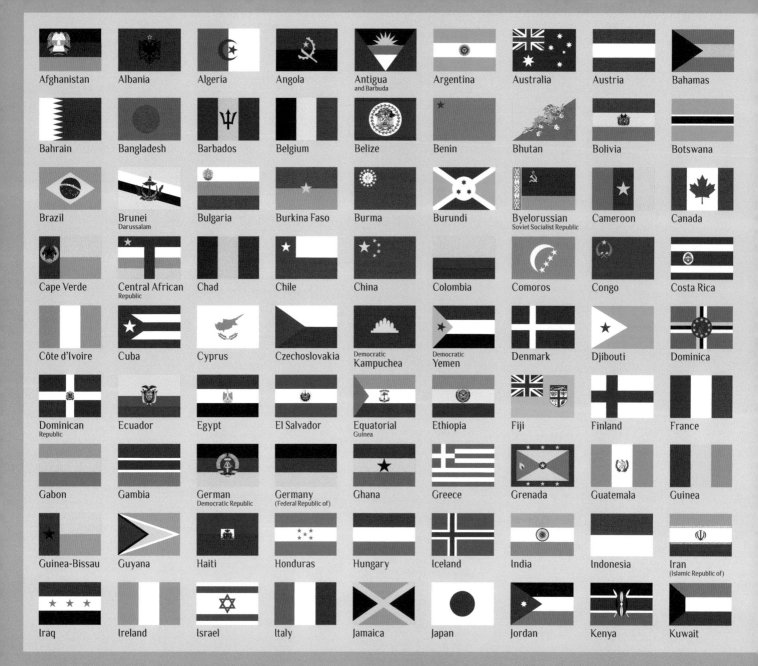

Afghanistan · Albania · Algeria · Angola · Antigua and Barbuda · Argentina · Australia · Austria · Bahamas

Bahrain · Bangladesh · Barbados · Belgium · Belize · Benin · Bhutan · Bolivia · Botswana

Brazil · Brunei Darussalam · Bulgaria · Burkina Faso · Burma · Burundi · Byelorussian Soviet Socialist Republic · Cameroon · Canada

Cape Verde · Central African Republic · Chad · Chile · China · Colombia · Comoros · Congo · Costa Rica

Côte d'Ivoire · Cuba · Cyprus · Czechoslovakia · Democratic Kampuchea · Democratic Yemen · Denmark · Djibouti · Dominica

Dominican Republic · Ecuador · Egypt · El Salvador · Equatorial Guinea · Ethiopia · Fiji · Finland · France

Gabon · Gambia · German Democratic Republic · Germany (Federal Republic of) · Ghana · Greece · Grenada · Guatemala · Guinea

Guinea-Bissau · Guyana · Haiti · Honduras · Hungary · Iceland · India · Indonesia · Iran (Islamic Republic of)

Iraq · Ireland · Israel · Italy · Jamaica · Japan · Jordan · Kenya · Kuwait

1986 — Year

United Nations

159 — Member states

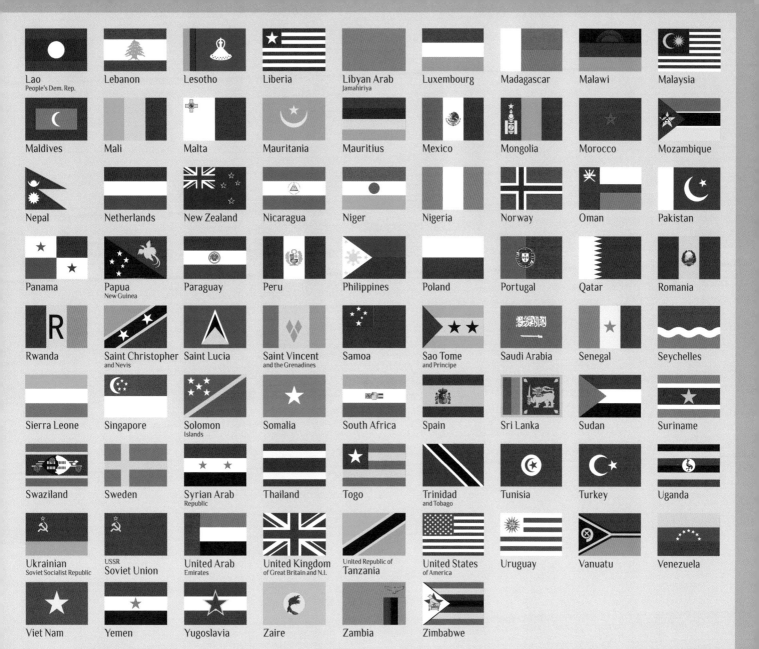

Lao
People's Dem. Rep.

Lebanon

Lesotho

Liberia

Libyan Arab
Jamahiriya

Luxembourg

Madagascar

Malawi

Malaysia

Maldives

Mali

Malta

Mauritania

Mauritius

Mexico

Mongolia

Morocco

Mozambique

Nepal

Netherlands

New Zealand

Nicaragua

Niger

Nigeria

Norway

Oman

Pakistan

Panama

Papua
New Guinea

Paraguay

Peru

Philippines

Poland

Portugal

Qatar

Romania

Rwanda

Saint Christopher
and Nevis

Saint Lucia

Saint Vincent
and the Grenadines

Samoa

Sao Tome
and Principe

Saudi Arabia

Senegal

Seychelles

Sierra Leone

Singapore

Solomon
Islands

Somalia

South Africa

Spain

Sri Lanka

Sudan

Suriname

Swaziland

Sweden

Syrian Arab
Republic

Thailand

Togo

Trinidad
and Tobago

Tunisia

Turkey

Uganda

Ukrainian
Soviet Socialist Republic

USSR
Soviet Union

United Arab
Emirates

United Kingdom
of Great Britain and N.I.

United Republic of
Tanzania

United States
of America

Uruguay

Vanuatu

Venezuela

Viet Nam

Yemen

Yugoslavia

Zaire

Zambia

Zimbabwe

Name change

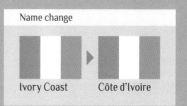

Ivory Coast

Côte d'Ivoire

Flag change

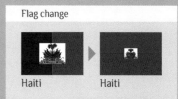

Haiti

Haiti

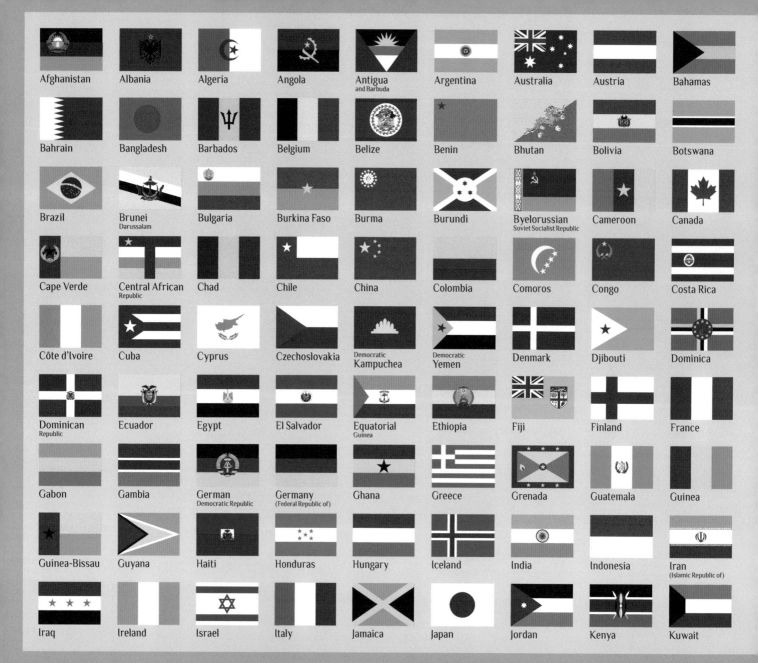

Afghanistan • Albania • Algeria • Angola • Antigua and Barbuda • Argentina • Australia • Austria • Bahamas

Bahrain • Bangladesh • Barbados • Belgium • Belize • Benin • Bhutan • Bolivia • Botswana

Brazil • Brunei Darussalam • Bulgaria • Burkina Faso • Burma • Burundi • Byelorussian Soviet Socialist Republic • Cameroon • Canada

Cape Verde • Central African Republic • Chad • Chile • China • Colombia • Comoros • Congo • Costa Rica

Côte d'Ivoire • Cuba • Cyprus • Czechoslovakia • Democratic Kampuchea • Democratic Yemen • Denmark • Djibouti • Dominica

Dominican Republic • Ecuador • Egypt • El Salvador • Equatorial Guinea • Ethiopia • Fiji • Finland • France

Gabon • Gambia • German Democratic Republic • Germany (Federal Republic of) • Ghana • Greece • Grenada • Guatemala • Guinea

Guinea-Bissau • Guyana • Haiti • Honduras • Hungary • Iceland • India • Indonesia • Iran (Islamic Republic of)

Iraq • Ireland • Israel • Italy • Jamaica • Japan • Jordan • Kenya • Kuwait

1987
Year

United Nations

159
Member states

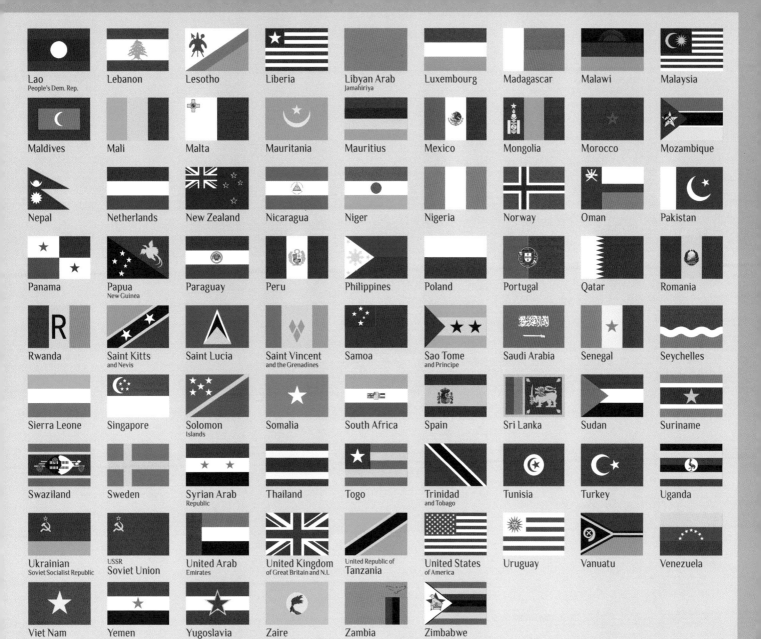

Lao
People's Dem. Rep.

Lebanon

Lesotho

Liberia

Libyan Arab
Jamahiriya

Luxembourg

Madagascar

Malawi

Malaysia

Maldives

Mali

Malta

Mauritania

Mauritius

Mexico

Mongolia

Morocco

Mozambique

Nepal

Netherlands

New Zealand

Nicaragua

Niger

Nigeria

Norway

Oman

Pakistan

Panama

Papua
New Guinea

Paraguay

Peru

Philippines

Poland

Portugal

Qatar

Romania

Rwanda

Saint Kitts
and Nevis

Saint Lucia

Saint Vincent
and the Grenadines

Samoa

Sao Tome
and Principe

Saudi Arabia

Senegal

Seychelles

Sierra Leone

Singapore

Solomon
Islands

Somalia

South Africa

Spain

Sri Lanka

Sudan

Suriname

Swaziland

Sweden

Syrian Arab
Republic

Thailand

Togo

Trinidad
and Tobago

Tunisia

Turkey

Uganda

Ukrainian
Soviet Socialist Republic

USSR
Soviet Union

United Arab
Emirates

United Kingdom
of Great Britain and N.I.

United Republic of
Tanzania

United States
of America

Uruguay

Vanuatu

Venezuela

Viet Nam

Yemen

Yugoslavia

Zaire

Zambia

Zimbabwe

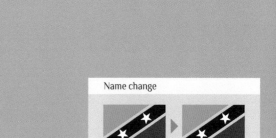

Name change

Saint Christopher
and Nevis

Saint Kitts
and Nevis

Flag change

Afghanistan

Afghanistan

Flag change

Ethiopia

Ethiopia

Flag change

Lesotho

Lesotho

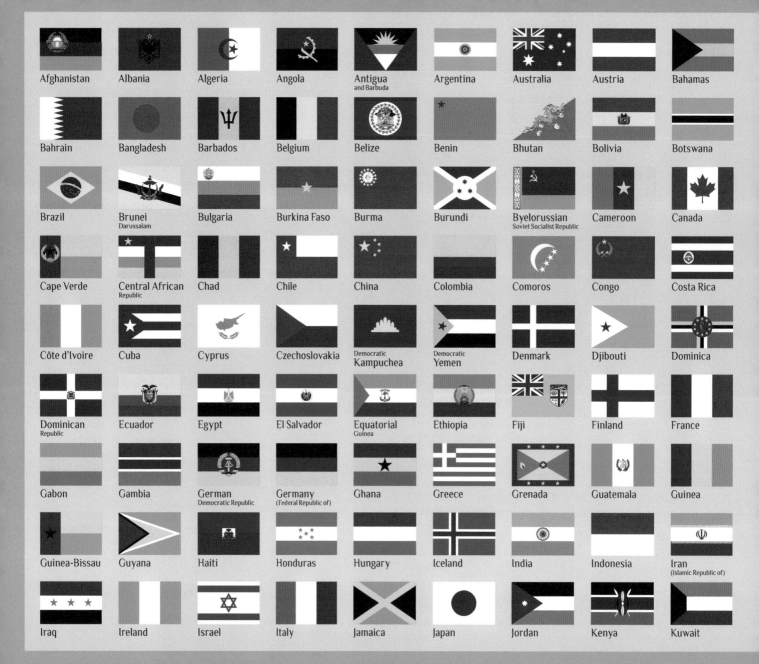

Afghanistan | Albania | Algeria | Angola | Antigua and Barbuda | Argentina | Australia | Austria | Bahamas

Bahrain | Bangladesh | Barbados | Belgium | Belize | Benin | Bhutan | Bolivia | Botswana

Brazil | Brunei Darussalam | Bulgaria | Burkina Faso | Burma | Burundi | Byelorussian Soviet Socialist Republic | Cameroon | Canada

Cape Verde | Central African Republic | Chad | Chile | China | Colombia | Comoros | Congo | Costa Rica

Côte d'Ivoire | Cuba | Cyprus | Czechoslovakia | Democratic Kampuchea | Democratic Yemen | Denmark | Djibouti | Dominica

Dominican Republic | Ecuador | Egypt | El Salvador | Equatorial Guinea | Ethiopia | Fiji | Finland | France

Gabon | Gambia | German Democratic Republic | Germany (Federal Republic of) | Ghana | Greece | Grenada | Guatemala | Guinea

Guinea-Bissau | Guyana | Haiti | Honduras | Hungary | Iceland | India | Indonesia | Iran (Islamic Republic of)

Iraq | Ireland | Israel | Italy | Jamaica | Japan | Jordan | Kenya | Kuwait

1988 | United Nations | 159
Year | | Member states

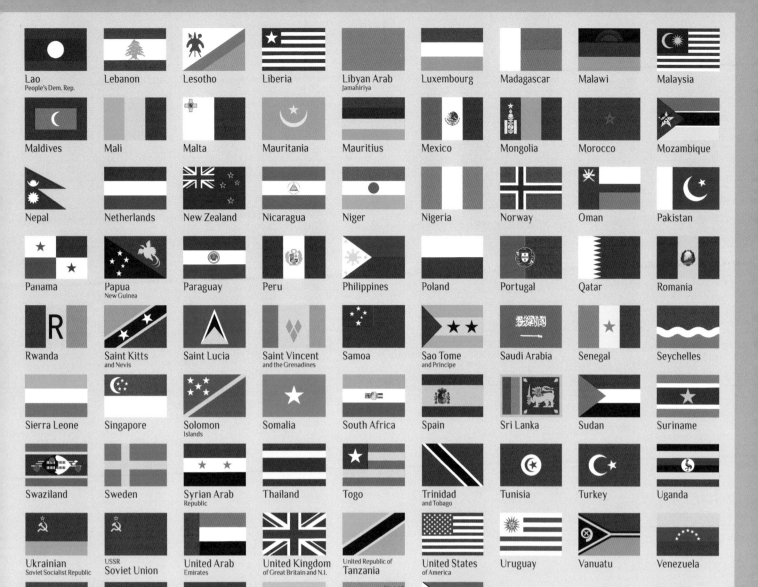

| | | | | | | | | |
|---|---|---|---|---|---|---|---|---|
| Lao People's Dem. Rep. | Lebanon | Lesotho | Liberia | Libyan Arab Jamahiriya | Luxembourg | Madagascar | Malawi | Malaysia |
| Maldives | Mali | Malta | Mauritania | Mauritius | Mexico | Mongolia | Morocco | Mozambique |
| Nepal | Netherlands | New Zealand | Nicaragua | Niger | Nigeria | Norway | Oman | Pakistan |
| Panama | Papua New Guinea | Paraguay | Peru | Philippines | Poland | Portugal | Qatar | Romania |
| Rwanda | Saint Kitts and Nevis | Saint Lucia | Saint Vincent and the Grenadines | Samoa | Sao Tome and Principe | Saudi Arabia | Senegal | Seychelles |
| Sierra Leone | Singapore | Solomon Islands | Somalia | South Africa | Spain | Sri Lanka | Sudan | Suriname |
| Swaziland | Sweden | Syrian Arab Republic | Thailand | Togo | Trinidad and Tobago | Tunisia | Turkey | Uganda |
| Ukrainian Soviet Socialist Republic | USSR Soviet Union | United Arab Emirates | United Kingdom of Great Britain and N.I. | United Republic of Tanzania | United States of America | Uruguay | Vanuatu | Venezuela |
| Viet Nam | Yemen | Yugoslavia | Zaire | Zambia | Zimbabwe | | | |

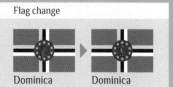

Flag change

Dominica → Dominica

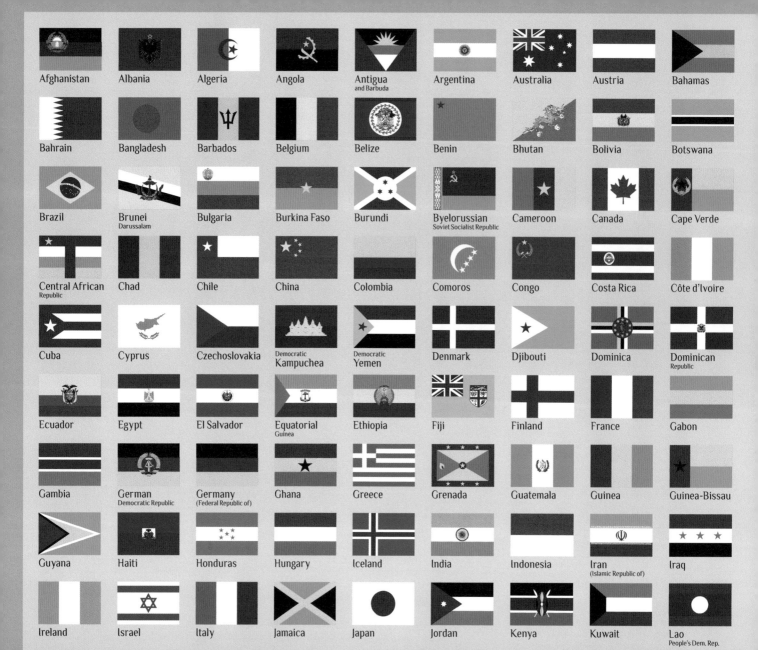

Afghanistan · Albania · Algeria · Angola · Antigua and Barbuda · Argentina · Australia · Austria · Bahamas

Bahrain · Bangladesh · Barbados · Belgium · Belize · Benin · Bhutan · Bolivia · Botswana

Brazil · Brunei Darussalam · Bulgaria · Burkina Faso · Burundi · Byelorussian Soviet Socialist Republic · Cameroon · Canada · Cape Verde

Central African Republic · Chad · Chile · China · Colombia · Comoros · Congo · Costa Rica · Côte d'Ivoire

Cuba · Cyprus · Czechoslovakia · Democratic Kampuchea · Democratic Yemen · Denmark · Djibouti · Dominica · Dominican Republic

Ecuador · Egypt · El Salvador · Equatorial Guinea · Ethiopia · Fiji · Finland · France · Gabon

Gambia · German Democratic Republic · Germany (Federal Republic of) · Ghana · Greece · Grenada · Guatemala · Guinea · Guinea-Bissau

Guyana · Haiti · Honduras · Hungary · Iceland · India · Indonesia · Iran (Islamic Republic of) · Iraq

Ireland · Israel · Italy · Jamaica · Japan · Jordan · Kenya · Kuwait · Lao People's Dem. Rep.

1989 — Year

United Nations

159 — Member states

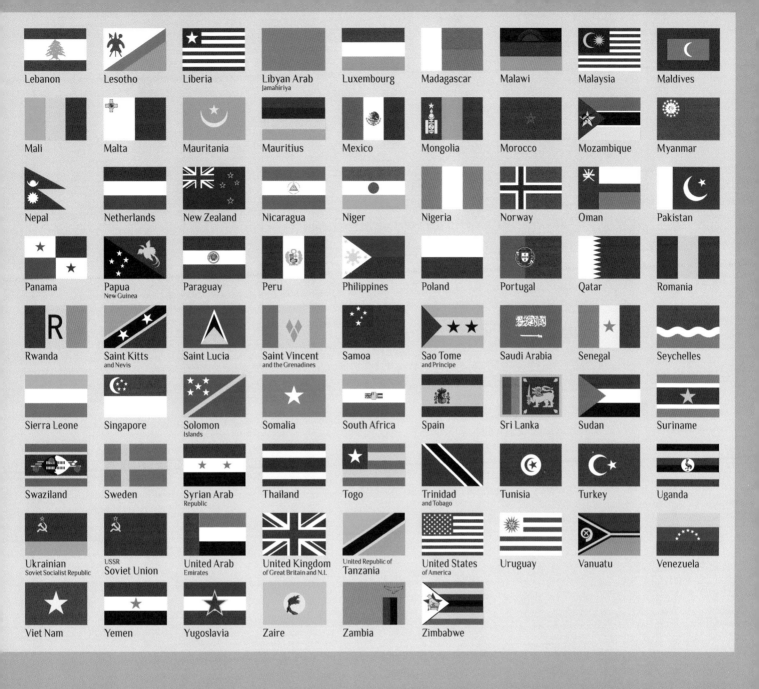

Lebanon

Lesotho

Liberia

Libyan Arab
Jamahiriya

Luxembourg

Madagascar

Malawi

Malaysia

Maldives

Mali

Malta

Mauritania

Mauritius

Mexico

Mongolia

Morocco

Mozambique

Myanmar

Nepal

Netherlands

New Zealand

Nicaragua

Niger

Nigeria

Norway

Oman

Pakistan

Panama

Papua
New Guinea

Paraguay

Peru

Philippines

Poland

Portugal

Qatar

Romania

Rwanda

Saint Kitts
and Nevis

Saint Lucia

Saint Vincent
and the Grenadines

Samoa

Sao Tome
and Principe

Saudi Arabia

Senegal

Seychelles

Sierra Leone

Singapore

Solomon
Islands

Somalia

South Africa

Spain

Sri Lanka

Sudan

Suriname

Swaziland

Sweden

Syrian Arab
Republic

Thailand

Togo

Trinidad
and Tobago

Tunisia

Turkey

Uganda

Ukrainian
Soviet Socialist Republic

USSR
Soviet Union

United Arab
Emirates

United Kingdom
of Great Britain and N.I.

United Republic of
Tanzania

United States
of America

Uruguay

Vanuatu

Venezuela

Viet Nam

Yemen

Yugoslavia

Zaire

Zambia

Zimbabwe

Name change

Burma

Myanmar

Flag change

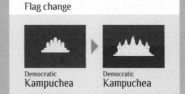

Democratic
Kampuchea

Democratic
Kampuchea

Flag change

Romania

Romania

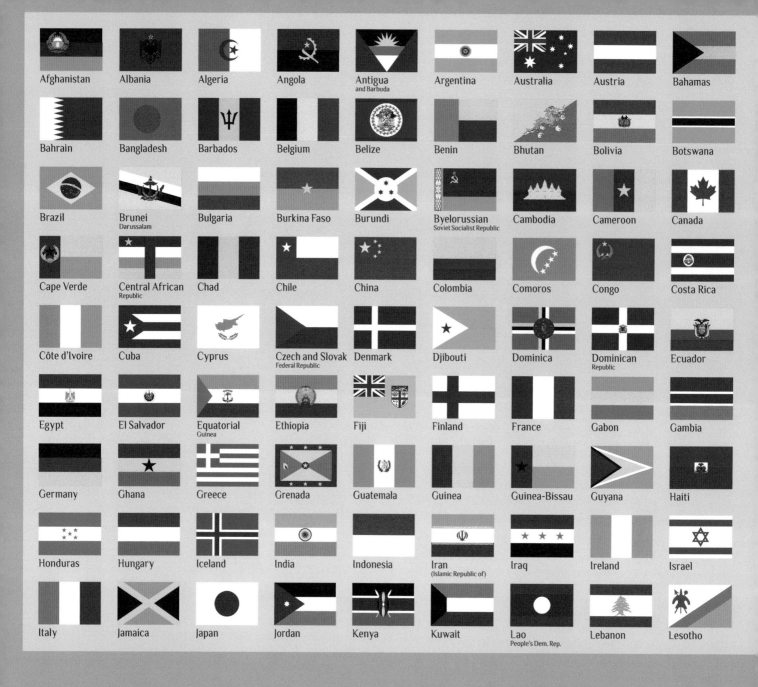

| | | | | | | | | |
|---|---|---|---|---|---|---|---|---|
| Afghanistan | Albania | Algeria | Angola | Antigua and Barbuda | Argentina | Australia | Austria | Bahamas |
| Bahrain | Bangladesh | Barbados | Belgium | Belize | Benin | Bhutan | Bolivia | Botswana |
| Brazil | Brunei Darussalam | Bulgaria | Burkina Faso | Burundi | Byelorussian Soviet Socialist Republic | Cambodia | Cameroon | Canada |
| Cape Verde | Central African Republic | Chad | Chile | China | Colombia | Comoros | Congo | Costa Rica |
| Côte d'Ivoire | Cuba | Cyprus | Czech and Slovak Federal Republic | Denmark | Djibouti | Dominica | Dominican Republic | Ecuador |
| Egypt | El Salvador | Equatorial Guinea | Ethiopia | Fiji | Finland | France | Gabon | Gambia |
| Germany | Ghana | Greece | Grenada | Guatemala | Guinea | Guinea-Bissau | Guyana | Haiti |
| Honduras | Hungary | Iceland | India | Indonesia | Iran (Islamic Republic of) | Iraq | Ireland | Israel |
| Italy | Jamaica | Japan | Jordan | Kenya | Kuwait | Lao People's Dem. Rep. | Lebanon | Lesotho |

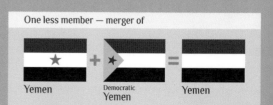

One less member — merger of

Yemen + Democratic Yemen = Yemen

Timeline                          page 94

1990
Year

United Nations

159
Member states

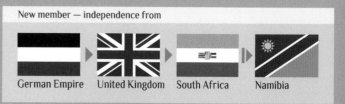

New member — independence from

German Empire ▶ United Kingdom ▶ South Africa ▷ Namibia

Liberia
Libyan Arab Jamahiriya
Liechtenstein
Luxembourg
Madagascar
Malawi
Malaysia
Maldives
Mali

Malta
Mauritania
Mauritius
Mexico
Mongolia
Morocco
Mozambique
Myanmar
Namibia

Nepal
Netherlands
New Zealand
Nicaragua
Niger
Nigeria
Norway
Oman
Pakistan

Panama
Papua New Guinea
Paraguay
Peru
Philippines
Poland
Portugal
Qatar
Romania

Rwanda
Saint Kitts and Nevis
Saint Lucia
Saint Vincent and the Grenadines
Samoa
Sao Tome and Principe
Saudi Arabia
Senegal
Seychelles

Sierra Leone
Singapore
Solomon Islands
Somalia
South Africa
Spain
Sri Lanka
Sudan
Suriname

Swaziland
Sweden
Syrian Arab Republic
Thailand
Togo
Trinidad and Tobago
Tunisia
Turkey
Uganda

Ukrainian Soviet Socialist Republic
USSR Soviet Union
United Arab Emirates
United Kingdom of Great Britain and N.I.
United Republic of Tanzania
United States of America
Uruguay
Vanuatu
Venezuela

Viet Nam
Yemen
Yugoslavia
Zaire
Zambia
Zimbabwe

New member

Liechtenstein

One less member — accession to

German Democratic Republic ▶ Germany (Federal Republic of)

Name change (UN listing)

Germany (Federal Republic of) ▶ Germany

Name change

Czechoslovakia ▶ Czech and Slovak Federal Republic

Name change

Democratic Kampuchea ▶ Cambodia

Flag change

Benin ▶ Benin

Flag change

Bulgaria ▶ Bulgaria

Flag change

Dominica ▶ Dominica

Flag change

Paraguay ▶ Paraguay

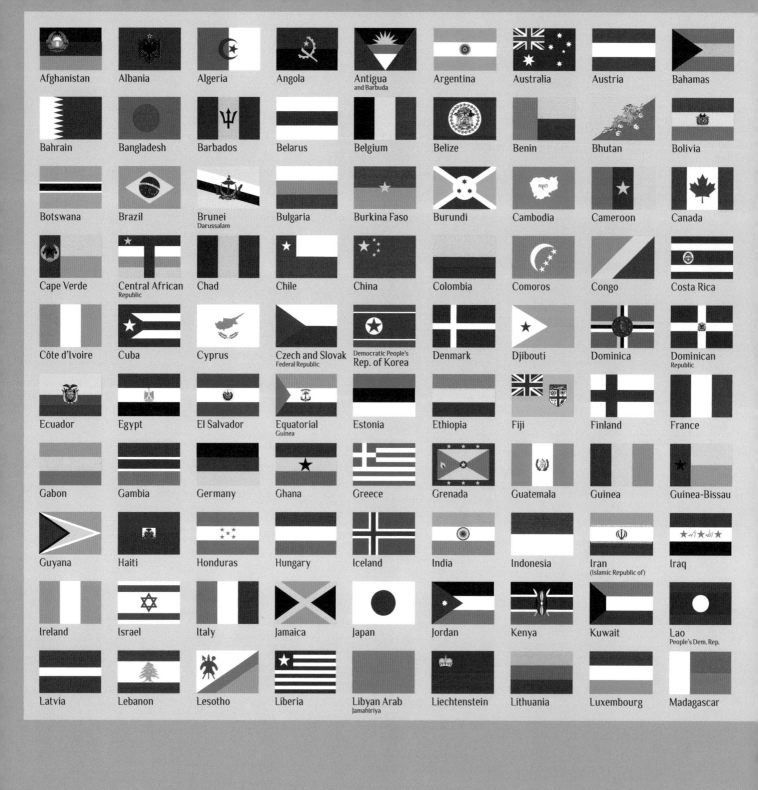

| | | | | | | | | |
|---|---|---|---|---|---|---|---|---|
| Afghanistan | Albania | Algeria | Angola | Antigua and Barbuda | Argentina | Australia | Austria | Bahamas |
| Bahrain | Bangladesh | Barbados | Belarus | Belgium | Belize | Benin | Bhutan | Bolivia |
| Botswana | Brazil | Brunei Darussalam | Bulgaria | Burkina Faso | Burundi | Cambodia | Cameroon | Canada |
| Cape Verde | Central African Republic | Chad | Chile | China | Colombia | Comoros | Congo | Costa Rica |
| Côte d'Ivoire | Cuba | Cyprus | Czech and Slovak Federal Republic | Democratic People's Rep. of Korea | Denmark | Djibouti | Dominica | Dominican Republic |
| Ecuador | Egypt | El Salvador | Equatorial Guinea | Estonia | Ethiopia | Fiji | Finland | France |
| Gabon | Gambia | Germany | Ghana | Greece | Grenada | Guatemala | Guinea | Guinea-Bissau |
| Guyana | Haiti | Honduras | Hungary | Iceland | India | Indonesia | Iran (Islamic Republic of) | Iraq |
| Ireland | Israel | Italy | Jamaica | Japan | Jordan | Kenya | Kuwait | Lao People's Dem. Rep. |
| Latvia | Lebanon | Lesotho | Liberia | Libyan Arab Jamahiriya | Liechtenstein | Lithuania | Luxembourg | Madagascar |

**Two new members**

Democratic People's Rep. of Korea — Republic of Korea

**Two new members — independence from**

United States of America ▶ Marshall Islands — Micronesia (Federated States of)

**Timeline** page 96

1991 Year — United Nations — 166 Member states

**Flag and name change**

USSR Soviet Union ▶ Russian Federation

**Flag change**

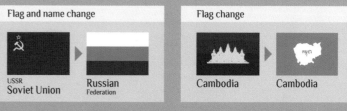

Cambodia ▶ Cambodia

Malawi · Malaysia · Maldives · Mali · Malta · Marshall Islands · Mauritania · Mauritius · Mexico

Micronesia (Federated States of) · Mongolia · Morocco · Mozambique · Myanmar · Namibia · Nepal · Netherlands · New Zealand

Nicaragua · Niger · Nigeria · Norway · Oman · Pakistan · Panama · Papua New Guinea · Paraguay

Peru · Philippines · Poland · Portugal · Qatar · Republic of Korea · Romania · Russian Federation · Rwanda

Saint Kitts and Nevis · Saint Lucia · Saint Vincent and the Grenadines · Samoa · Sao Tome and Principe · Saudi Arabia · Senegal · Seychelles · Sierra Leone

Singapore · Solomon Islands · Somalia · South Africa · Spain · Sri Lanka · Sudan · Suriname · Swaziland

Sweden · Syrian Arab Republic · Thailand · Togo · Trinidad and Tobago · Tunisia · Turkey · Uganda · Ukraine

United Arab Emirates · United Kingdom of Great Britain and N.I. · United Republic of Tanzania · United States of America · Uruguay · Vanuatu · Venezuela · Viet Nam · Yemen

Yugoslavia · Zaire · Zambia · Zimbabwe

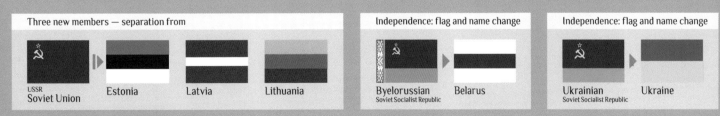

Three new members — separation from

USSR Soviet Union ▶ Estonia · Latvia · Lithuania

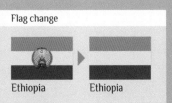

Independence: flag and name change

Byelorussian Soviet Socialist Republic ▶ Belarus

Independence: flag and name change

Ukrainian Soviet Socialist Republic ▶ Ukraine

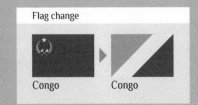

Flag change

Congo ▶ Congo

Flag change

Ethiopia ▶ Ethiopia

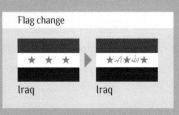

Flag change

Iraq ▶ Iraq

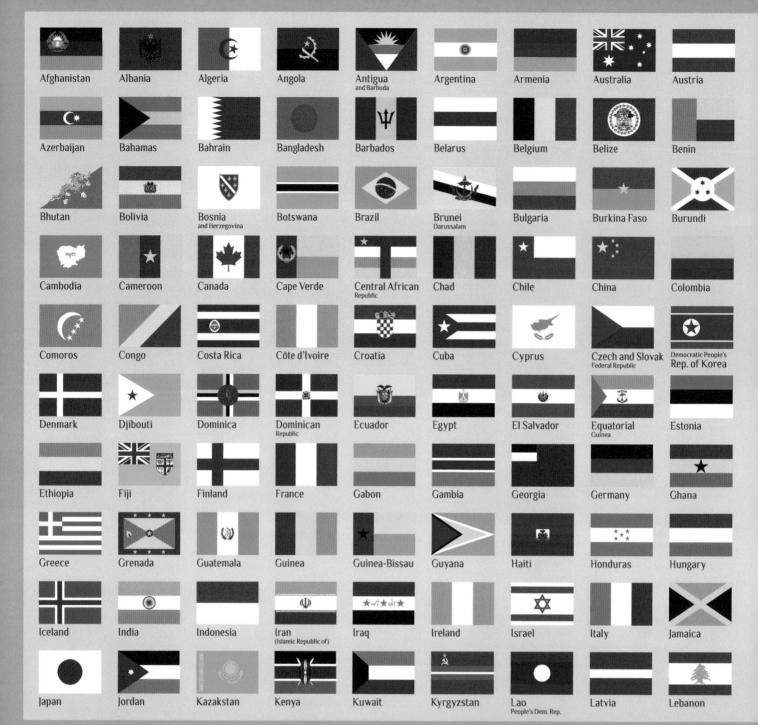

Afghanistan · Albania · Algeria · Angola · Antigua and Barbuda · Argentina · Armenia · Australia · Austria

Azerbaijan · Bahamas · Bahrain · Bangladesh · Barbados · Belarus · Belgium · Belize · Benin

Bhutan · Bolivia · Bosnia and Herzegovina · Botswana · Brazil · Brunei Darussalam · Bulgaria · Burkina Faso · Burundi

Cambodia · Cameroon · Canada · Cape Verde · Central African Republic · Chad · Chile · China · Colombia

Comoros · Congo · Costa Rica · Côte d'Ivoire · Croatia · Cuba · Cyprus · Czech and Slovak Federal Republic · Democratic People's Rep. of Korea

Denmark · Djibouti · Dominica · Dominican Republic · Ecuador · Egypt · El Salvador · Equatorial Guinea · Estonia

Ethiopia · Fiji · Finland · France · Gabon · Gambia · Georgia · Germany · Ghana

Greece · Grenada · Guatemala · Guinea · Guinea-Bissau · Guyana · Haiti · Honduras · Hungary

Iceland · India · Indonesia · Iran (Islamic Republic of) · Iraq · Ireland · Israel · Italy · Jamaica

Japan · Jordan · Kazakstan · Kenya · Kuwait · Kyrgyzstan · Lao People's Dem. Rep. · Latvia · Lebanon

Timeline                                    page 98

1992 PART ONE
Year

United Nations

179
Member states

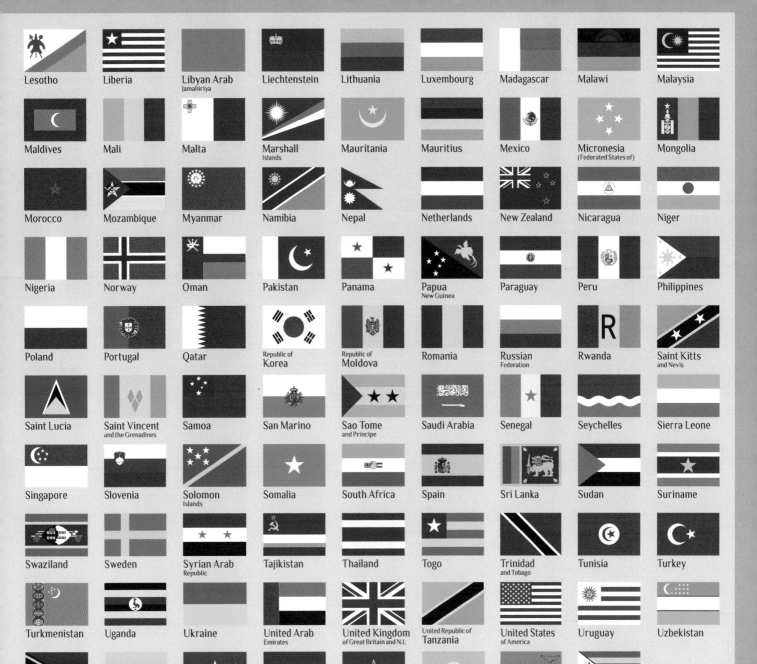

| | | | | | | | | |
|---|---|---|---|---|---|---|---|---|
| Lesotho | Liberia | Libyan Arab Jamahiriya | Liechtenstein | Lithuania | Luxembourg | Madagascar | Malawi | Malaysia |
| Maldives | Mali | Malta | Marshall Islands | Mauritania | Mauritius | Mexico | Micronesia (Federated States of) | Mongolia |
| Morocco | Mozambique | Myanmar | Namibia | Nepal | Netherlands | New Zealand | Nicaragua | Niger |
| Nigeria | Norway | Oman | Pakistan | Panama | Papua New Guinea | Paraguay | Peru | Philippines |
| Poland | Portugal | Qatar | Republic of Korea | Republic of Moldova | Romania | Russian Federation | Rwanda | Saint Kitts and Nevis |
| Saint Lucia | Saint Vincent and the Grenadines | Samoa | San Marino | Sao Tome and Principe | Saudi Arabia | Senegal | Seychelles | Sierra Leone |
| Singapore | Slovenia | Solomon Islands | Somalia | South Africa | Spain | Sri Lanka | Sudan | Suriname |
| Swaziland | Sweden | Syrian Arab Republic | Tajikistan | Thailand | Togo | Trinidad and Tobago | Tunisia | Turkey |
| Turkmenistan | Uganda | Ukraine | United Arab Emirates | United Kingdom of Great Britain and N.I. | United Republic of Tanzania | United States of America | Uruguay | Uzbekistan |
| Vanuatu | Venezuela | Viet Nam | Yemen | Yugoslavia | Zaire | Zambia | Zimbabwe | |

**New member**

San Marino

**Three new members — separation from**

| Yugoslavia | Bosnia and Herzegovina | Croatia | Slovenia |
|---|---|---|---|

**Nine new members — separation from**

| USSR Soviet Union | Armenia | Azerbaijan | Georgia | Kazakstan |
|---|---|---|---|---|
| Kyrgyzstan | Republic of Moldova | Tajikistan | Turkmenistan | Uzbekistan |

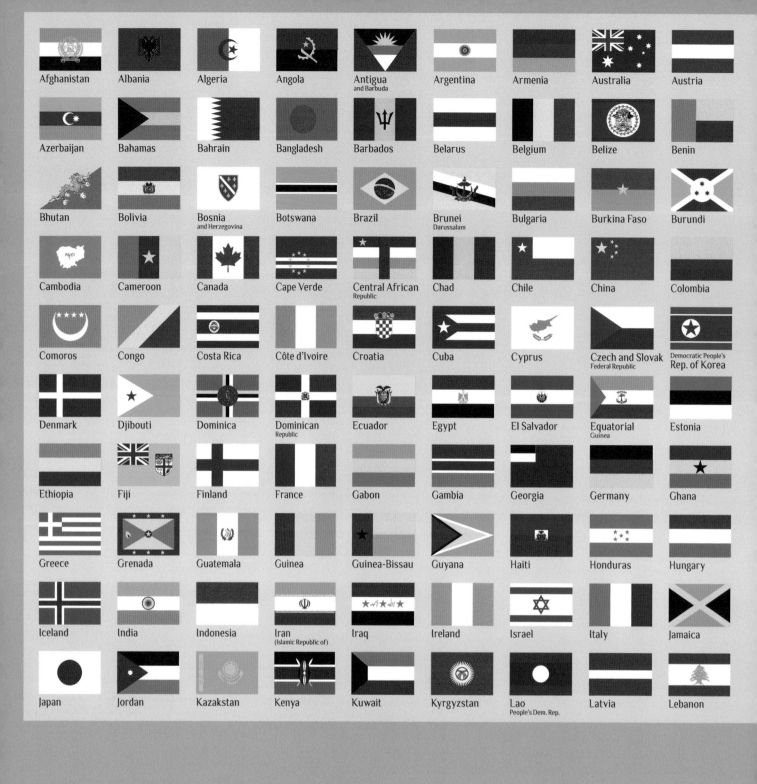

Afghanistan  Albania  Algeria  Angola  Antigua and Barbuda  Argentina  Armenia  Australia  Austria

Azerbaijan  Bahamas  Bahrain  Bangladesh  Barbados  Belarus  Belgium  Belize  Benin

Bhutan  Bolivia  Bosnia and Herzegovina  Botswana  Brazil  Brunei Darussalam  Bulgaria  Burkina Faso  Burundi

Cambodia  Cameroon  Canada  Cape Verde  Central African Republic  Chad  Chile  China  Colombia

Comoros  Congo  Costa Rica  Côte d'Ivoire  Croatia  Cuba  Cyprus  Czech and Slovak Federal Republic  Democratic People's Rep. of Korea

Denmark  Djibouti  Dominica  Dominican Republic  Ecuador  Egypt  El Salvador  Equatorial Guinea  Estonia

Ethiopia  Fiji  Finland  France  Gabon  Gambia  Georgia  Germany  Ghana

Greece  Grenada  Guatemala  Guinea  Guinea-Bissau  Guyana  Haiti  Honduras  Hungary

Iceland  India  Indonesia  Iran (Islamic Republic of)  Iraq  Ireland  Israel  Italy  Jamaica

Japan  Jordan  Kazakstan  Kenya  Kuwait  Kyrgyzstan  Lao People's Dem. Rep.  Latvia  Lebanon

Timeline  page 100

1992 PART TWO
Year

United Nations

179
Member states

Flag change

Afghanistan ▶ Afghanistan

Flag change

Albania ▶ Albania

Flag change

Comoros ▶ Comoros

Flag change

Mongolia ▶ Mongolia

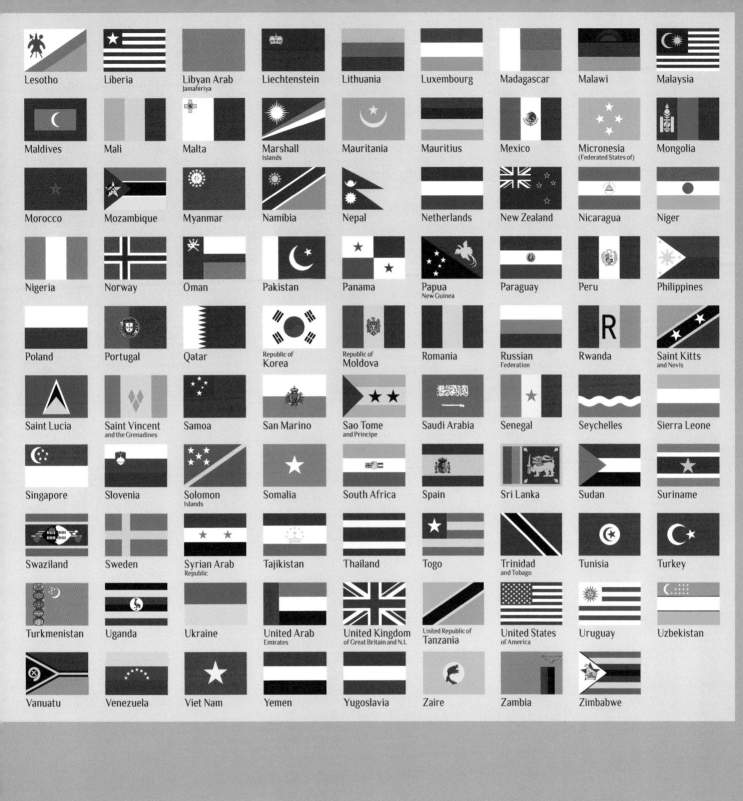

| | | | | | | | | |
|---|---|---|---|---|---|---|---|---|
| Lesotho | Liberia | Libyan Arab Jamahiriya | Liechtenstein | Lithuania | Luxembourg | Madagascar | Malawi | Malaysia |
| Maldives | Mali | Malta | Marshall Islands | Mauritania | Mauritius | Mexico | Micronesia (Federated States of) | Mongolia |
| Morocco | Mozambique | Myanmar | Namibia | Nepal | Netherlands | New Zealand | Nicaragua | Niger |
| Nigeria | Norway | Oman | Pakistan | Panama | Papua New Guinea | Paraguay | Peru | Philippines |
| Poland | Portugal | Qatar | Republic of Korea | Republic of Moldova | Romania | Russian Federation | Rwanda | Saint Kitts and Nevis |
| Saint Lucia | Saint Vincent and the Grenadines | Samoa | San Marino | Sao Tome and Principe | Saudi Arabia | Senegal | Seychelles | Sierra Leone |
| Singapore | Slovenia | Solomon Islands | Somalia | South Africa | Spain | Sri Lanka | Sudan | Suriname |
| Swaziland | Sweden | Syrian Arab Republic | Tajikistan | Thailand | Togo | Trinidad and Tobago | Tunisia | Turkey |
| Turkmenistan | Uganda | Ukraine | United Arab Emirates | United Kingdom of Great Britain and N.I. | United Republic of Tanzania | United States of America | Uruguay | Uzbekistan |
| Vanuatu | Venezuela | Viet Nam | Yemen | Yugoslavia | Zaire | Zambia | Zimbabwe | |

Flag change

Brazil ▸ Brazil

Flag change

Democratic People's Rep. of Korea ▸ Democratic People's Rep. of Korea

Flag change

Cape Verde ▸ Cape Verde

Flag change

Yugoslavia ▸ Yugoslavia

Two flag changes

Kyrgyzstan ▸ Kyrgyzstan ▸ Kyrgyzstan

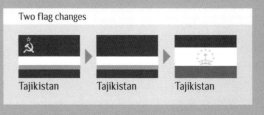

Two flag changes

Tajikistan ▸ Tajikistan ▸ Tajikistan

Afghanistan · Albania · Algeria · Andorra · Angola · Antigua and Barbuda · Argentina · Armenia · Australia

Austria · Azerbaijan · Bahamas · Bahrain · Bangladesh · Barbados · Belarus · Belgium · Belize

Benin · Bhutan · Bolivia · Bosnia and Herzegovina · Botswana · Brazil · Brunei Darussalam · Bulgaria · Burkina Faso

Burundi · Cambodia · Cameroon · Canada · Cape Verde · Central African Republic · Chad · Chile · China

Colombia · Comoros · Congo · Costa Rica · Côte d'Ivoire · Croatia · Cuba · Cyprus · Czech Republic

Democratic People's Rep. of Korea · Denmark · Djibouti · Dominica · Dominican Republic · Ecuador · Egypt · El Salvador · Equatorial Guinea

Eritrea · Estonia · Ethiopia · Fiji · Finland · France · Gabon · Gambia · Georgia

Germany · Ghana · Greece · Grenada · Guatemala · Guinea · Guinea-Bissau · Guyana · Haiti

Honduras · Hungary · Iceland · India · Indonesia · Iran (Islamic Republic of) · Iraq · Ireland · Israel

Italy · Jamaica · Japan · Jordan · Kazakstan · Kenya · Kuwait · Kyrgyzstan · Lao People's Dem. Rep.

Latvia · Lebanon · Lesotho · Liberia · Libyan Arab Jamahiriya · Liechtenstein · Lithuania · Luxembourg · Madagascar

Timeline                    page 102

1993 — Year

United Nations

184 — Member states

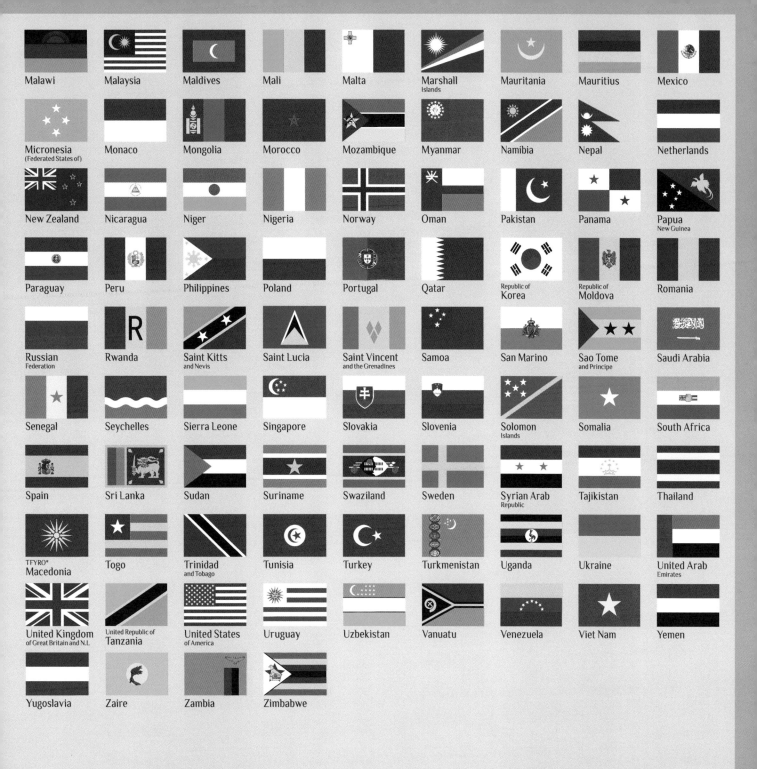

Malawi | Malaysia | Maldives | Mali | Malta | Marshall Islands | Mauritania | Mauritius | Mexico

Micronesia (Federated States of) | Monaco | Mongolia | Morocco | Mozambique | Myanmar | Namibia | Nepal | Netherlands

New Zealand | Nicaragua | Niger | Nigeria | Norway | Oman | Pakistan | Panama | Papua New Guinea

Paraguay | Peru | Philippines | Poland | Portugal | Qatar | Republic of Korea | Republic of Moldova | Romania

Russian Federation | Rwanda | Saint Kitts and Nevis | Saint Lucia | Saint Vincent and the Grenadines | Samoa | San Marino | Sao Tome and Principe | Saudi Arabia

Senegal | Seychelles | Sierra Leone | Singapore | Slovakia | Slovenia | Solomon Islands | Somalia | South Africa

Spain | Sri Lanka | Sudan | Suriname | Swaziland | Sweden | Syrian Arab Republic | Tajikistan | Thailand

TFYRO* Macedonia | Togo | Trinidad and Tobago | Tunisia | Turkey | Turkmenistan | Uganda | Ukraine | United Arab Emirates

United Kingdom of Great Britain and N.I. | United Republic of Tanzania | United States of America | Uruguay | Uzbekistan | Vanuatu | Venezuela | Viet Nam | Yemen

Yugoslavia | Zaire | Zambia | Zimbabwe

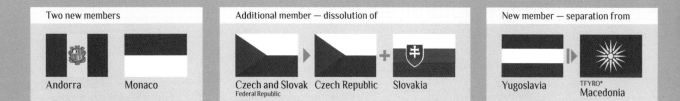

**Two new members**
Andorra | Monaco

**Additional member — dissolution of**
Czech and Slovak Federal Republic ▸ Czech Republic + Slovakia

**New member — separation from**
Yugoslavia ▸ TFYRO* Macedonia

*The Former Yugoslav Republic of

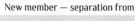

**New member — separation from**
Kingdom of Italy | United Kingdom of Great Britain and N.I. | Ethiopia ▸ Eritrea

**Flag change**
Cambodia ▸ Cambodia

**Flag change**
Russian Federation ▸ Russian Federation

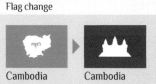

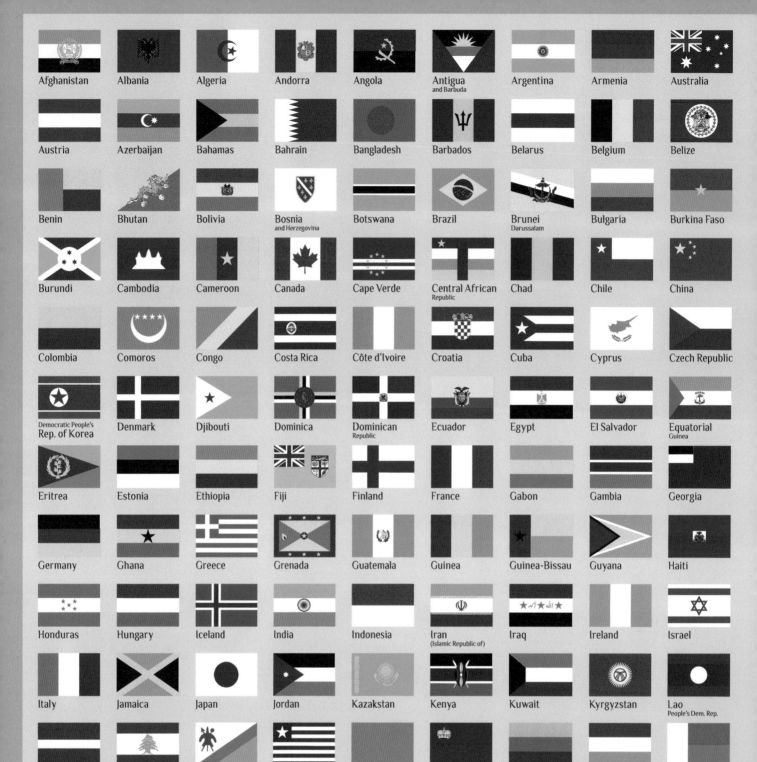

| | | | | | | | | |
|---|---|---|---|---|---|---|---|---|
| Afghanistan | Albania | Algeria | Andorra | Angola | Antigua and Barbuda | Argentina | Armenia | Australia |
| Austria | Azerbaijan | Bahamas | Bahrain | Bangladesh | Barbados | Belarus | Belgium | Belize |
| Benin | Bhutan | Bolivia | Bosnia and Herzegovina | Botswana | Brazil | Brunei Darussalam | Bulgaria | Burkina Faso |
| Burundi | Cambodia | Cameroon | Canada | Cape Verde | Central African Republic | Chad | Chile | China |
| Colombia | Comoros | Congo | Costa Rica | Côte d'Ivoire | Croatia | Cuba | Cyprus | Czech Republic |
| Democratic People's Rep. of Korea | Denmark | Djibouti | Dominica | Dominican Republic | Ecuador | Egypt | El Salvador | Equatorial Guinea |
| Eritrea | Estonia | Ethiopia | Fiji | Finland | France | Gabon | Gambia | Georgia |
| Germany | Ghana | Greece | Grenada | Guatemala | Guinea | Guinea-Bissau | Guyana | Haiti |
| Honduras | Hungary | Iceland | India | Indonesia | Iran (Islamic Republic of) | Iraq | Ireland | Israel |
| Italy | Jamaica | Japan | Jordan | Kazakstan | Kenya | Kuwait | Kyrgyzstan | Lao People's Dem. Rep. |
| Latvia | Lebanon | Lesotho | Liberia | Libyan Arab Jamahiriya | Liechtenstein | Lithuania | Luxembourg | Madagascar |

| 1994 | | 185 |
|---|---|---|
| Year | United Nations | Member states |

Malawi   Malaysia   Maldives   Mali   Malta   Marshall Islands   Mauritania   Mauritius   Mexico

Micronesia (Federated States of)   Monaco   Mongolia   Morocco   Mozambique   Myanmar   Namibia   Nepal   Netherlands

New Zealand   Nicaragua   Niger   Nigeria   Norway   Oman   Pakistan   Palau   Panama

Papua New Guinea   Paraguay   Peru   Philippines   Poland   Portugal   Qatar   Republic of Korea   Republic of Moldova

Romania   Russian Federation   Rwanda   Saint Kitts and Nevis   Saint Lucia   Saint Vincent and the Grenadines   Samoa   San Marino   Sao Tome and Principe

Saudi Arabia   Senegal   Seychelles   Sierra Leone   Singapore   Slovakia   Slovenia   Solomon Islands   Somalia

South Africa   Spain   Sri Lanka   Sudan   Suriname   Swaziland   Sweden   Syrian Arab Republic   Tajikistan

Thailand   TFYRO Macedonia   Togo   Trinidad and Tobago   Tunisia   Turkey   Turkmenistan   Uganda   Ukraine

United Arab Emirates   United Kingdom of Great Britain and N.I.   United Republic of Tanzania   United States of America   Uruguay   Uzbekistan   Vanuatu   Venezuela   Viet Nam

Yemen   Yugoslavia   Zaire   Zambia   Zimbabwe

New member — independence from

United States of America   ▶   Palau

Flag change

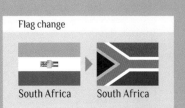

South Africa   ▶   South Africa

| | | | | | | | |
|---|---|---|---|---|---|---|---|
| Afghanistan | Albania | Algeria | Andorra | Angola | Antigua and Barbuda | Argentina | Armenia | Australia |
| Austria | Azerbaijan | Bahamas | Bahrain | Bangladesh | Barbados | Belarus | Belgium | Belize |
| Benin | Bhutan | Bolivia | Bosnia and Herzegovina | Botswana | Brazil | Brunei Darussalam | Bulgaria | Burkina Faso |
| Burundi | Cambodia | Cameroon | Canada | Cape Verde | Central African Republic | Chad | Chile | China |
| Colombia | Comoros | Congo | Costa Rica | Côte d'Ivoire | Croatia | Cuba | Cyprus | Czech Republic |
| Democratic People's Rep. of Korea | Denmark | Djibouti | Dominica | Dominican Republic | Ecuador | Egypt | El Salvador | Equatorial Guinea |
| Eritrea | Estonia | Ethiopia | Fiji | Finland | France | Gabon | Gambia | Georgia |
| Germany | Ghana | Greece | Grenada | Guatemala | Guinea | Guinea-Bissau | Guyana | Haiti |
| Honduras | Hungary | Iceland | India | Indonesia | Iran (Islamic Republic of) | Iraq | Ireland | Israel |
| Italy | Jamaica | Japan | Jordan | Kazakstan | Kenya | Kuwait | Kyrgyzstan | Lao People's Dem. Rep. |
| Latvia | Lebanon | Lesotho | Liberia | Libyan Arab Jamahiriya | Liechtenstein | Lithuania | Luxembourg | Madagascar |

Timeline                    page 106

**1995**
Year

United Nations

**185**
Member states

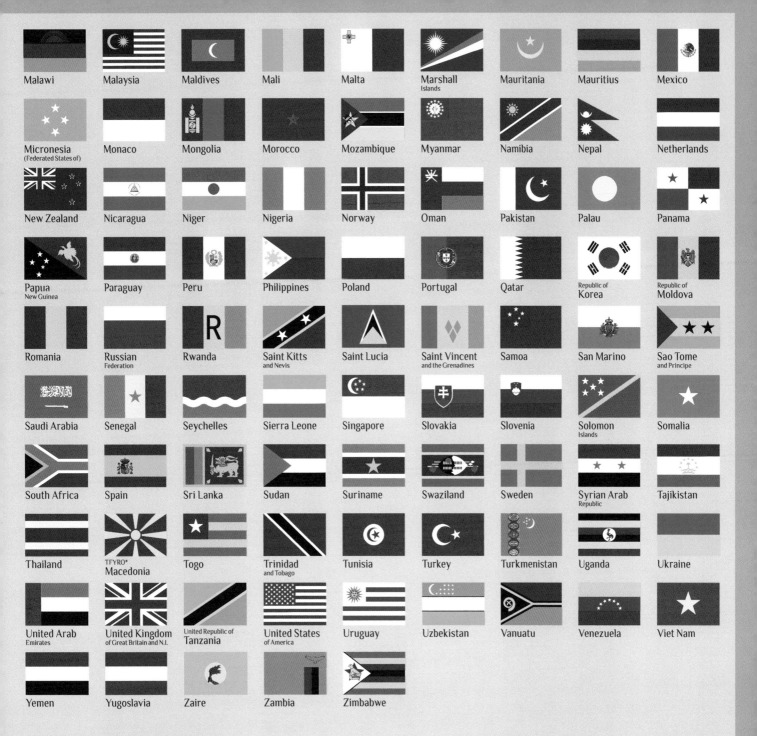

Malawi | Malaysia | Maldives | Mali | Malta | Marshall Islands | Mauritania | Mauritius | Mexico

Micronesia (Federated States of) | Monaco | Mongolia | Morocco | Mozambique | Myanmar | Namibia | Nepal | Netherlands

New Zealand | Nicaragua | Niger | Nigeria | Norway | Oman | Pakistan | Palau | Panama

Papua New Guinea | Paraguay | Peru | Philippines | Poland | Portugal | Qatar | Republic of Korea | Republic of Moldova

Romania | Russian Federation | Rwanda | Saint Kitts and Nevis | Saint Lucia | Saint Vincent and the Grenadines | Samoa | San Marino | Sao Tome and Principe

Saudi Arabia | Senegal | Seychelles | Sierra Leone | Singapore | Slovakia | Slovenia | Solomon Islands | Somalia

South Africa | Spain | Sri Lanka | Sudan | Suriname | Swaziland | Sweden | Syrian Arab Republic | Tajikistan

Thailand | TFYRO* Macedonia | Togo | Trinidad and Tobago | Tunisia | Turkey | Turkmenistan | Uganda | Ukraine

United Arab Emirates | United Kingdom of Great Britain and N.I. | United Republic of Tanzania | United States of America | Uruguay | Uzbekistan | Vanuatu | Venezuela | Viet Nam

Yemen | Yugoslavia | Zaire | Zambia | Zimbabwe

*The Former Yugoslav Republic of

Flag change

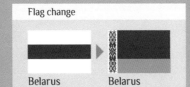

Belarus ▸ Belarus

Flag change

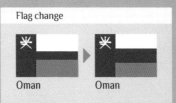

Oman ▸ Oman

Flag change

TFYRO* Macedonia ▸ TFYRO* Macedonia

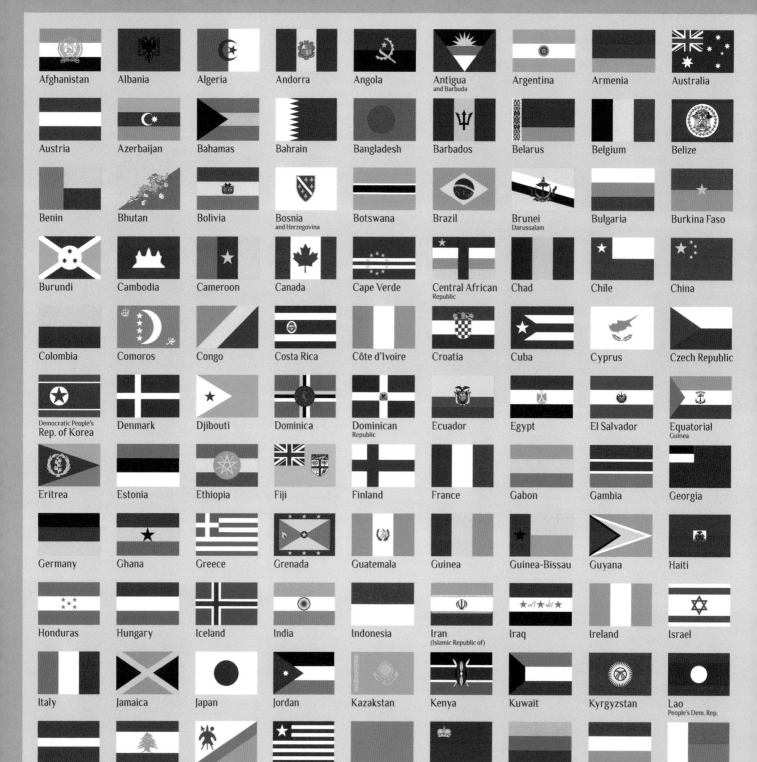

Afghanistan · Albania · Algeria · Andorra · Angola · Antigua and Barbuda · Argentina · Armenia · Australia

Austria · Azerbaijan · Bahamas · Bahrain · Bangladesh · Barbados · Belarus · Belgium · Belize

Benin · Bhutan · Bolivia · Bosnia and Herzegovina · Botswana · Brazil · Brunei Darussalam · Bulgaria · Burkina Faso

Burundi · Cambodia · Cameroon · Canada · Cape Verde · Central African Republic · Chad · Chile · China

Colombia · Comoros · Congo · Costa Rica · Côte d'Ivoire · Croatia · Cuba · Cyprus · Czech Republic

Democratic People's Rep. of Korea · Denmark · Djibouti · Dominica · Dominican Republic · Ecuador · Egypt · El Salvador · Equatorial Guinea

Eritrea · Estonia · Ethiopia · Fiji · Finland · France · Gabon · Gambia · Georgia

Germany · Ghana · Greece · Grenada · Guatemala · Guinea · Guinea-Bissau · Guyana · Haiti

Honduras · Hungary · Iceland · India · Indonesia · Iran (Islamic Republic of) · Iraq · Ireland · Israel

Italy · Jamaica · Japan · Jordan · Kazakstan · Kenya · Kuwait · Kyrgyzstan · Lao People's Dem. Rep.

Latvia · Lebanon · Lesotho · Liberia · Libyan Arab Jamahiriya · Liechtenstein · Lithuania · Luxembourg · Madagascar

Timeline        page 108

**1996** — Year

United Nations

**185** — Member states

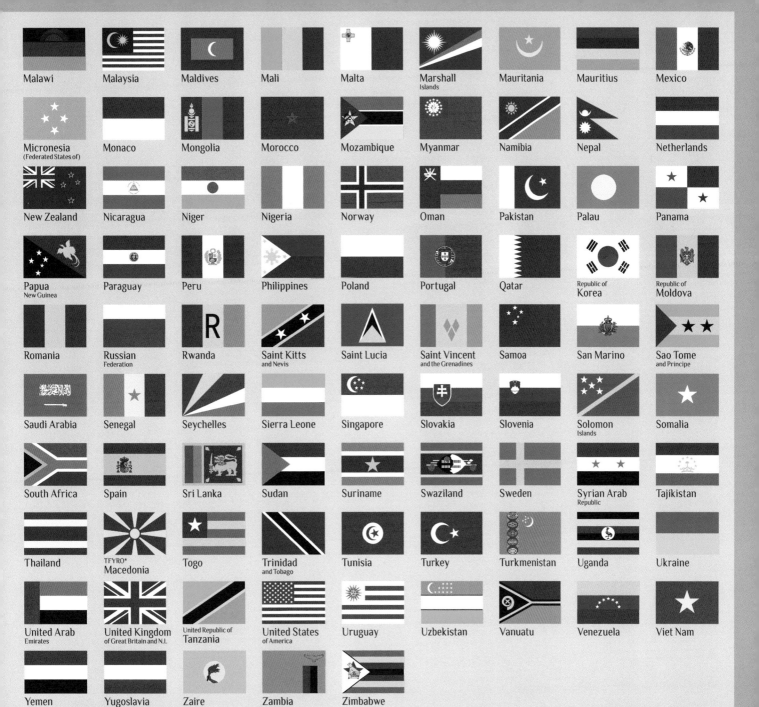

Malawi | Malaysia | Maldives | Mali | Malta | Marshall Islands | Mauritania | Mauritius | Mexico

Micronesia (Federated States of) | Monaco | Mongolia | Morocco | Mozambique | Myanmar | Namibia | Nepal | Netherlands

New Zealand | Nicaragua | Niger | Nigeria | Norway | Oman | Pakistan | Palau | Panama

Papua New Guinea | Paraguay | Peru | Philippines | Poland | Portugal | Qatar | Republic of Korea | Republic of Moldova

Romania | Russian Federation | Rwanda | Saint Kitts and Nevis | Saint Lucia | Saint Vincent and the Grenadines | Samoa | San Marino | Sao Tome and Principe

Saudi Arabia | Senegal | Seychelles | Sierra Leone | Singapore | Slovakia | Slovenia | Solomon Islands | Somalia

South Africa | Spain | Sri Lanka | Sudan | Suriname | Swaziland | Sweden | Syrian Arab Republic | Tajikistan

Thailand | TFYRO* Macedonia | Togo | Trinidad and Tobago | Tunisia | Turkey | Turkmenistan | Uganda | Ukraine

United Arab Emirates | United Kingdom of Great Britain and N.I. | United Republic of Tanzania | United States of America | Uruguay | Uzbekistan | Vanuatu | Venezuela | Viet Nam

Yemen | Yugoslavia | Zaire | Zambia | Zimbabwe

Flag change

Comoros ▸ Comoros

Flag change

Ethiopia ▸ Ethiopia

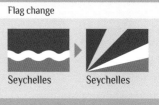

Flag change

Seychelles ▸ Seychelles

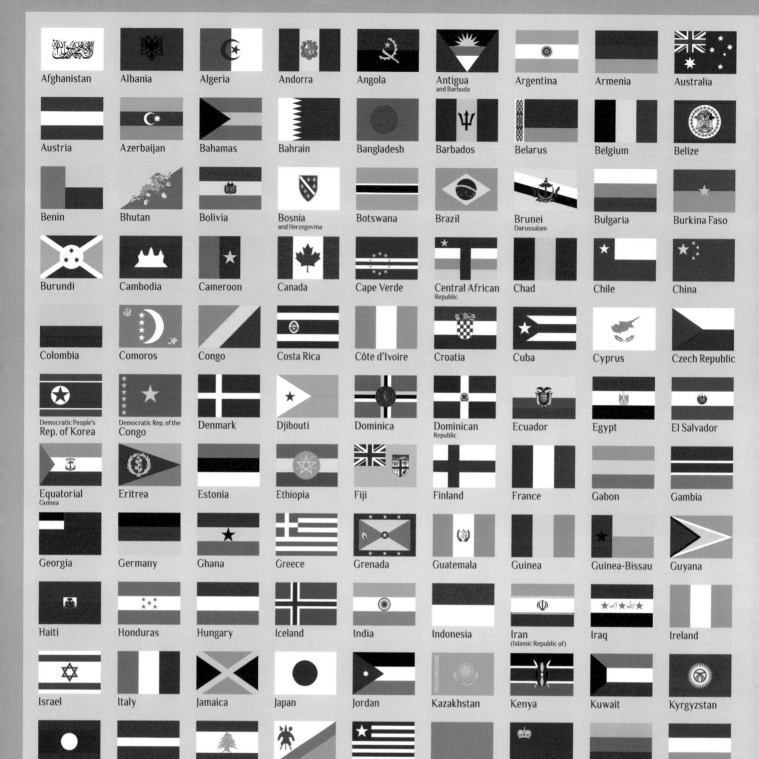

Afghanistan  Albania  Algeria  Andorra  Angola  Antigua and Barbuda  Argentina  Armenia  Australia

Austria  Azerbaijan  Bahamas  Bahrain  Bangladesh  Barbados  Belarus  Belgium  Belize

Benin  Bhutan  Bolivia  Bosnia and Herzegovina  Botswana  Brazil  Brunei Darussalam  Bulgaria  Burkina Faso

Burundi  Cambodia  Cameroon  Canada  Cape Verde  Central African Republic  Chad  Chile  China

Colombia  Comoros  Congo  Costa Rica  Côte d'Ivoire  Croatia  Cuba  Cyprus  Czech Republic

Democratic People's Rep. of Korea  Democratic Rep. of the Congo  Denmark  Djibouti  Dominica  Dominican Republic  Ecuador  Egypt  El Salvador

Equatorial Guinea  Eritrea  Estonia  Ethiopia  Fiji  Finland  France  Gabon  Gambia

Georgia  Germany  Ghana  Greece  Grenada  Guatemala  Guinea  Guinea-Bissau  Guyana

Haiti  Honduras  Hungary  Iceland  India  Indonesia  Iran (Islamic Republic of)  Iraq  Ireland

Israel  Italy  Jamaica  Japan  Jordan  Kazakhstan  Kenya  Kuwait  Kyrgyzstan

Lao People's Dem. Rep.  Latvia  Lebanon  Lesotho  Liberia  Libyan Arab Jamahiriya  Liechtenstein  Lithuania  Luxembourg

1997
Year

United Nations

185
Member states

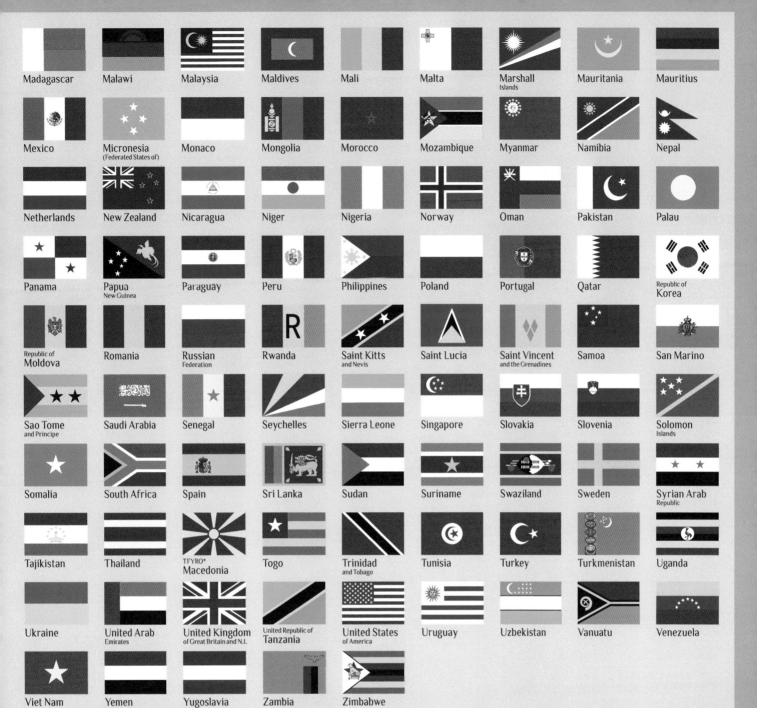

Madagascar | Malawi | Malaysia | Maldives | Mali | Malta | Marshall Islands | Mauritania | Mauritius

Mexico | Micronesia (Federated States of) | Monaco | Mongolia | Morocco | Mozambique | Myanmar | Namibia | Nepal

Netherlands | New Zealand | Nicaragua | Niger | Nigeria | Norway | Oman | Pakistan | Palau

Panama | Papua New Guinea | Paraguay | Peru | Philippines | Poland | Portugal | Qatar | Republic of Korea

Republic of Moldova | Romania | Russian Federation | Rwanda | Saint Kitts and Nevis | Saint Lucia | Saint Vincent and the Grenadines | Samoa | San Marino

Sao Tome and Principe | Saudi Arabia | Senegal | Seychelles | Sierra Leone | Singapore | Slovakia | Slovenia | Solomon Islands

Somalia | South Africa | Spain | Sri Lanka | Sudan | Suriname | Swaziland | Sweden | Syrian Arab Republic

Tajikistan | Thailand | TFYRO* Macedonia | Togo | Trinidad and Tobago | Tunisia | Turkey | Turkmenistan | Uganda

Ukraine | United Arab Emirates | United Kingdom of Great Britain and N.I. | United Republic of Tanzania | United States of America | Uruguay | Uzbekistan | Vanuatu | Venezuela

Viet Nam | Yemen | Yugoslavia | Zambia | Zimbabwe

### Flag and name change

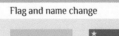

Zaire

Democratic Rep. of the Congo

### Name change

Kazakstan    Kazakhstan

### Flag change

Afghanistan

Afghanistan

### Flag change

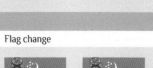

Turkmenistan

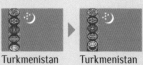

Turkmenistan

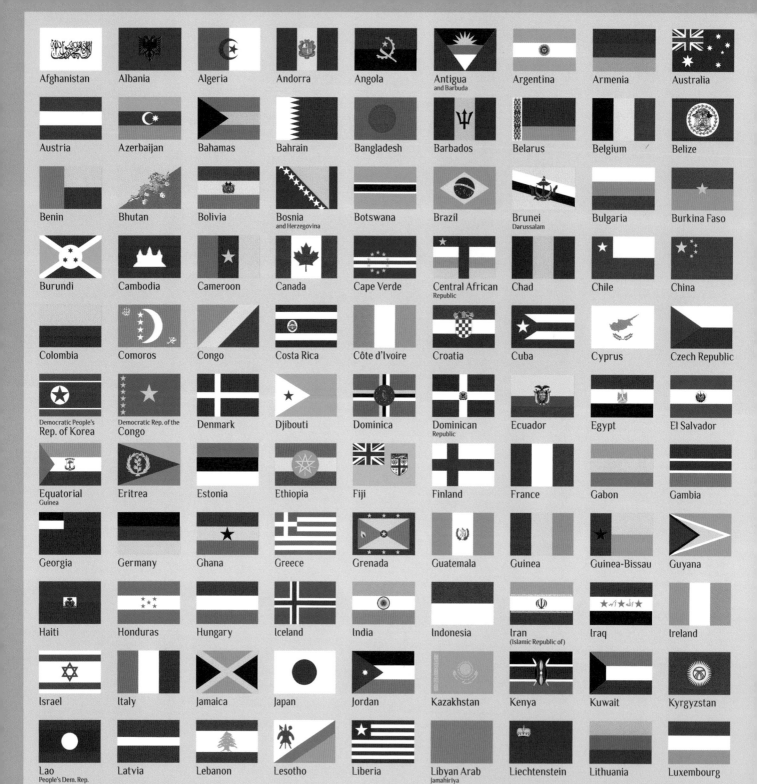

Afghanistan | Albania | Algeria | Andorra | Angola | Antigua and Barbuda | Argentina | Armenia | Australia

Austria | Azerbaijan | Bahamas | Bahrain | Bangladesh | Barbados | Belarus | Belgium | Belize

Benin | Bhutan | Bolivia | Bosnia and Herzegovina | Botswana | Brazil | Brunei Darussalam | Bulgaria | Burkina Faso

Burundi | Cambodia | Cameroon | Canada | Cape Verde | Central African Republic | Chad | Chile | China

Colombia | Comoros | Congo | Costa Rica | Côte d'Ivoire | Croatia | Cuba | Cyprus | Czech Republic

Democratic People's Rep. of Korea | Democratic Rep. of the Congo | Denmark | Djibouti | Dominica | Dominican Republic | Ecuador | Egypt | El Salvador

Equatorial Guinea | Eritrea | Estonia | Ethiopia | Fiji | Finland | France | Gabon | Gambia

Georgia | Germany | Ghana | Greece | Grenada | Guatemala | Guinea | Guinea-Bissau | Guyana

Haiti | Honduras | Hungary | Iceland | India | Indonesia | Iran (Islamic Republic of) | Iraq | Ireland

Israel | Italy | Jamaica | Japan | Jordan | Kazakhstan | Kenya | Kuwait | Kyrgyzstan

Lao People's Dem. Rep. | Latvia | Lebanon | Lesotho | Liberia | Libyan Arab Jamahiriya | Liechtenstein | Lithuania | Luxembourg

1998
Year

United Nations

185
Member states

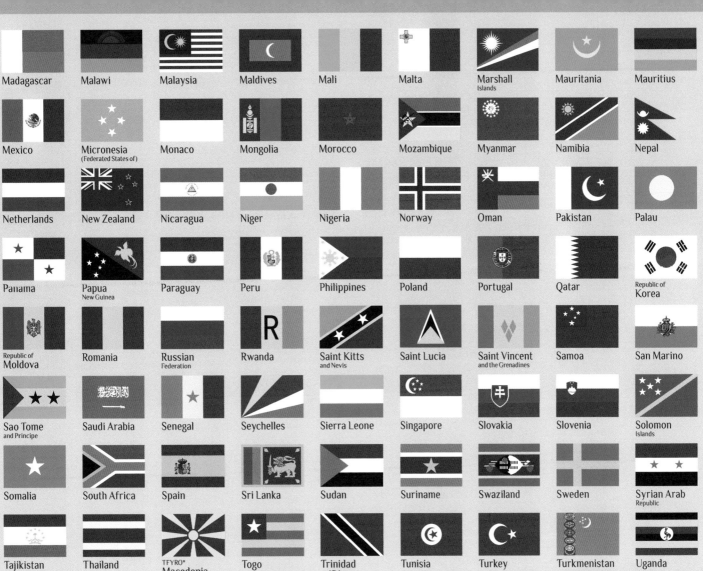

| | | | | | | | | |
|---|---|---|---|---|---|---|---|---|
| Madagascar | Malawi | Malaysia | Maldives | Mali | Malta | Marshall Islands | Mauritania | Mauritius |
| Mexico | Micronesia (Federated States of) | Monaco | Mongolia | Morocco | Mozambique | Myanmar | Namibia | Nepal |
| Netherlands | New Zealand | Nicaragua | Niger | Nigeria | Norway | Oman | Pakistan | Palau |
| Panama | Papua New Guinea | Paraguay | Peru | Philippines | Poland | Portugal | Qatar | Republic of Korea |
| Republic of Moldova | Romania | Russian Federation | Rwanda | Saint Kitts and Nevis | Saint Lucia | Saint Vincent and the Grenadines | Samoa | San Marino |
| Sao Tome and Principe | Saudi Arabia | Senegal | Seychelles | Sierra Leone | Singapore | Slovakia | Slovenia | Solomon Islands |
| Somalia | South Africa | Spain | Sri Lanka | Sudan | Suriname | Swaziland | Sweden | Syrian Arab Republic |
| Tajikistan | Thailand | TFYRO* Macedonia | Togo | Trinidad and Tobago | Tunisia | Turkey | Turkmenistan | Uganda |
| Ukraine | United Arab Emirates | United Kingdom of Great Britain and N.I. | United Republic of Tanzania | United States of America | Uruguay | Uzbekistan | Vanuatu | Venezuela |
| Viet Nam | Yemen | Yugoslavia | Zambia | Zimbabwe | | | | |

Flag change

Bosnia and Herzegovina ▶ Bosnia and Herzegovina

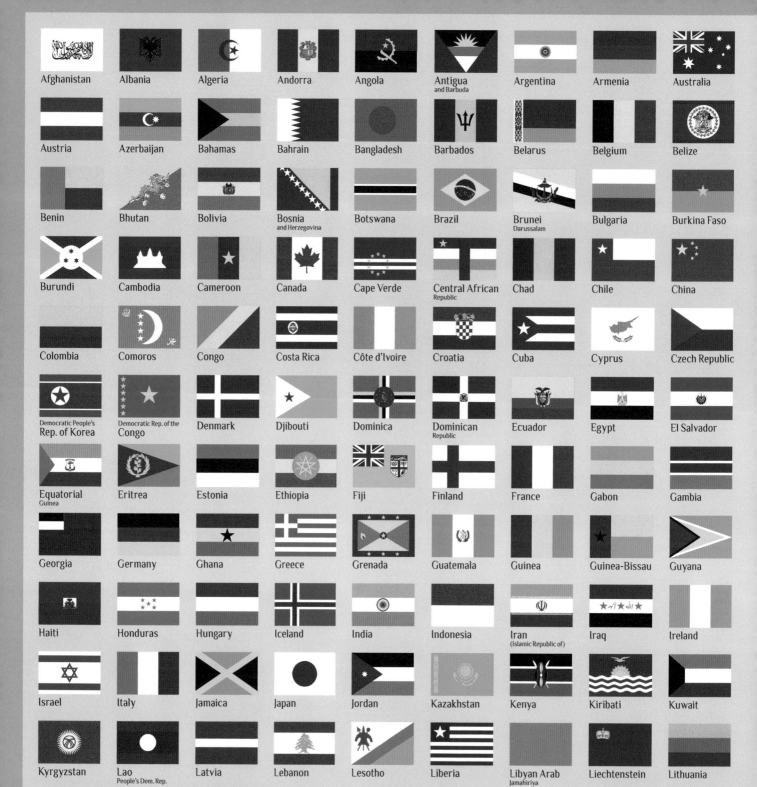

Afghanistan | Albania | Algeria | Andorra | Angola | Antigua and Barbuda | Argentina | Armenia | Australia

Austria | Azerbaijan | Bahamas | Bahrain | Bangladesh | Barbados | Belarus | Belgium | Belize

Benin | Bhutan | Bolivia | Bosnia and Herzegovina | Botswana | Brazil | Brunei Darussalam | Bulgaria | Burkina Faso

Burundi | Cambodia | Cameroon | Canada | Cape Verde | Central African Republic | Chad | Chile | China

Colombia | Comoros | Congo | Costa Rica | Côte d'Ivoire | Croatia | Cuba | Cyprus | Czech Republic

Democratic People's Rep. of Korea | Democratic Rep. of the Congo | Denmark | Djibouti | Dominica | Dominican Republic | Ecuador | Egypt | El Salvador

Equatorial Guinea | Eritrea | Estonia | Ethiopia | Fiji | Finland | France | Gabon | Gambia

Georgia | Germany | Ghana | Greece | Grenada | Guatemala | Guinea | Guinea-Bissau | Guyana

Haiti | Honduras | Hungary | Iceland | India | Indonesia | Iran (Islamic Republic of) | Iraq | Ireland

Israel | Italy | Jamaica | Japan | Jordan | Kazakhstan | Kenya | Kiribati | Kuwait

Kyrgyzstan | Lao People's Dem. Rep. | Latvia | Lebanon | Lesotho | Liberia | Libyan Arab Jamahiriya | Liechtenstein | Lithuania

1999
Year

United Nations

188
Member states

| | | | | | | | | |
|---|---|---|---|---|---|---|---|---|
| Luxembourg | Madagascar | Malawi | Malaysia | Maldives | Mali | Malta | Marshall Islands | Mauritania |
| Mauritius | Mexico | Micronesia (Federated States of) | Monaco | Mongolia | Morocco | Mozambique | Myanmar | Namibia |
| Nauru | Nepal | Netherlands | New Zealand | Nicaragua | Niger | Nigeria | Norway | Oman |
| Pakistan | Palau | Panama | Papua New Guinea | Paraguay | Peru | Philippines | Poland | Portugal |
| Qatar | Republic of Korea | Republic of Moldova | Romania | Russian Federation | Rwanda | Saint Kitts and Nevis | Saint Lucia | Saint Vincent and the Grenadines |
| Samoa | San Marino | Sao Tome and Principe | Saudi Arabia | Senegal | Seychelles | Sierra Leone | Singapore | Slovakia |
| Slovenia | Solomon Islands | Somalia | South Africa | Spain | Sri Lanka | Sudan | Suriname | Swaziland |
| Sweden | Syrian Arab Republic | Tajikistan | Thailand | TFYRO Macedonia | Togo | Tonga | Trinidad and Tobago | Tunisia |
| Turkey | Turkmenistan | Uganda | Ukraine | United Arab Emirates | United Kingdom of Great Britain and N.I | United Republic of Tanzania | United States of America | Uruguay |
| Uzbekistan | Vanuatu | Venezuela | Viet Nam | Yemen | Yugoslavia | Zambia | Zimbabwe | |

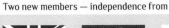

Two new members — independence from

United Kingdom of Great Britain and N.I

Kiribati

Tonga

New member — independence from

Australia

Nauru

Flag change

Tunisia

Tunisia

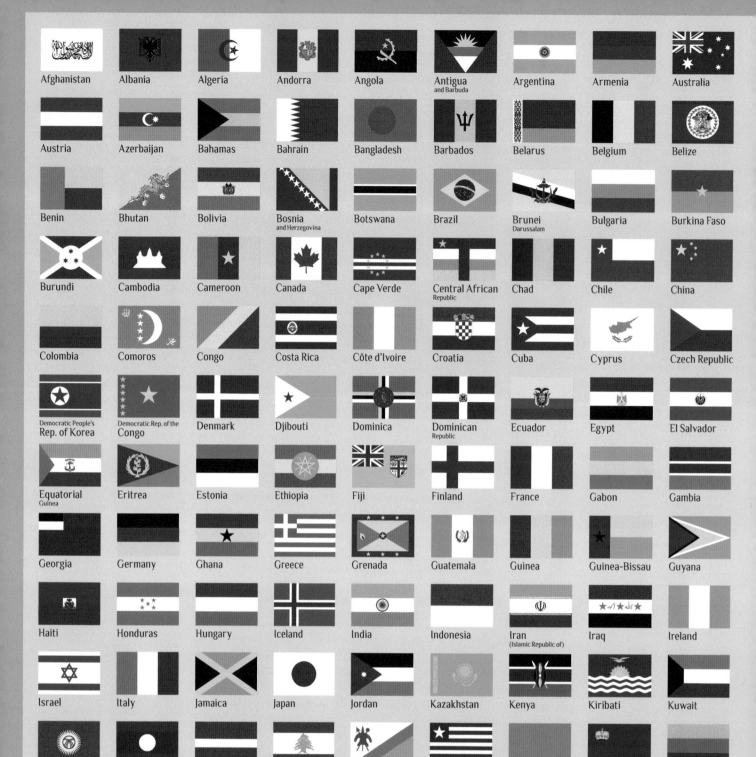

Afghanistan | Albania | Algeria | Andorra | Angola | Antigua and Barbuda | Argentina | Armenia | Australia

Austria | Azerbaijan | Bahamas | Bahrain | Bangladesh | Barbados | Belarus | Belgium | Belize

Benin | Bhutan | Bolivia | Bosnia and Herzegovina | Botswana | Brazil | Brunei Darussalam | Bulgaria | Burkina Faso

Burundi | Cambodia | Cameroon | Canada | Cape Verde | Central African Republic | Chad | Chile | China

Colombia | Comoros | Congo | Costa Rica | Côte d'Ivoire | Croatia | Cuba | Cyprus | Czech Republic

Democratic People's Rep. of Korea | Democratic Rep. of the Congo | Denmark | Djibouti | Dominica | Dominican Republic | Ecuador | Egypt | El Salvador

Equatorial Guinea | Eritrea | Estonia | Ethiopia | Fiji | Finland | France | Gabon | Gambia

Georgia | Germany | Ghana | Greece | Grenada | Guatemala | Guinea | Guinea-Bissau | Guyana

Haiti | Honduras | Hungary | Iceland | India | Indonesia | Iran (Islamic Republic of) | Iraq | Ireland

Israel | Italy | Jamaica | Japan | Jordan | Kazakhstan | Kenya | Kiribati | Kuwait

Kyrgyzstan | Lao People's Dem. Rep. | Latvia | Lebanon | Lesotho | Liberia | Libyan Arab Jamahiriya | Liechtenstein | Lithuania

| 2000 | | 189 |
| Year | United Nations | Member states |

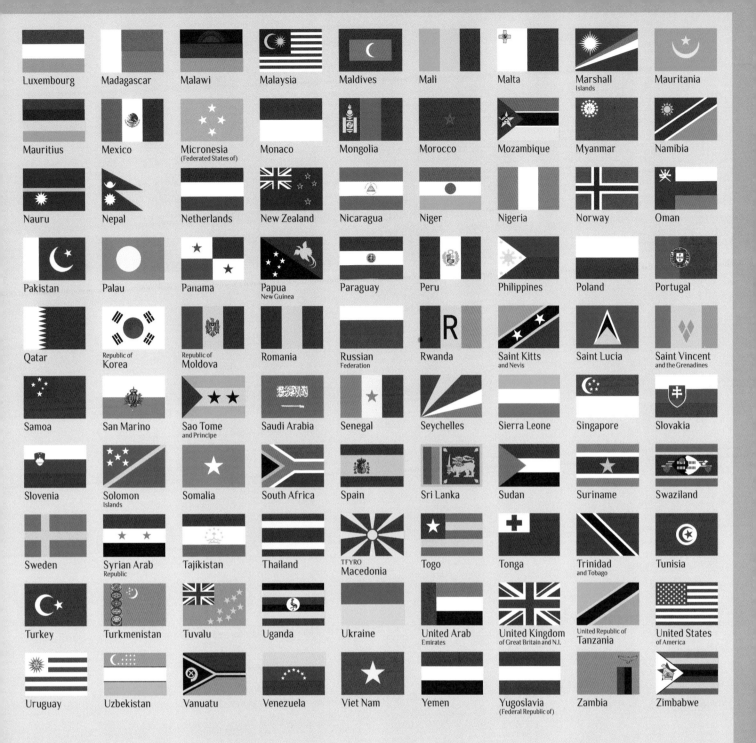

| | | | | | | | | |
|---|---|---|---|---|---|---|---|---|
| Luxembourg | Madagascar | Malawi | Malaysia | Maldives | Mali | Malta | Marshall Islands | Mauritania |
| Mauritius | Mexico | Micronesia (Federated States of) | Monaco | Mongolia | Morocco | Mozambique | Myanmar | Namibia |
| Nauru | Nepal | Netherlands | New Zealand | Nicaragua | Niger | Nigeria | Norway | Oman |
| Pakistan | Palau | Panama | Papua New Guinea | Paraguay | Peru | Philippines | Poland | Portugal |
| Qatar | Republic of Korea | Republic of Moldova | Romania | Russian Federation | Rwanda | Saint Kitts and Nevis | Saint Lucia | Saint Vincent and the Grenadines |
| Samoa | San Marino | Sao Tome and Principe | Saudi Arabia | Senegal | Seychelles | Sierra Leone | Singapore | Slovakia |
| Slovenia | Solomon Islands | Somalia | South Africa | Spain | Sri Lanka | Sudan | Suriname | Swaziland |
| Sweden | Syrian Arab Republic | Tajikistan | Thailand | TFYRO Macedonia | Togo | Tonga | Trinidad and Tobago | Tunisia |
| Turkey | Turkmenistan | Tuvalu | Uganda | Ukraine | United Arab Emirates | United Kingdom of Great Britain and N.I. | United Republic of Tanzania | United States of America |
| Uruguay | Uzbekistan | Vanuatu | Venezuela | Viet Nam | Yemen | Yugoslavia (Federal Republic of) | Zambia | Zimbabwe |

Formal readmission of member

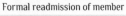

Yugoslavia → Yugoslavia (Federal Republic of)

New member — separation from

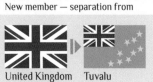

United Kingdom of Great Britain and N.I. → Tuvalu

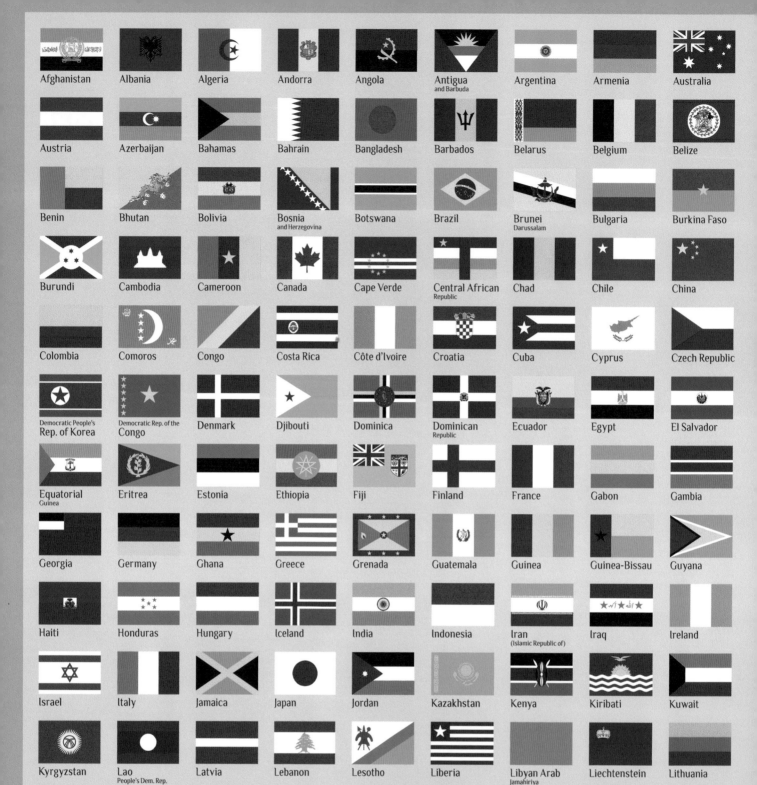

Afghanistan | Albania | Algeria | Andorra | Angola | Antigua and Barbuda | Argentina | Armenia | Australia

Austria | Azerbaijan | Bahamas | Bahrain | Bangladesh | Barbados | Belarus | Belgium | Belize

Benin | Bhutan | Bolivia | Bosnia and Herzegovina | Botswana | Brazil | Brunei Darussalam | Bulgaria | Burkina Faso

Burundi | Cambodia | Cameroon | Canada | Cape Verde | Central African Republic | Chad | Chile | China

Colombia | Comoros | Congo | Costa Rica | Côte d'Ivoire | Croatia | Cuba | Cyprus | Czech Republic

Democratic People's Rep. of Korea | Democratic Rep. of the Congo | Denmark | Djibouti | Dominica | Dominican Republic | Ecuador | Egypt | El Salvador

Equatorial Guinea | Eritrea | Estonia | Ethiopia | Fiji | Finland | France | Gabon | Gambia

Georgia | Germany | Ghana | Greece | Grenada | Guatemala | Guinea | Guinea-Bissau | Guyana

Haiti | Honduras | Hungary | Iceland | India | Indonesia | Iran (Islamic Republic of) | Iraq | Ireland

Israel | Italy | Jamaica | Japan | Jordan | Kazakhstan | Kenya | Kiribati | Kuwait

Kyrgyzstan | Lao People's Dem. Rep. | Latvia | Lebanon | Lesotho | Liberia | Libyan Arab Jamahiriya | Liechtenstein | Lithuania

Timeline                    page 118

**2001**
Year

**United Nations**

**189**
Member states

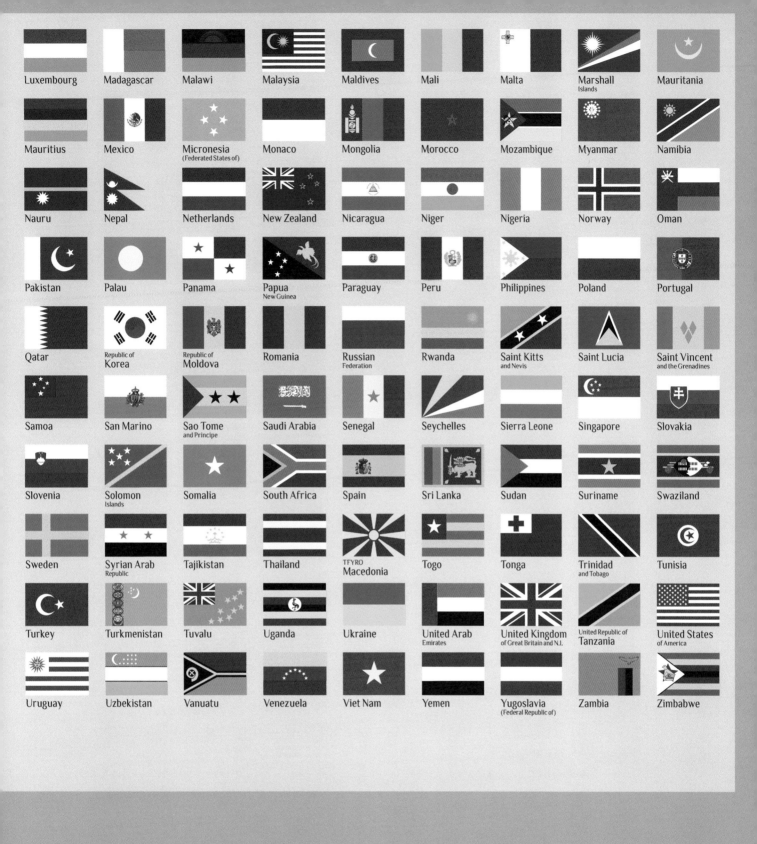

Luxembourg
Madagascar
Malawi
Malaysia
Maldives
Mali
Malta
Marshall Islands
Mauritania

Mauritius
Mexico
Micronesia (Federated States of)
Monaco
Mongolia
Morocco
Mozambique
Myanmar
Namibia

Nauru
Nepal
Netherlands
New Zealand
Nicaragua
Niger
Nigeria
Norway
Oman

Pakistan
Palau
Panama
Papua New Guinea
Paraguay
Peru
Philippines
Poland
Portugal

Qatar
Republic of Korea
Republic of Moldova
Romania
Russian Federation
Rwanda
Saint Kitts and Nevis
Saint Lucia
Saint Vincent and the Grenadines

Samoa
San Marino
Sao Tome and Principe
Saudi Arabia
Senegal
Seychelles
Sierra Leone
Singapore
Slovakia

Slovenia
Solomon Islands
Somalia
South Africa
Spain
Sri Lanka
Sudan
Suriname
Swaziland

Sweden
Syrian Arab Republic
Tajikistan
Thailand
TFYRO Macedonia
Togo
Tonga
Trinidad and Tobago
Tunisia

Turkey
Turkmenistan
Tuvalu
Uganda
Ukraine
United Arab Emirates
United Kingdom of Great Britain and N.I.
United Republic of Tanzania
United States of America

Uruguay
Uzbekistan
Vanuatu
Venezuela
Viet Nam
Yemen
Yugoslavia (Federal Republic of)
Zambia
Zimbabwe

Flag change

Afghanistan ▸ Afghanistan

Flag change

Rwanda ▸ Rwanda

Flag change

Turkmenistan ▸ Turkmenistan

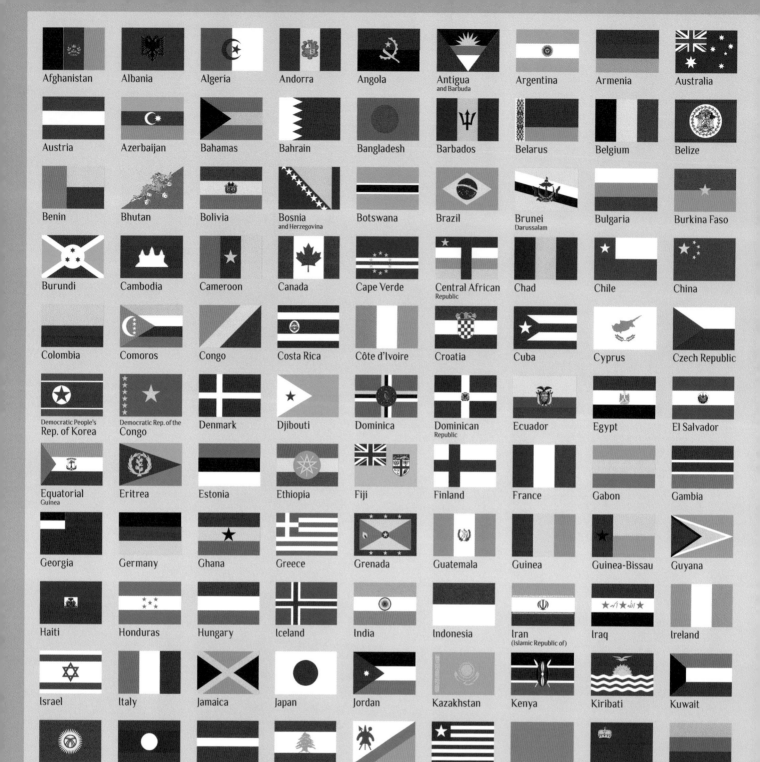

Afghanistan • Albania • Algeria • Andorra • Angola • Antigua and Barbuda • Argentina • Armenia • Australia

Austria • Azerbaijan • Bahamas • Bahrain • Bangladesh • Barbados • Belarus • Belgium • Belize

Benin • Bhutan • Bolivia • Bosnia and Herzegovina • Botswana • Brazil • Brunei Darussalam • Bulgaria • Burkina Faso

Burundi • Cambodia • Cameroon • Canada • Cape Verde • Central African Republic • Chad • Chile • China

Colombia • Comoros • Congo • Costa Rica • Côte d'Ivoire • Croatia • Cuba • Cyprus • Czech Republic

Democratic People's Rep. of Korea • Democratic Rep. of the Congo • Denmark • Djibouti • Dominica • Dominican Republic • Ecuador • Egypt • El Salvador

Equatorial Guinea • Eritrea • Estonia • Ethiopia • Fiji • Finland • France • Gabon • Gambia

Georgia • Germany • Ghana • Greece • Grenada • Guatemala • Guinea • Guinea-Bissau • Guyana

Haiti • Honduras • Hungary • Iceland • India • Indonesia • Iran (Islamic Republic of) • Iraq • Ireland

Israel • Italy • Jamaica • Japan • Jordan • Kazakhstan • Kenya • Kiribati • Kuwait

Kyrgyzstan • Lao People's Dem. Rep. • Latvia • Lebanon • Lesotho • Liberia • Libyan Arab Jamahiriya • Liechtenstein • Lithuania

Timeline                         page 120

2002
Year

United Nations

191
Member states

| Luxembourg | Madagascar | Malawi | Malaysia | Maldives | Mali | Malta | Marshall Islands | Mauritania |

| Mauritius | Mexico | Micronesia (Federated States of) | Monaco | Mongolia | Morocco | Mozambique | Myanmar | Namibia |

| Nauru | Nepal | Netherlands | New Zealand | Nicaragua | Niger | Nigeria | Norway | Oman |

| Pakistan | Palau | Panama | Papua New Guinea | Paraguay | Peru | Philippines | Poland | Portugal |

| Qatar | Republic of Korea | Republic of Moldova | Romania | Russian Federation | Rwanda | Saint Kitts and Nevis | Saint Lucia | Saint Vincent and the Grenadines |

| Samoa | San Marino | Sao Tome and Principe | Saudi Arabia | Senegal | Seychelles | Sierra Leone | Singapore | Slovakia |

| Slovenia | Solomon Islands | Somalia | South Africa | Spain | Sri Lanka | Sudan | Suriname | Swaziland |

| Sweden | Switzerland | Syrian Arab Republic | Tajikistan | Thailand | TFYRO Macedonia | Timor-Leste | Togo | Tonga |

| Trinidad and Tobago | Tunisia | Turkey | Turkmenistan | Tuvalu | Uganda | Ukraine | United Arab Emirates | United Kingdom of Great Britain and N.I. |

| United Republic of Tanzania | United States of America | Uruguay | Uzbekistan | Vanuatu | Venezuela | Viet Nam | Yemen | Yugoslavia (Federal Republic of) |

| Zambia | Zimbabwe |

New member

Switzerland

New member — independence from

Portugal ▶ Indonesia ▶▶ United Nations ▶ Timor-Leste

Two flag changes

Afghanistan ▶ Afghanistan ▶ Afghanistan

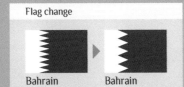

Flag change

Bahrain ▶ Bahrain

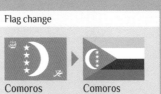

Flag change

Comoros ▶ Comoros

Flag change

Saint Lucia ▶ Saint Lucia

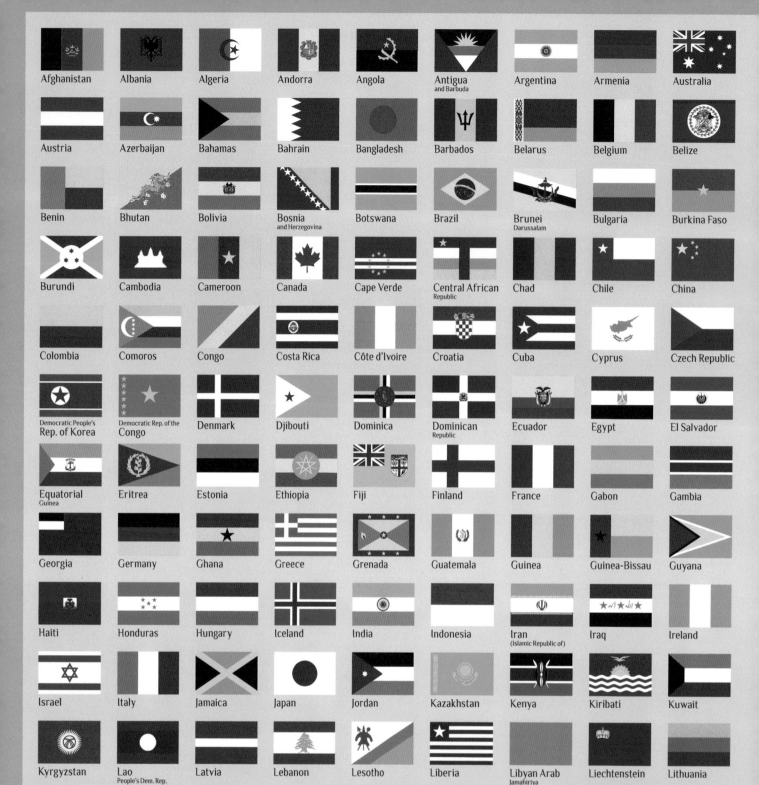

| | | | | | | | | |
|---|---|---|---|---|---|---|---|---|
| Afghanistan | Albania | Algeria | Andorra | Angola | Antigua and Barbuda | Argentina | Armenia | Australia |
| Austria | Azerbaijan | Bahamas | Bahrain | Bangladesh | Barbados | Belarus | Belgium | Belize |
| Benin | Bhutan | Bolivia | Bosnia and Herzegovina | Botswana | Brazil | Brunei Darussalam | Bulgaria | Burkina Faso |
| Burundi | Cambodia | Cameroon | Canada | Cape Verde | Central African Republic | Chad | Chile | China |
| Colombia | Comoros | Congo | Costa Rica | Côte d'Ivoire | Croatia | Cuba | Cyprus | Czech Republic |
| Democratic People's Rep. of Korea | Democratic Rep. of the Congo | Denmark | Djibouti | Dominica | Dominican Republic | Ecuador | Egypt | El Salvador |
| Equatorial Guinea | Eritrea | Estonia | Ethiopia | Fiji | Finland | France | Gabon | Gambia |
| Georgia | Germany | Ghana | Greece | Grenada | Guatemala | Guinea | Guinea-Bissau | Guyana |
| Haiti | Honduras | Hungary | Iceland | India | Indonesia | Iran (Islamic Republic of) | Iraq | Ireland |
| Israel | Italy | Jamaica | Japan | Jordan | Kazakhstan | Kenya | Kiribati | Kuwait |
| Kyrgyzstan | Lao People's Dem. Rep. | Latvia | Lebanon | Lesotho | Liberia | Libyan Arab Jamahiriya | Liechtenstein | Lithuania |

| 2003 | | 191 |
|---|---|---|
| Year | United Nations | Member states |

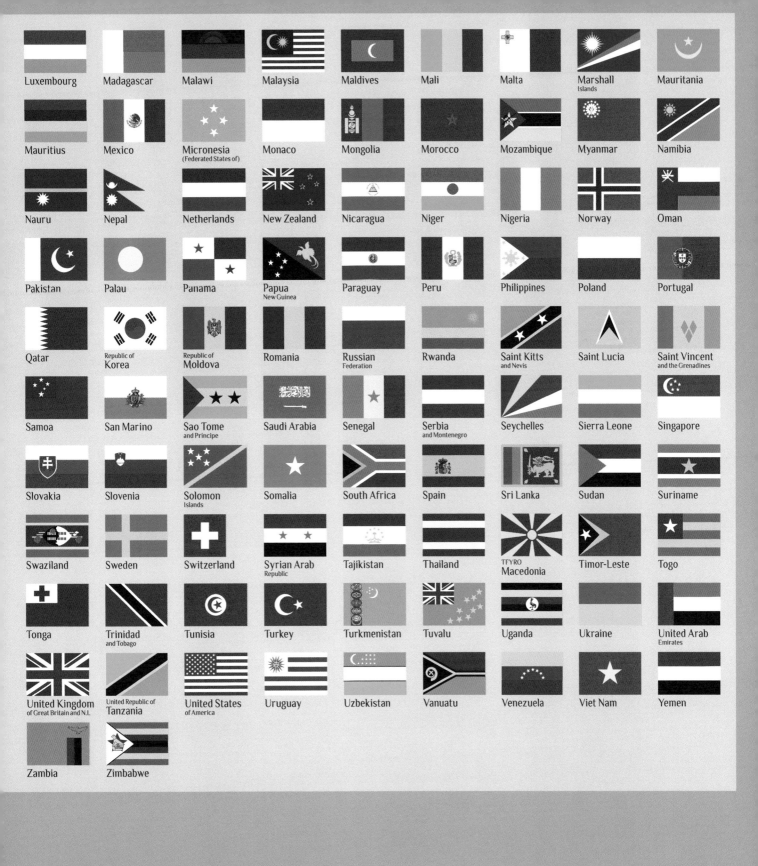

Luxembourg
Madagascar
Malawi
Malaysia
Maldives
Mali
Malta
Marshall Islands
Mauritania

Mauritius
Mexico
Micronesia (Federated States of)
Monaco
Mongolia
Morocco
Mozambique
Myanmar
Namibia

Nauru
Nepal
Netherlands
New Zealand
Nicaragua
Niger
Nigeria
Norway
Oman

Pakistan
Palau
Panama
Papua New Guinea
Paraguay
Peru
Philippines
Poland
Portugal

Qatar
Republic of Korea
Republic of Moldova
Romania
Russian Federation
Rwanda
Saint Kitts and Nevis
Saint Lucia
Saint Vincent and the Grenadines

Samoa
San Marino
Sao Tome and Principe
Saudi Arabia
Senegal
Serbia and Montenegro
Seychelles
Sierra Leone
Singapore

Slovakia
Slovenia
Solomon Islands
Somalia
South Africa
Spain
Sri Lanka
Sudan
Suriname

Swaziland
Sweden
Switzerland
Syrian Arab Republic
Tajikistan
Thailand
TFYRO Macedonia
Timor-Leste
Togo

Tonga
Trinidad and Tobago
Tunisia
Turkey
Turkmenistan
Tuvalu
Uganda
Ukraine
United Arab Emirates

United Kingdom of Great Britain and N.I.
United Republic of Tanzania
United States of America
Uruguay
Uzbekistan
Vanuatu
Venezuela
Viet Nam
Yemen

Zambia
Zimbabwe

Name change

Yugoslavia (Federal Republic of)
Serbia and Montenegro

Flag change

Democratic Rep. of the Congo
Democratic Rep. of the Congo

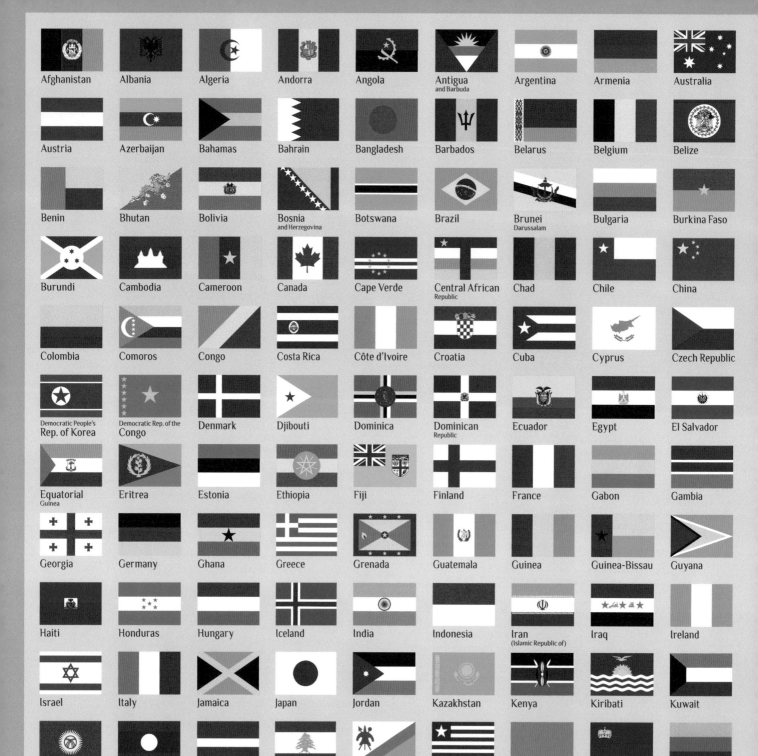

Afghanistan | Albania | Algeria | Andorra | Angola | Antigua and Barbuda | Argentina | Armenia | Australia

Austria | Azerbaijan | Bahamas | Bahrain | Bangladesh | Barbados | Belarus | Belgium | Belize

Benin | Bhutan | Bolivia | Bosnia and Herzegovina | Botswana | Brazil | Brunei Darussalam | Bulgaria | Burkina Faso

Burundi | Cambodia | Cameroon | Canada | Cape Verde | Central African Republic | Chad | Chile | China

Colombia | Comoros | Congo | Costa Rica | Côte d'Ivoire | Croatia | Cuba | Cyprus | Czech Republic

Democratic People's Rep. of Korea | Democratic Rep. of the Congo | Denmark | Djibouti | Dominica | Dominican Republic | Ecuador | Egypt | El Salvador

Equatorial Guinea | Eritrea | Estonia | Ethiopia | Fiji | Finland | France | Gabon | Gambia

Georgia | Germany | Ghana | Greece | Grenada | Guatemala | Guinea | Guinea-Bissau | Guyana

Haiti | Honduras | Hungary | Iceland | India | Indonesia | Iran (Islamic Republic of) | Iraq | Ireland

Israel | Italy | Jamaica | Japan | Jordan | Kazakhstan | Kenya | Kiribati | Kuwait

Kyrgyzstan | Lao People's Dem. Rep. | Latvia | Lebanon | Lesotho | Liberia | Libyan Arab Jamahiriya | Liechtenstein | Lithuania

Timeline                    page 124

2004
Year

United Nations

191
Member states

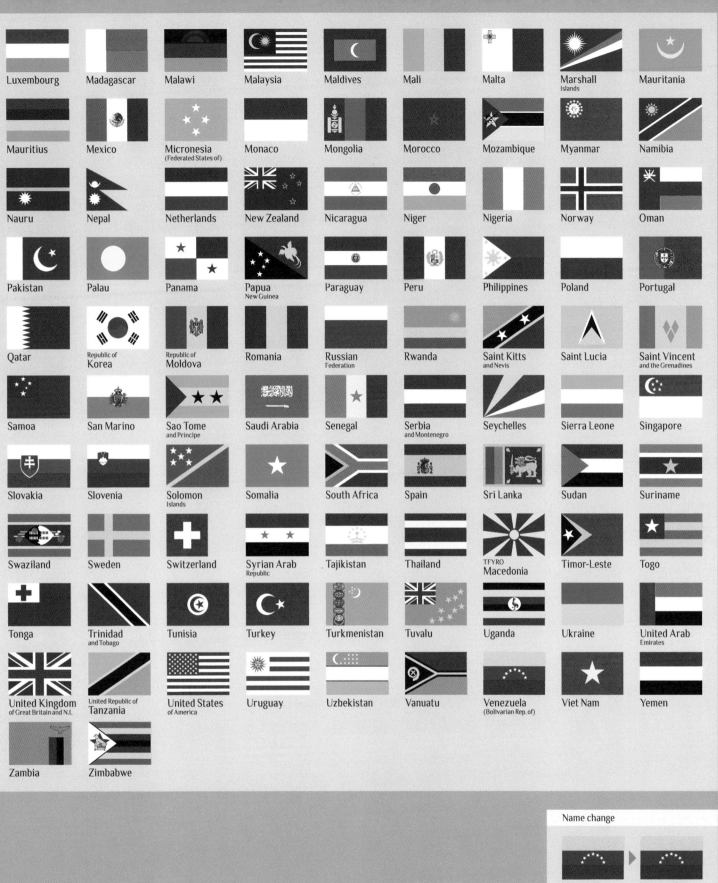

Luxembourg · Madagascar · Malawi · Malaysia · Maldives · Mali · Malta · Marshall Islands · Mauritania

Mauritius · Mexico · Micronesia (Federated States of) · Monaco · Mongolia · Morocco · Mozambique · Myanmar · Namibia

Nauru · Nepal · Netherlands · New Zealand · Nicaragua · Niger · Nigeria · Norway · Oman

Pakistan · Palau · Panama · Papua New Guinea · Paraguay · Peru · Philippines · Poland · Portugal

Qatar · Republic of Korea · Republic of Moldova · Romania · Russian Federation · Rwanda · Saint Kitts and Nevis · Saint Lucia · Saint Vincent and the Grenadines

Samoa · San Marino · Sao Tome and Principe · Saudi Arabia · Senegal · Serbia and Montenegro · Seychelles · Sierra Leone · Singapore

Slovakia · Slovenia · Solomon Islands · Somalia · South Africa · Spain · Sri Lanka · Sudan · Suriname

Swaziland · Sweden · Switzerland · Syrian Arab Republic · Tajikistan · Thailand · TFYRO Macedonia · Timor-Leste · Togo

Tonga · Trinidad and Tobago · Tunisia · Turkey · Turkmenistan · Tuvalu · Uganda · Ukraine · United Arab Emirates

United Kingdom of Great Britain and N.I. · United Republic of Tanzania · United States of America · Uruguay · Uzbekistan · Vanuatu · Venezuela (Bolivarian Rep. of) · Viet Nam · Yemen

Zambia · Zimbabwe

Name change

Venezuela → Venezuela (Bolivarian Rep. of)

Flag change

Afghanistan → Afghanistan

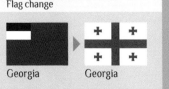

Flag change

Georgia → Georgia

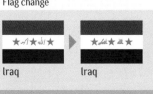

Flag change

Iraq → Iraq

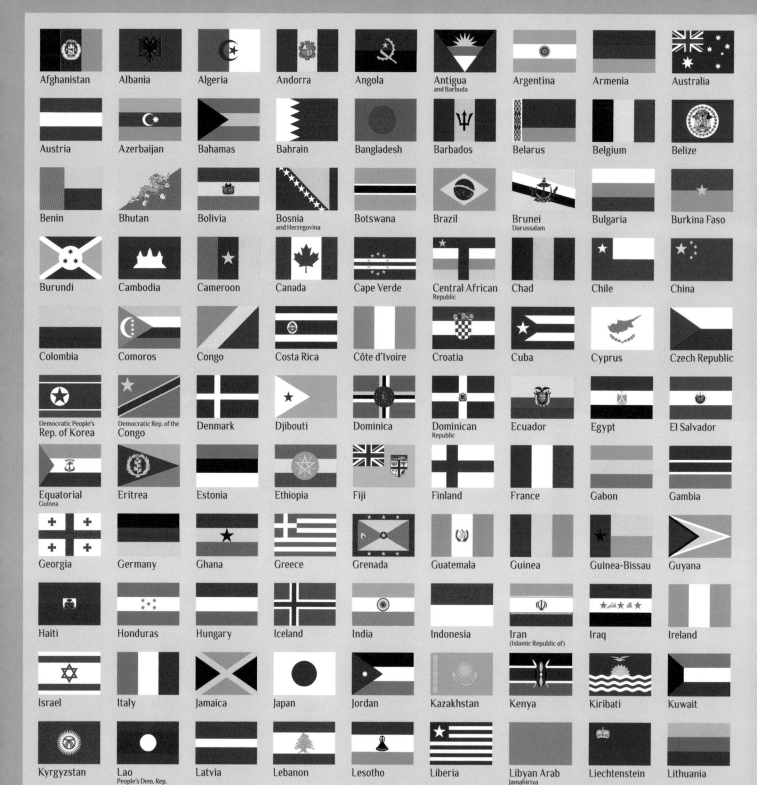

Afghanistan | Albania | Algeria | Andorra | Angola | Antigua and Barbuda | Argentina | Armenia | Australia

Austria | Azerbaijan | Bahamas | Bahrain | Bangladesh | Barbados | Belarus | Belgium | Belize

Benin | Bhutan | Bolivia | Bosnia and Herzegovina | Botswana | Brazil | Brunei Darussalam | Bulgaria | Burkina Faso

Burundi | Cambodia | Cameroon | Canada | Cape Verde | Central African Republic | Chad | Chile | China

Colombia | Comoros | Congo | Costa Rica | Côte d'Ivoire | Croatia | Cuba | Cyprus | Czech Republic

Democratic People's Rep. of Korea | Democratic Rep. of the Congo | Denmark | Djibouti | Dominica | Dominican Republic | Ecuador | Egypt | El Salvador

Equatorial Guinea | Eritrea | Estonia | Ethiopia | Fiji | Finland | France | Gabon | Gambia

Georgia | Germany | Ghana | Greece | Grenada | Guatemala | Guinea | Guinea-Bissau | Guyana

Haiti | Honduras | Hungary | Iceland | India | Indonesia | Iran (Islamic Republic of) | Iraq | Ireland

Israel | Italy | Jamaica | Japan | Jordan | Kazakhstan | Kenya | Kiribati | Kuwait

Kyrgyzstan | Lao People's Dem. Rep. | Latvia | Lebanon | Lesotho | Liberia | Libyan Arab Jamahiriya | Liechtenstein | Lithuania

## No changes in 2005

Timeline                                    page 126

2006  192

Year | United Nations | Member states

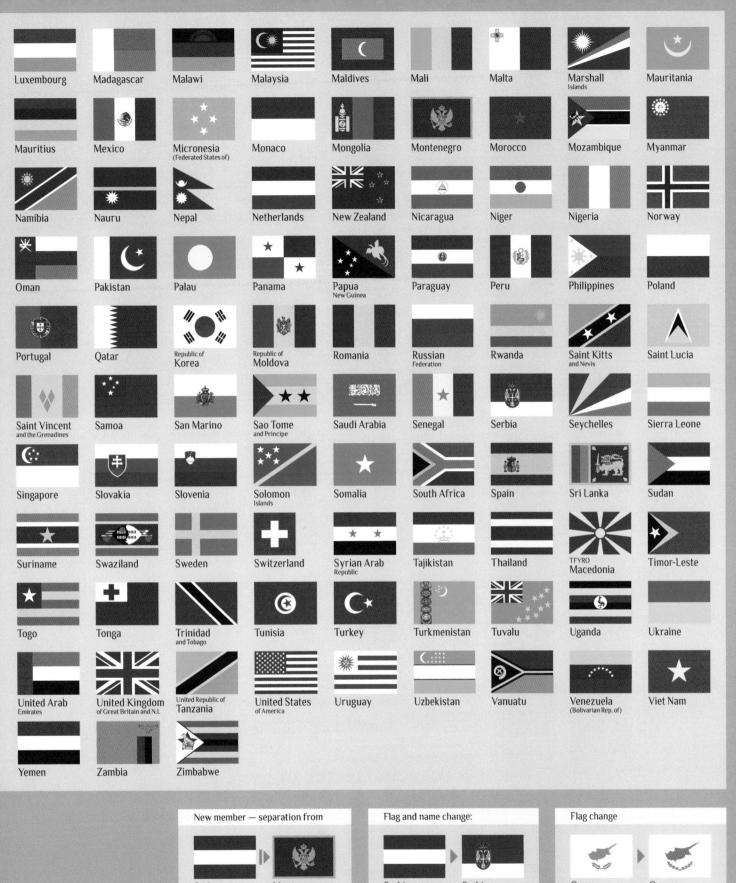

| | | | | | | | | |
|---|---|---|---|---|---|---|---|---|
| Luxembourg | Madagascar | Malawi | Malaysia | Maldives | Mali | Malta | Marshall Islands | Mauritania |
| Mauritius | Mexico | Micronesia (Federated States of) | Monaco | Mongolia | Montenegro | Morocco | Mozambique | Myanmar |
| Namibia | Nauru | Nepal | Netherlands | New Zealand | Nicaragua | Niger | Nigeria | Norway |
| Oman | Pakistan | Palau | Panama | Papua New Guinea | Paraguay | Peru | Philippines | Poland |
| Portugal | Qatar | Republic of Korea | Republic of Moldova | Romania | Russian Federation | Rwanda | Saint Kitts and Nevis | Saint Lucia |
| Saint Vincent and the Grenadines | Samoa | San Marino | Sao Tome and Principe | Saudi Arabia | Senegal | Serbia | Seychelles | Sierra Leone |
| Singapore | Slovakia | Slovenia | Solomon Islands | Somalia | South Africa | Spain | Sri Lanka | Sudan |
| Suriname | Swaziland | Sweden | Switzerland | Syrian Arab Republic | Tajikistan | Thailand | TFYRO Macedonia | Timor-Leste |
| Togo | Tonga | Trinidad and Tobago | Tunisia | Turkey | Turkmenistan | Tuvalu | Uganda | Ukraine |
| United Arab Emirates | United Kingdom of Great Britain and N.I. | United Republic of Tanzania | United States of America | Uruguay | Uzbekistan | Vanuatu | Venezuela (Bolivarian Rep. of) | Viet Nam |
| Yemen | Zambia | Zimbabwe | | | | | | |

New member — separation from
Serbia and Montenegro ▶ Montenegro

Flag and name change:
Serbia and Montenegro ▶ Serbia

Flag change
Cyprus ▶ Cyprus

Flag change
Democratic Rep. of the Congo ▶ Democratic Rep. of the Congo

Flag change
Lesotho ▶ Lesotho

Flag change
Venezuela (Bolivarian Rep. of) ▶ Venezuela (Bolivarian Rep. of)

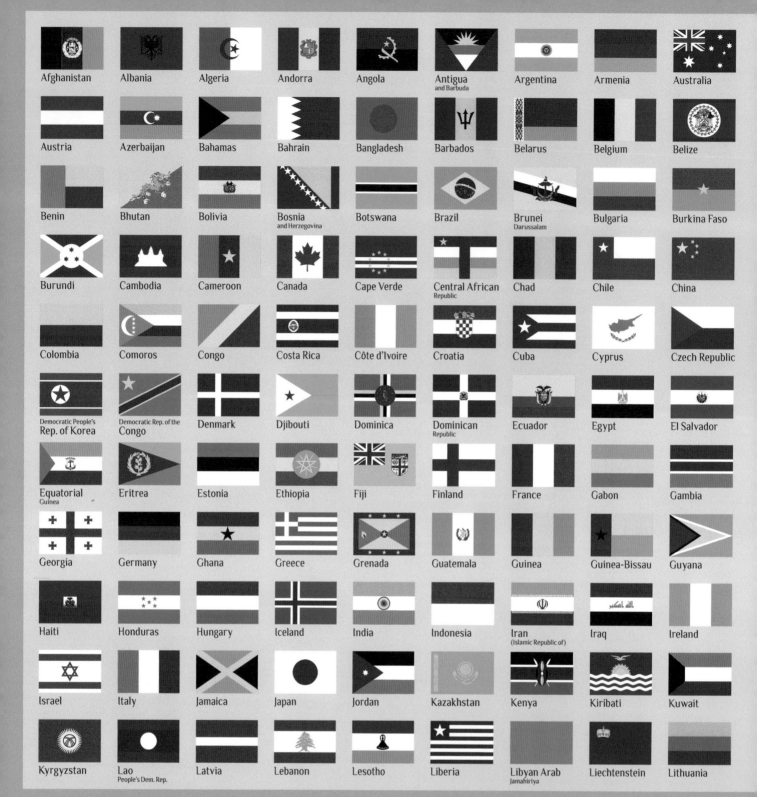

Afghanistan · Albania · Algeria · Andorra · Angola · Antigua and Barbuda · Argentina · Armenia · Australia

Austria · Azerbaijan · Bahamas · Bahrain · Bangladesh · Barbados · Belarus · Belgium · Belize

Benin · Bhutan · Bolivia · Bosnia and Herzegovina · Botswana · Brazil · Brunei Darussalam · Bulgaria · Burkina Faso

Burundi · Cambodia · Cameroon · Canada · Cape Verde · Central African Republic · Chad · Chile · China

Colombia · Comoros · Congo · Costa Rica · Côte d'Ivoire · Croatia · Cuba · Cyprus · Czech Republic

Democratic People's Rep. of Korea · Democratic Rep. of the Congo · Denmark · Djibouti · Dominica · Dominican Republic · Ecuador · Egypt · El Salvador

Equatorial Guinea · Eritrea · Estonia · Ethiopia · Fiji · Finland · France · Gabon · Gambia

Georgia · Germany · Ghana · Greece · Grenada · Guatemala · Guinea · Guinea-Bissau · Guyana

Haiti · Honduras · Hungary · Iceland · India · Indonesia · Iran (Islamic Republic of) · Iraq · Ireland

Israel · Italy · Jamaica · Japan · Jordan · Kazakhstan · Kenya · Kiribati · Kuwait

Kyrgyzstan · Lao People's Dem. Rep. · Latvia · Lebanon · Lesotho · Liberia · Libyan Arab Jamahiriya · Liechtenstein · Lithuania

No changes in 2007

Timeline page 128

2008 Year · United Nations · 192 Member states

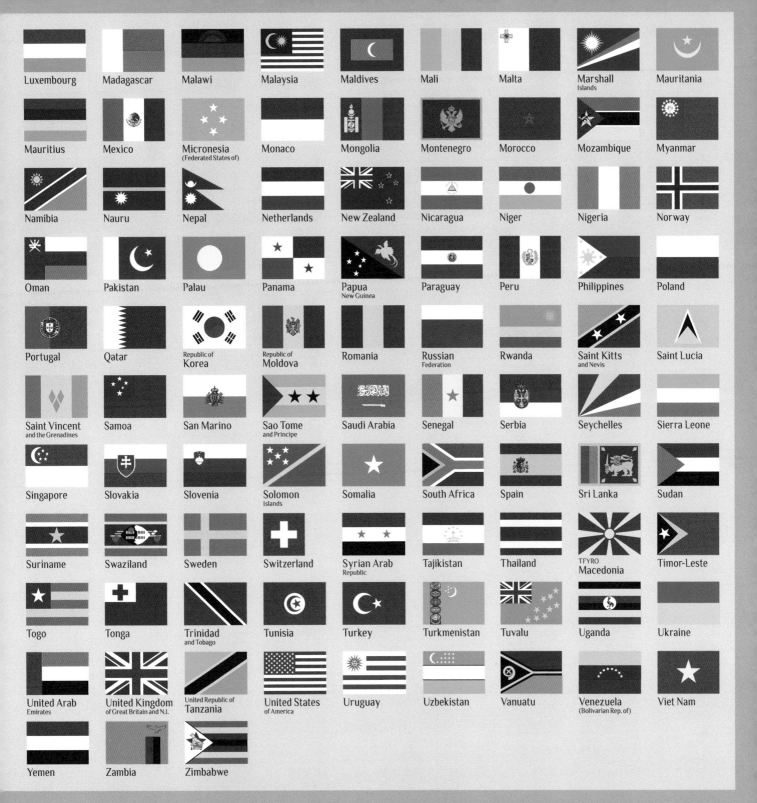

Luxembourg
Madagascar
Malawi
Malaysia
Maldives
Mali
Malta
Marshall Islands
Mauritania

Mauritius
Mexico
Micronesia (Federated States of)
Monaco
Mongolia
Montenegro
Morocco
Mozambique
Myanmar

Namibia
Nauru
Nepal
Netherlands
New Zealand
Nicaragua
Niger
Nigeria
Norway

Oman
Pakistan
Palau
Panama
Papua New Guinea
Paraguay
Peru
Philippines
Poland

Portugal
Qatar
Republic of Korea
Republic of Moldova
Romania
Russian Federation
Rwanda
Saint Kitts and Nevis
Saint Lucia

Saint Vincent and the Grenadines
Samoa
San Marino
Sao Tome and Principe
Saudi Arabia
Senegal
Serbia
Seychelles
Sierra Leone

Singapore
Slovakia
Slovenia
Solomon Islands
Somalia
South Africa
Spain
Sri Lanka
Sudan

Suriname
Swaziland
Sweden
Switzerland
Syrian Arab Republic
Tajikistan
Thailand
TFYRO Macedonia
Timor-Leste

Togo
Tonga
Trinidad and Tobago
Tunisia
Turkey
Turkmenistan
Tuvalu
Uganda
Ukraine

United Arab Emirates
United Kingdom of Great Britain and N.I.
United Republic of Tanzania
United States of America
Uruguay
Uzbekistan
Vanuatu
Venezuela (Bolivarian Rep. of)
Viet Nam

Yemen
Zambia
Zimbabwe

Flag change

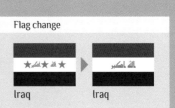

Iraq      Iraq

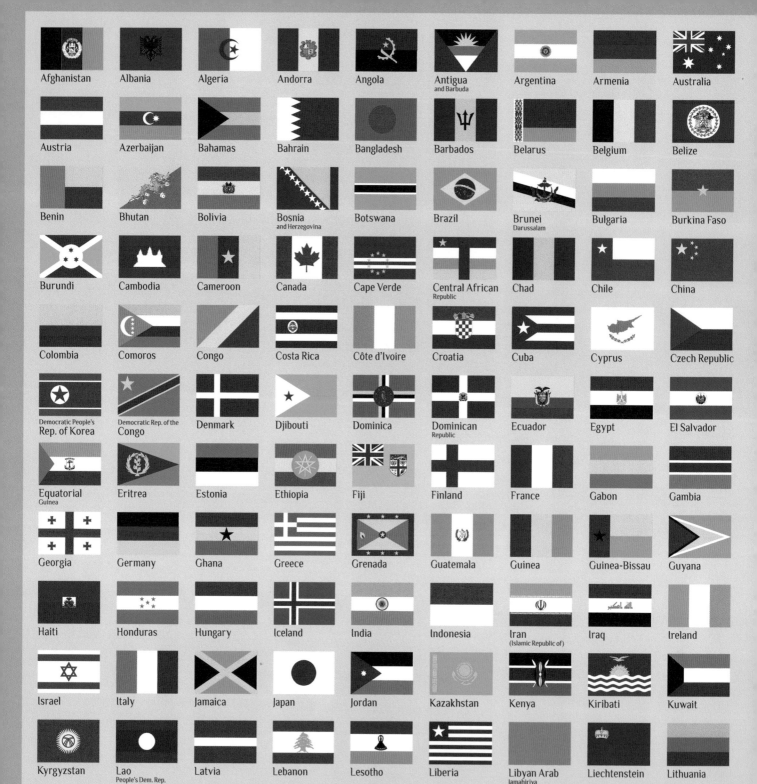

Afghanistan | Albania | Algeria | Andorra | Angola | Antigua and Barbuda | Argentina | Armenia | Australia

Austria | Azerbaijan | Bahamas | Bahrain | Bangladesh | Barbados | Belarus | Belgium | Belize

Benin | Bhutan | Bolivia | Bosnia and Herzegovina | Botswana | Brazil | Brunei Darussalam | Bulgaria | Burkina Faso

Burundi | Cambodia | Cameroon | Canada | Cape Verde | Central African Republic | Chad | Chile | China

Colombia | Comoros | Congo | Costa Rica | Côte d'Ivoire | Croatia | Cuba | Cyprus | Czech Republic

Democratic People's Rep. of Korea | Democratic Rep. of the Congo | Denmark | Djibouti | Dominica | Dominican Republic | Ecuador | Egypt | El Salvador

Equatorial Guinea | Eritrea | Estonia | Ethiopia | Fiji | Finland | France | Gabon | Gambia

Georgia | Germany | Ghana | Greece | Grenada | Guatemala | Guinea | Guinea-Bissau | Guyana

Haiti | Honduras | Hungary | Iceland | India | Indonesia | Iran (Islamic Republic of) | Iraq | Ireland

Israel | Italy | Jamaica | Japan | Jordan | Kazakhstan | Kenya | Kiribati | Kuwait

Kyrgyzstan | Lao People's Dem. Rep. | Latvia | Lebanon | Lesotho | Liberia | Libyan Arab Jamahiriya | Liechtenstein | Lithuania

## No changes in 2009

Timeline                                     page 130

| 2010 |  | 192 |
| Year | United Nations | Member states |

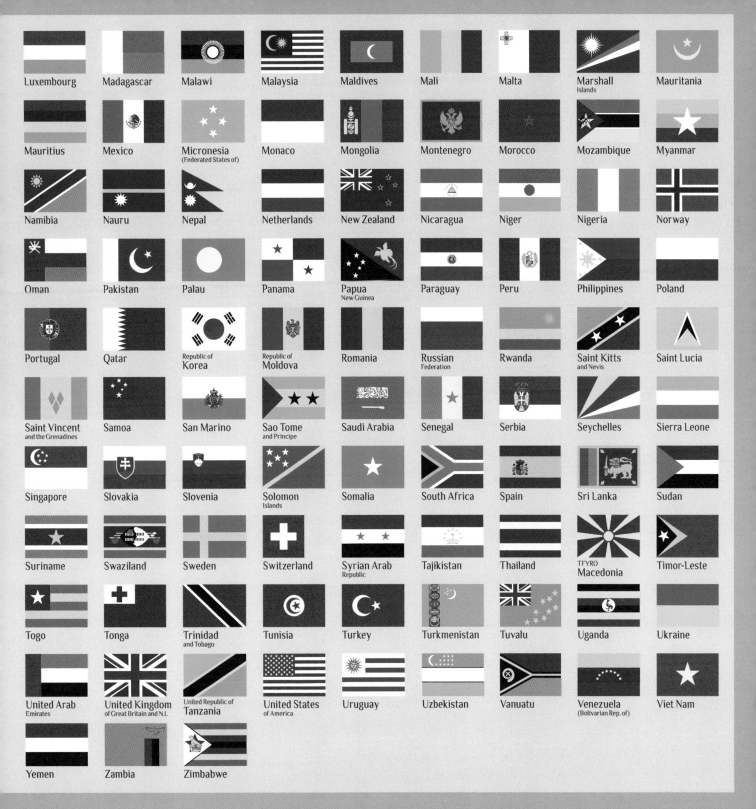

| Luxembourg | Madagascar | Malawi | Malaysia | Maldives | Mali | Malta | Marshall Islands | Mauritania |
| Mauritius | Mexico | Micronesia (Federated States of) | Monaco | Mongolia | Montenegro | Morocco | Mozambique | Myanmar |
| Namibia | Nauru | Nepal | Netherlands | New Zealand | Nicaragua | Niger | Nigeria | Norway |
| Oman | Pakistan | Palau | Panama | Papua New Guinea | Paraguay | Peru | Philippines | Poland |
| Portugal | Qatar | Republic of Korea | Republic of Moldova | Romania | Russian Federation | Rwanda | Saint Kitts and Nevis | Saint Lucia |
| Saint Vincent and the Grenadines | Samoa | San Marino | Sao Tome and Principe | Saudi Arabia | Senegal | Serbia | Seychelles | Sierra Leone |
| Singapore | Slovakia | Slovenia | Solomon Islands | Somalia | South Africa | Spain | Sri Lanka | Sudan |
| Suriname | Swaziland | Sweden | Switzerland | Syrian Arab Republic | Tajikistan | Thailand | TFYRO Macedonia | Timor-Leste |
| Togo | Tonga | Trinidad and Tobago | Tunisia | Turkey | Turkmenistan | Tuvalu | Uganda | Ukraine |
| United Arab Emirates | United Kingdom of Great Britain and N.I. | United Republic of Tanzania | United States of America | Uruguay | Uzbekistan | Vanuatu | Venezuela (Bolivarian Rep. of) | Viet Nam |
| Yemen | Zambia | Zimbabwe | | | | | | |

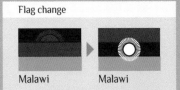

Flag change

Malawi ▶ Malawi

Flag change

Myanmar ▶ Myanmar

Flag change

Serbia ▶ Serbia

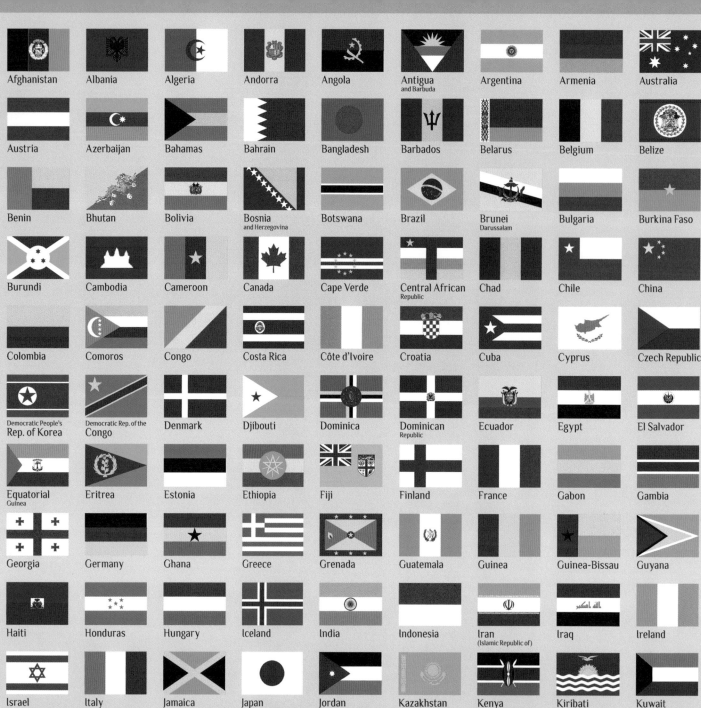

Afghanistan | Albania | Algeria | Andorra | Angola | Antigua and Barbuda | Argentina | Armenia | Australia

Austria | Azerbaijan | Bahamas | Bahrain | Bangladesh | Barbados | Belarus | Belgium | Belize

Benin | Bhutan | Bolivia | Bosnia and Herzegovina | Botswana | Brazil | Brunei Darussalam | Bulgaria | Burkina Faso

Burundi | Cambodia | Cameroon | Canada | Cape Verde | Central African Republic | Chad | Chile | China

Colombia | Comoros | Congo | Costa Rica | Côte d'Ivoire | Croatia | Cuba | Cyprus | Czech Republic

Democratic People's Rep. of Korea | Democratic Rep. of the Congo | Denmark | Djibouti | Dominica | Dominican Republic | Ecuador | Egypt | El Salvador

Equatorial Guinea | Eritrea | Estonia | Ethiopia | Fiji | Finland | France | Gabon | Gambia

Georgia | Germany | Ghana | Greece | Grenada | Guatemala | Guinea | Guinea-Bissau | Guyana

Haiti | Honduras | Hungary | Iceland | India | Indonesia | Iran (Islamic Republic of) | Iraq | Ireland

Israel | Italy | Jamaica | Japan | Jordan | Kazakhstan | Kenya | Kiribati | Kuwait

Kyrgyzstan | Lao People's Dem. Rep. | Latvia | Lebanon | Lesotho | Liberia | Libya | Liechtenstein | Lithuania

2011
Year

United Nations

193
Member states

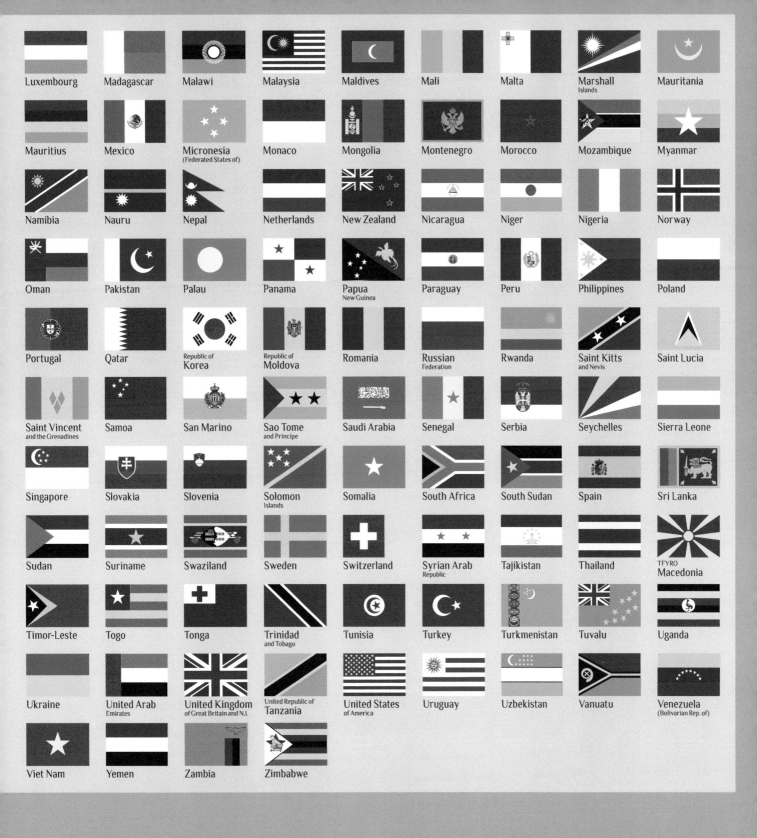

Luxembourg · Madagascar · Malawi · Malaysia · Maldives · Mali · Malta · Marshall Islands · Mauritania

Mauritius · Mexico · Micronesia (Federated States of) · Monaco · Mongolia · Montenegro · Morocco · Mozambique · Myanmar

Namibia · Nauru · Nepal · Netherlands · New Zealand · Nicaragua · Niger · Nigeria · Norway

Oman · Pakistan · Palau · Panama · Papua New Guinea · Paraguay · Peru · Philippines · Poland

Portugal · Qatar · Republic of Korea · Republic of Moldova · Romania · Russian Federation · Rwanda · Saint Kitts and Nevis · Saint Lucia

Saint Vincent and the Grenadines · Samoa · San Marino · Sao Tome and Principe · Saudi Arabia · Senegal · Serbia · Seychelles · Sierra Leone

Singapore · Slovakia · Slovenia · Solomon Islands · Somalia · South Africa · South Sudan · Spain · Sri Lanka

Sudan · Suriname · Swaziland · Sweden · Switzerland · Syrian Arab Republic · Tajikistan · Thailand · TFYRO Macedonia

Timor-Leste · Togo · Tonga · Trinidad and Tobago · Tunisia · Turkey · Turkmenistan · Tuvalu · Uganda

Ukraine · United Arab Emirates · United Kingdom of Great Britain and N.I. · United Republic of Tanzania · United States of America · Uruguay · Uzbekistan · Vanuatu · Venezuela (Bolivarian Rep. of)

Viet Nam · Yemen · Zambia · Zimbabwe

New member — separation from

Sudan · South Sudan

Flag and name change

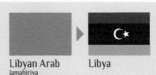

Libyan Arab Jamahiriya · Libya

Flag change

San Marino · San Marino

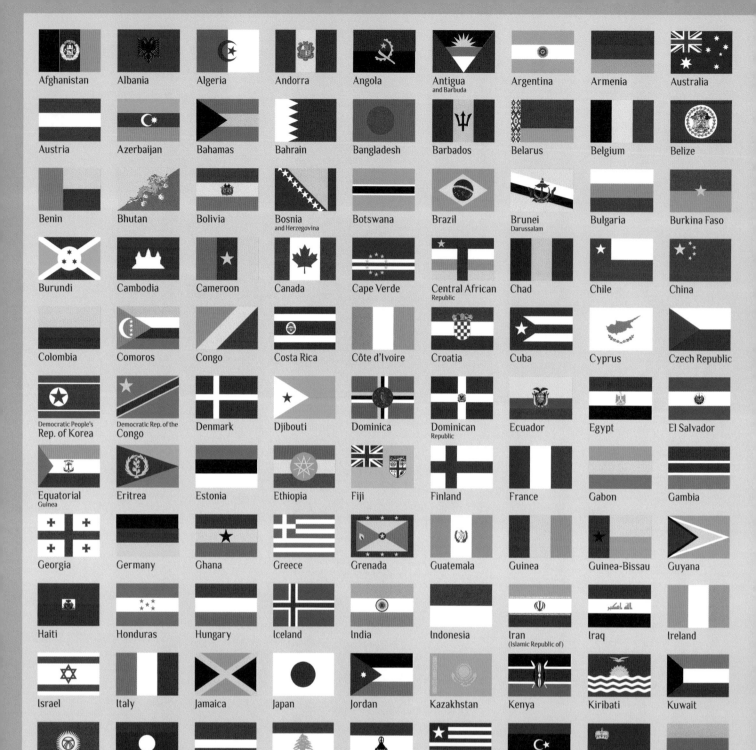

| Afghanistan | Albania | Algeria | Andorra | Angola | Antigua and Barbuda | Argentina | Armenia | Australia |
| Austria | Azerbaijan | Bahamas | Bahrain | Bangladesh | Barbados | Belarus | Belgium | Belize |
| Benin | Bhutan | Bolivia | Bosnia and Herzegovina | Botswana | Brazil | Brunei Darussalam | Bulgaria | Burkina Faso |
| Burundi | Cambodia | Cameroon | Canada | Cape Verde | Central African Republic | Chad | Chile | China |
| Colombia | Comoros | Congo | Costa Rica | Côte d'Ivoire | Croatia | Cuba | Cyprus | Czech Republic |
| Democratic People's Rep. of Korea | Democratic Rep. of the Congo | Denmark | Djibouti | Dominica | Dominican Republic | Ecuador | Egypt | El Salvador |
| Equatorial Guinea | Eritrea | Estonia | Ethiopia | Fiji | Finland | France | Gabon | Gambia |
| Georgia | Germany | Ghana | Greece | Grenada | Guatemala | Guinea | Guinea-Bissau | Guyana |
| Haiti | Honduras | Hungary | Iceland | India | Indonesia | Iran (Islamic Republic of) | Iraq | Ireland |
| Israel | Italy | Jamaica | Japan | Jordan | Kazakhstan | Kenya | Kiribati | Kuwait |
| Kyrgyzstan | Lao People's Dem. Rep. | Latvia | Lebanon | Lesotho | Liberia | Libya | Liechtenstein | Lithuania |

Timeline                          page 134

2012
Year

United Nations

193
Member states

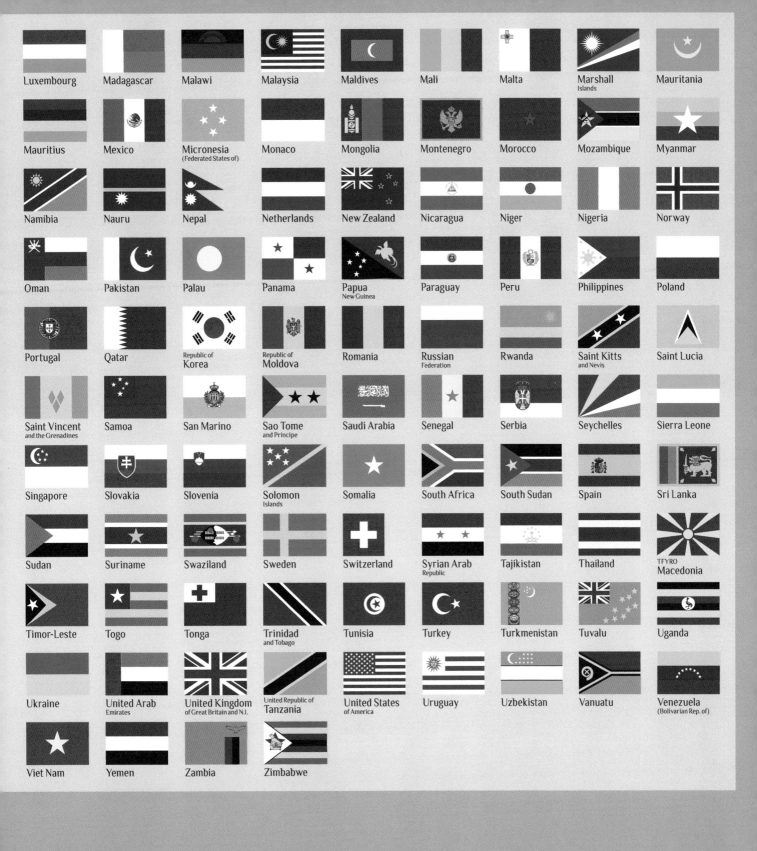

Luxembourg | Madagascar | Malawi | Malaysia | Maldives | Mali | Malta | Marshall Islands | Mauritania

Mauritius | Mexico | Micronesia (Federated States of) | Monaco | Mongolia | Montenegro | Morocco | Mozambique | Myanmar

Namibia | Nauru | Nepal | Netherlands | New Zealand | Nicaragua | Niger | Nigeria | Norway

Oman | Pakistan | Palau | Panama | Papua New Guinea | Paraguay | Peru | Philippines | Poland

Portugal | Qatar | Republic of Korea | Republic of Moldova | Romania | Russian Federation | Rwanda | Saint Kitts and Nevis | Saint Lucia

Saint Vincent and the Grenadines | Samoa | San Marino | Sao Tome and Principe | Saudi Arabia | Senegal | Serbia | Seychelles | Sierra Leone

Singapore | Slovakia | Slovenia | Solomon Islands | Somalia | South Africa | South Sudan | Spain | Sri Lanka

Sudan | Suriname | Swaziland | Sweden | Switzerland | Syrian Arab Republic | Tajikistan | Thailand | TFYRO Macedonia

Timor-Leste | Togo | Tonga | Trinidad and Tobago | Tunisia | Turkey | Turkmenistan | Tuvalu | Uganda

Ukraine | United Arab Emirates | United Kingdom of Great Britain and N.I. | United Republic of Tanzania | United States of America | Uruguay | Uzbekistan | Vanuatu | Venezuela (Bolivarian Rep. of)

Viet Nam | Yemen | Zambia | Zimbabwe

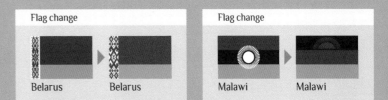

Flag change

Belarus ▶ Belarus

Flag change

Malawi ▶ Malawi

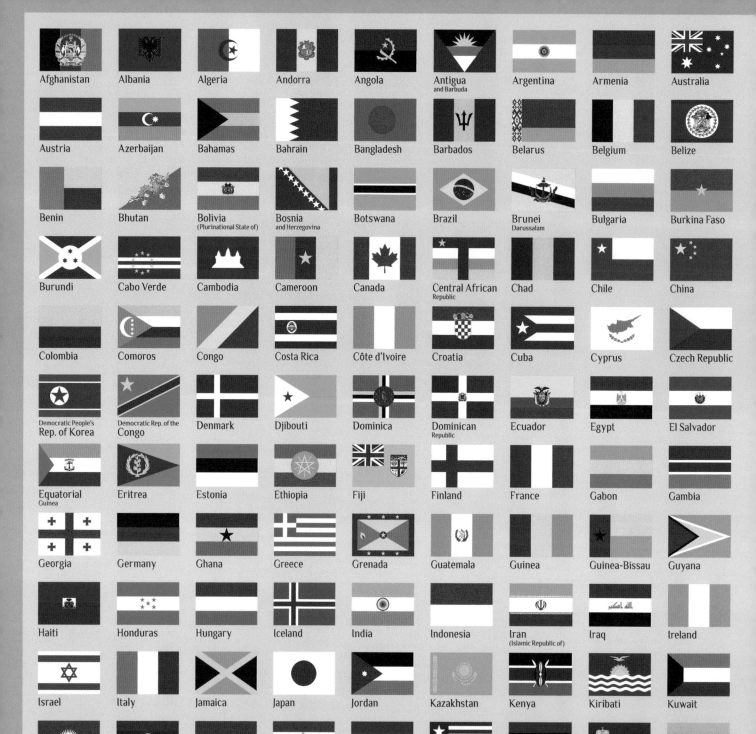

Afghanistan
Albania
Algeria
Andorra
Angola
Antigua and Barbuda
Argentina
Armenia
Australia

Austria
Azerbaijan
Bahamas
Bahrain
Bangladesh
Barbados
Belarus
Belgium
Belize

Benin
Bhutan
Bolivia (Plurinational State of)
Bosnia and Herzegovina
Botswana
Brazil
Brunei Darussalam
Bulgaria
Burkina Faso

Burundi
Cabo Verde
Cambodia
Cameroon
Canada
Central African Republic
Chad
Chile
China

Colombia
Comoros
Congo
Costa Rica
Côte d'Ivoire
Croatia
Cuba
Cyprus
Czech Republic

Democratic People's Rep. of Korea
Democratic Rep. of the Congo
Denmark
Djibouti
Dominica
Dominican Republic
Ecuador
Egypt
El Salvador

Equatorial Guinea
Eritrea
Estonia
Ethiopia
Fiji
Finland
France
Gabon
Gambia

Georgia
Germany
Ghana
Greece
Grenada
Guatemala
Guinea
Guinea-Bissau
Guyana

Haiti
Honduras
Hungary
Iceland
India
Indonesia
Iran (Islamic Republic of)
Iraq
Ireland

Israel
Italy
Jamaica
Japan
Jordan
Kazakhstan
Kenya
Kiribati
Kuwait

Kyrgyzstan
Lao People's Dem. Rep.
Latvia
Lebanon
Lesotho
Liberia
Libya
Liechtenstein
Lithuania

2013
Year

United Nations

193
Member states

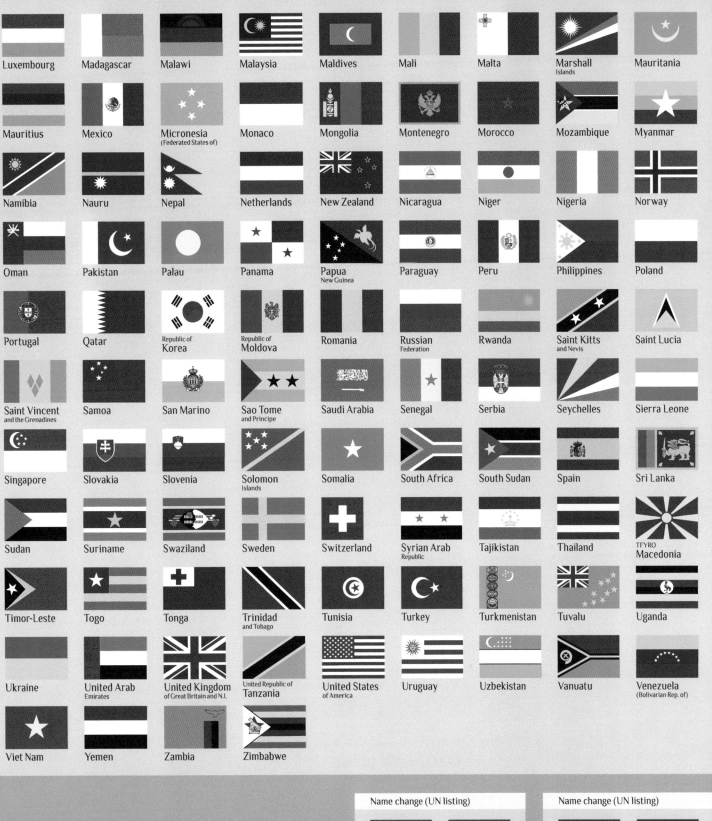

Luxembourg
Madagascar
Malawi
Malaysia
Maldives
Mali
Malta
Marshall Islands
Mauritania

Mauritius
Mexico
Micronesia (Federated States of)
Monaco
Mongolia
Montenegro
Morocco
Mozambique
Myanmar

Namibia
Nauru
Nepal
Netherlands
New Zealand
Nicaragua
Niger
Nigeria
Norway

Oman
Pakistan
Palau
Panama
Papua New Guinea
Paraguay
Peru
Philippines
Poland

Portugal
Qatar
Republic of Korea
Republic of Moldova
Romania
Russian Federation
Rwanda
Saint Kitts and Nevis
Saint Lucia

Saint Vincent and the Grenadines
Samoa
San Marino
Sao Tome and Principe
Saudi Arabia
Senegal
Serbia
Seychelles
Sierra Leone

Singapore
Slovakia
Slovenia
Solomon Islands
Somalia
South Africa
South Sudan
Spain
Sri Lanka

Sudan
Suriname
Swaziland
Sweden
Switzerland
Syrian Arab Republic
Tajikistan
Thailand
TFYRO Macedonia

Timor-Leste
Togo
Tonga
Trinidad and Tobago
Tunisia
Turkey
Turkmenistan
Tuvalu
Uganda

Ukraine
United Arab Emirates
United Kingdom of Great Britain and N.I.
United Republic of Tanzania
United States of America
Uruguay
Uzbekistan
Vanuatu
Venezuela (Bolivarian Rep. of)

Viet Nam
Yemen
Zambia
Zimbabwe

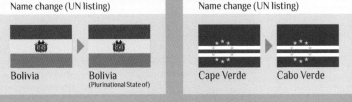

Name change (UN listing)

Bolivia  >  Bolivia (Plurinational State of)

Name change (UN listing)

Cape Verde  >  Cabo Verde

Flag change

Afghanistan  >  Afghanistan

Flag change

Paraguay  >  Paraguay

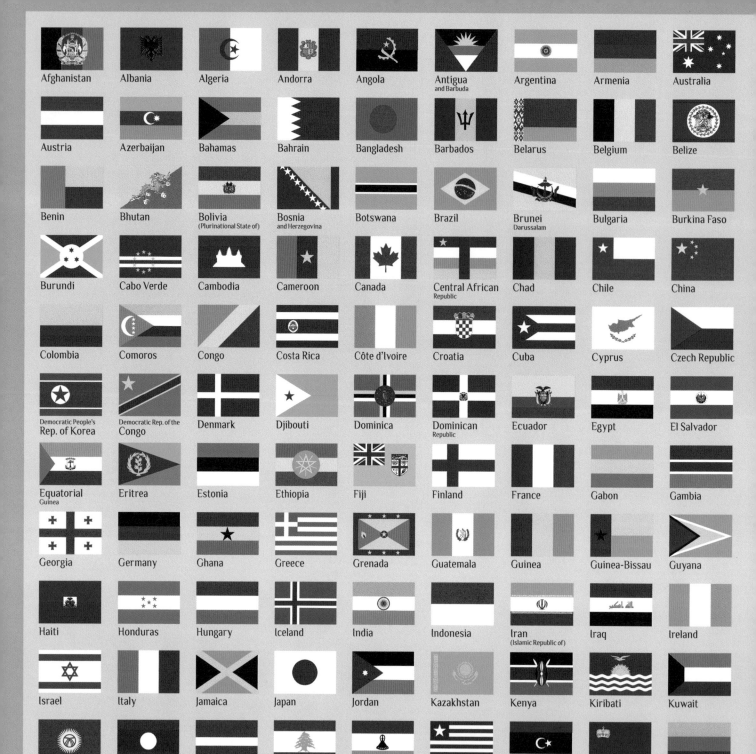

Afghanistan · Albania · Algeria · Andorra · Angola · Antigua and Barbuda · Argentina · Armenia · Australia

Austria · Azerbaijan · Bahamas · Bahrain · Bangladesh · Barbados · Belarus · Belgium · Belize

Benin · Bhutan · Bolivia (Plurinational State of) · Bosnia and Herzegovina · Botswana · Brazil · Brunei Darussalam · Bulgaria · Burkina Faso

Burundi · Cabo Verde · Cambodia · Cameroon · Canada · Central African Republic · Chad · Chile · China

Colombia · Comoros · Congo · Costa Rica · Côte d'Ivoire · Croatia · Cuba · Cyprus · Czech Republic

Democratic People's Rep. of Korea · Democratic Rep. of the Congo · Denmark · Djibouti · Dominica · Dominican Republic · Ecuador · Egypt · El Salvador

Equatorial Guinea · Eritrea · Estonia · Ethiopia · Fiji · Finland · France · Gabon · Gambia

Georgia · Germany · Ghana · Greece · Grenada · Guatemala · Guinea · Guinea-Bissau · Guyana

Haiti · Honduras · Hungary · Iceland · India · Indonesia · Iran (Islamic Republic of) · Iraq · Ireland

Israel · Italy · Jamaica · Japan · Jordan · Kazakhstan · Kenya · Kiribati · Kuwait

Kyrgyzstan · Lao People's Dem. Rep. · Latvia · Lebanon · Lesotho · Liberia · Libya · Liechtenstein · Lithuania

No changes in 2014

Timeline                                                    page 138

| 2015 | | 193 | 2 |
|------|--|-----|---|
| Year | United Nations | Member states | Observer states |

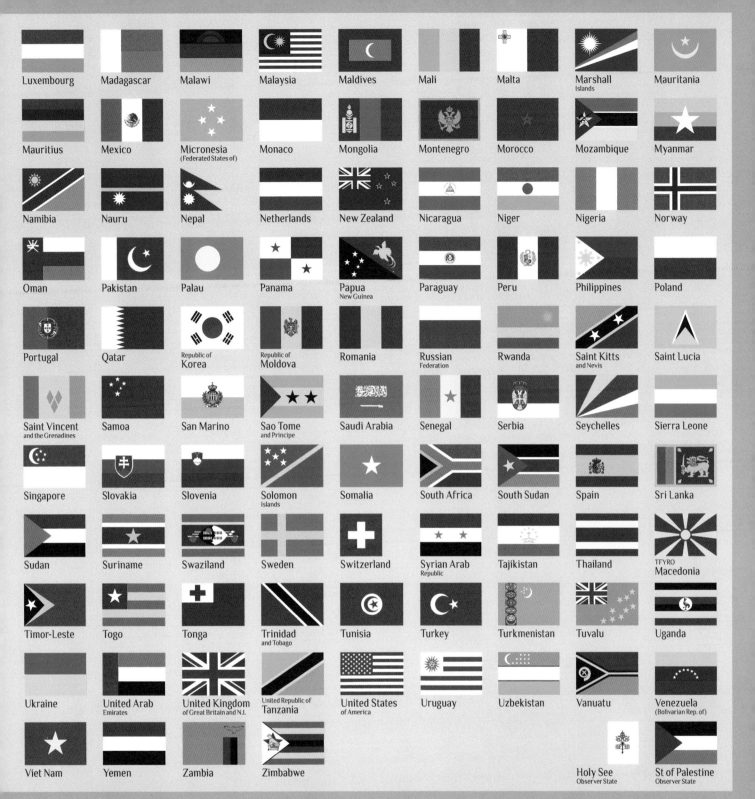

Luxembourg · Madagascar · Malawi · Malaysia · Maldives · Mali · Malta · Marshall Islands · Mauritania

Mauritius · Mexico · Micronesia (Federated States of) · Monaco · Mongolia · Montenegro · Morocco · Mozambique · Myanmar

Namibia · Nauru · Nepal · Netherlands · New Zealand · Nicaragua · Niger · Nigeria · Norway

Oman · Pakistan · Palau · Panama · Papua New Guinea · Paraguay · Peru · Philippines · Poland

Portugal · Qatar · Republic of Korea · Republic of Moldova · Romania · Russian Federation · Rwanda · Saint Kitts and Nevis · Saint Lucia

Saint Vincent and the Grenadines · Samoa · San Marino · Sao Tome and Principe · Saudi Arabia · Senegal · Serbia · Seychelles · Sierra Leone

Singapore · Slovakia · Slovenia · Solomon Islands · Somalia · South Africa · South Sudan · Spain · Sri Lanka

Sudan · Suriname · Swaziland · Sweden · Switzerland · Syrian Arab Republic · Tajikistan · Thailand · TFYRO Macedonia

Timor-Leste · Togo · Tonga · Trinidad and Tobago · Tunisia · Turkey · Turkmenistan · Tuvalu · Uganda

Ukraine · United Arab Emirates · United Kingdom of Great Britain and N.I. · United Republic of Tanzania · United States of America · Uruguay · Uzbekistan · Vanuatu · Venezuela (Bolivarian Rep. of)

Viet Nam · Yemen · Zambia · Zimbabwe · Holy See Observer State · St of Palestine Observer State

Addition of Observer States' flags

 Holy See Observer State

 St of Palestine Observer State

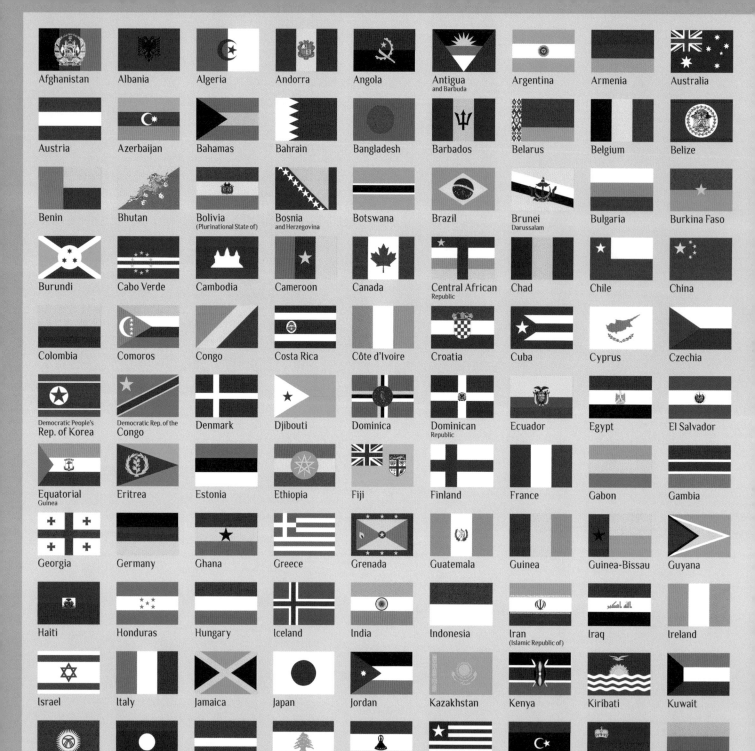

Afghanistan, Albania, Algeria, Andorra, Angola, Antigua and Barbuda, Argentina, Armenia, Australia

Austria, Azerbaijan, Bahamas, Bahrain, Bangladesh, Barbados, Belarus, Belgium, Belize

Benin, Bhutan, Bolivia (Plurinational State of), Bosnia and Herzegovina, Botswana, Brazil, Brunei Darussalam, Bulgaria, Burkina Faso

Burundi, Cabo Verde, Cambodia, Cameroon, Canada, Central African Republic, Chad, Chile, China

Colombia, Comoros, Congo, Costa Rica, Côte d'Ivoire, Croatia, Cuba, Cyprus, Czechia

Democratic People's Rep. of Korea, Democratic Rep. of the Congo, Denmark, Djibouti, Dominica, Dominican Republic, Ecuador, Egypt, El Salvador

Equatorial Guinea, Eritrea, Estonia, Ethiopia, Fiji, Finland, France, Gabon, Gambia

Georgia, Germany, Ghana, Greece, Grenada, Guatemala, Guinea, Guinea-Bissau, Guyana

Haiti, Honduras, Hungary, Iceland, India, Indonesia, Iran (Islamic Republic of), Iraq, Ireland

Israel, Italy, Jamaica, Japan, Jordan, Kazakhstan, Kenya, Kiribati, Kuwait

Kyrgyzstan, Lao People's Dem. Rep., Latvia, Lebanon, Lesotho, Liberia, Libya, Liechtenstein, Lithuania

| 2016 | | 193 | 2 |
|---|---|---|---|
| Year | United Nations | Member states | Observer states |

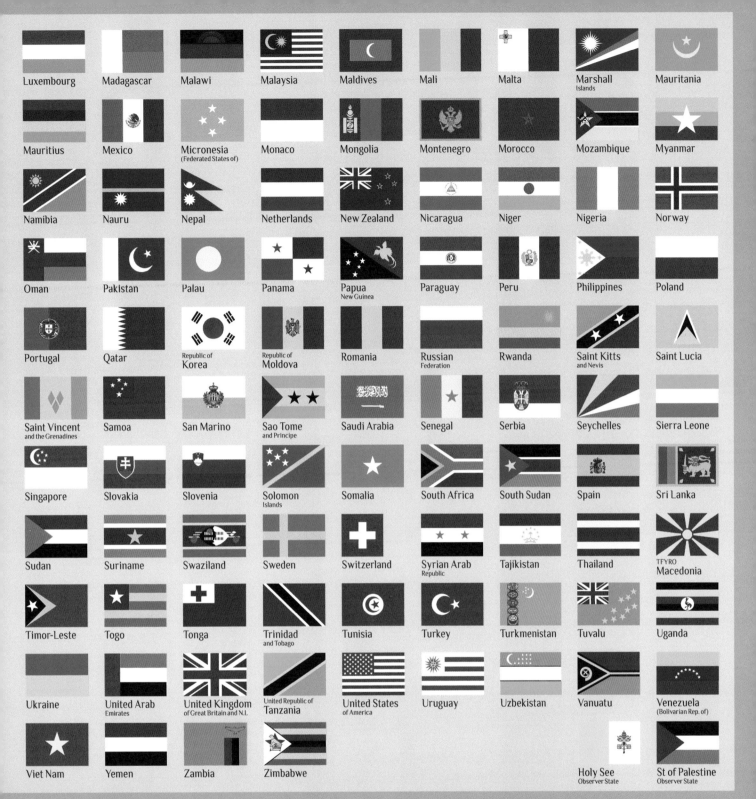

| | | | |
|---|---|---|---|
| Luxembourg | Madagascar | Malawi | Malaysia |
| Maldives | Mali | Malta | Marshall Islands |
| Mauritania | | | |
| Mauritius | Mexico | Micronesia (Federated States of) | Monaco |
| Mongolia | Montenegro | Morocco | Mozambique |
| Myanmar | | | |
| Namibia | Nauru | Nepal | Netherlands |
| New Zealand | Nicaragua | Niger | Nigeria |
| Norway | | | |
| Oman | Pakistan | Palau | Panama |
| Papua New Guinea | Paraguay | Peru | Philippines |
| Poland | | | |
| Portugal | Qatar | Republic of Korea | Republic of Moldova |
| Romania | Russian Federation | Rwanda | Saint Kitts and Nevis |
| Saint Lucia | | | |
| Saint Vincent and the Grenadines | Samoa | San Marino | Sao Tome and Principe |
| Saudi Arabia | Senegal | Serbia | Seychelles |
| Sierra Leone | | | |
| Singapore | Slovakia | Slovenia | Solomon Islands |
| Somalia | South Africa | South Sudan | Spain |
| Sri Lanka | | | |
| Sudan | Suriname | Swaziland | Sweden |
| Switzerland | Syrian Arab Republic | Tajikistan | Thailand |
| TFYRO Macedonia | | | |
| Timor-Leste | Togo | Tonga | Trinidad and Tobago |
| Tunisia | Turkey | Turkmenistan | Tuvalu |
| Uganda | | | |
| Ukraine | United Arab Emirates | United Kingdom of Great Britain and N.I. | United Republic of Tanzania |
| United States of America | Uruguay | Uzbekistan | Vanuatu |
| Venezuela (Bolivarian Rep. of) | | | |
| Viet Nam | Yemen | Zambia | Zimbabwe |
| Holy See Observer State | St of Palestine Observer State | | |

Name change (UN listing)

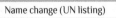

Czech Republic ▶ Czechia

Afghanistan • Albania • Algeria • Andorra • Angola • Antigua and Barbuda • Argentina • Armenia • Australia

Austria • Azerbaijan • Bahamas • Bahrain • Bangladesh • Barbados • Belarus • Belgium • Belize

Benin • Bhutan • Bolivia (Plurinational State of) • Bosnia and Herzegovina • Botswana • Brazil • Brunei Darussalam • Bulgaria • Burkina Faso

Burundi • Cabo Verde • Cambodia • Cameroon • Canada • Central African Republic • Chad • Chile • China

Colombia • Comoros • Congo • Costa Rica • Côte d'Ivoire • Croatia • Cuba • Cyprus • Czechia

Democratic People's Rep. of Korea • Democratic Rep. of the Congo • Denmark • Djibouti • Dominica • Dominican Republic • Ecuador • Egypt • El Salvador

Equatorial Guinea • Eritrea • Estonia • Ethiopia • Fiji • Finland • France • Gabon • Gambia

Georgia • Germany • Ghana • Greece • Grenada • Guatemala • Guinea • Guinea-Bissau • Guyana

Haiti • Honduras • Hungary • Iceland • India • Indonesia • Iran (Islamic Republic of) • Iraq • Ireland

Israel • Italy • Jamaica • Japan • Jordan • Kazakhstan • Kenya • Kiribati • Kuwait

Kyrgyzstan • Lao People's Dem. Rep. • Latvia • Lebanon • Lesotho • Liberia • Libya • Liechtenstein • Lithuania

| 2017 | | 193 | 2 |
| --- | --- | --- | --- |
| Year | United Nations | Member states | Observer states |

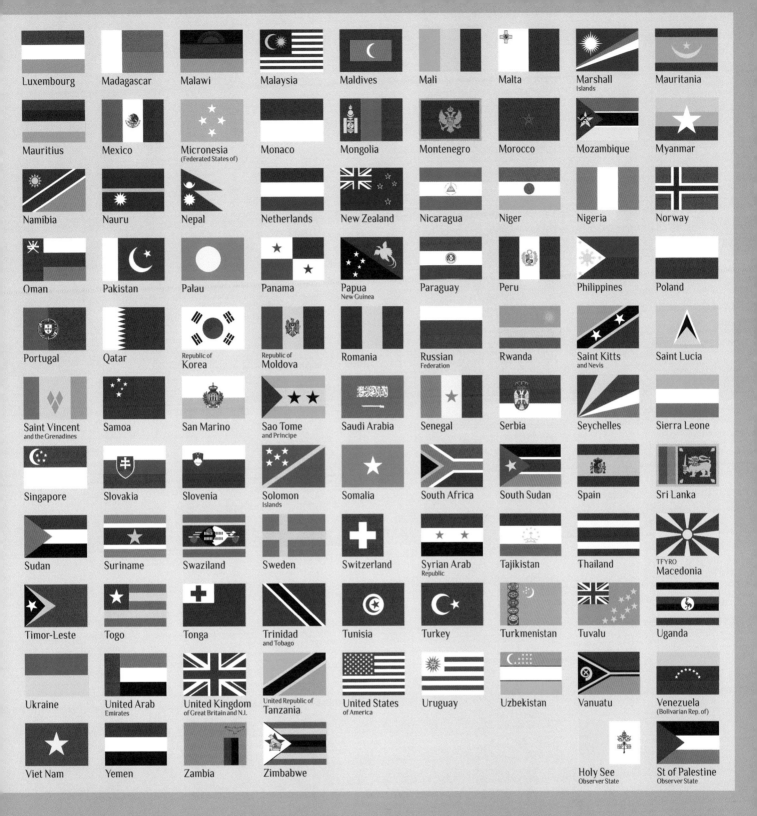

Luxembourg | Madagascar | Malawi | Malaysia | Maldives | Mali | Malta | Marshall Islands | Mauritania

Mauritius | Mexico | Micronesia (Federated States of) | Monaco | Mongolia | Montenegro | Morocco | Mozambique | Myanmar

Namibia | Nauru | Nepal | Netherlands | New Zealand | Nicaragua | Niger | Nigeria | Norway

Oman | Pakistan | Palau | Panama | Papua New Guinea | Paraguay | Peru | Philippines | Poland

Portugal | Qatar | Republic of Korea | Republic of Moldova | Romania | Russian Federation | Rwanda | Saint Kitts and Nevis | Saint Lucia

Saint Vincent and the Grenadines | Samoa | San Marino | Sao Tome and Principe | Saudi Arabia | Senegal | Serbia | Seychelles | Sierra Leone

Singapore | Slovakia | Slovenia | Solomon Islands | Somalia | South Africa | South Sudan | Spain | Sri Lanka

Sudan | Suriname | Swaziland | Sweden | Switzerland | Syrian Arab Republic | Tajikistan | Thailand | TFYRO Macedonia

Timor-Leste | Togo | Tonga | Trinidad and Tobago | Tunisia | Turkey | Turkmenistan | Tuvalu | Uganda

Ukraine | United Arab Emirates | United Kingdom of Great Britain and N.I. | United Republic of Tanzania | United States of America | Uruguay | Uzbekistan | Vanuatu | Venezuela (Bolivarian Rep. of)

Viet Nam | Yemen | Zambia | Zimbabwe | | | | Holy See Observer State | St of Palestine Observer State

Flag change

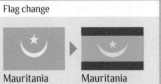

Mauritania | Mauritania

Afghanistan · Albania · Algeria · Andorra · Angola · Antigua and Barbuda · Argentina · Armenia · Australia

Austria · Azerbaijan · Bahamas · Bahrain · Bangladesh · Barbados · Belarus · Belgium · Belize

Benin · Bhutan · Bolivia (Plurinational State of) · Bosnia and Herzegovina · Botswana · Brazil · Brunei Darussalam · Bulgaria · Burkina Faso

Burundi · Cabo Verde · Cambodia · Cameroon · Canada · Central African Republic · Chad · Chile · China

Colombia · Comoros · Congo · Costa Rica · Côte d'Ivoire · Croatia · Cuba · Cyprus · Czechia

Democratic People's Rep. of Korea · Democratic Rep. of the Congo · Denmark · Djibouti · Dominica · Dominican Republic · Ecuador · Egypt · El Salvador

Equatorial Guinea · Eritrea · Estonia · Eswatini · Ethiopia · Fiji · Finland · France · Gabon

Gambia · Georgia · Germany · Ghana · Greece · Grenada · Guatemala · Guinea · Guinea-Bissau

Guyana · Haiti · Honduras · Hungary · Iceland · India · Indonesia · Iran (Islamic Republic of) · Iraq

Ireland · Israel · Italy · Jamaica · Japan · Jordan · Kazakhstan · Kenya · Kiribati

Kuwait · Kyrgyzstan · Lao People's Dem. Rep. · Latvia · Lebanon · Lesotho · Liberia · Libya · Liechtenstein

| 2018 | | 193 | 2 |
|------|------|-----|---|
| Year | United Nations | Member states | Observer states |

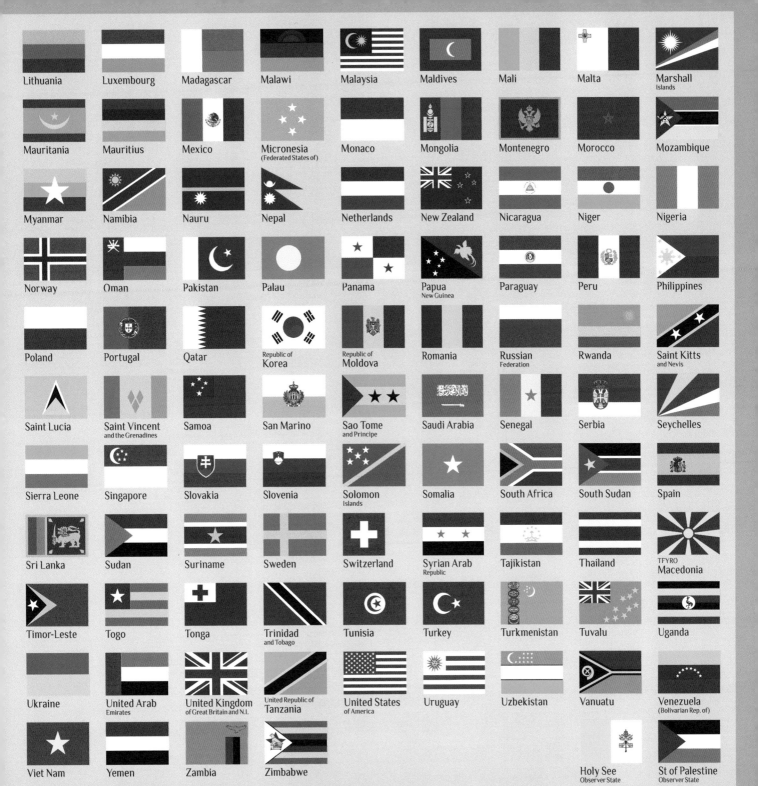

| Lithuania | Luxembourg | Madagascar | Malawi | Malaysia | Maldives | Mali | Malta | Marshall Islands |
|---|---|---|---|---|---|---|---|---|
| Mauritania | Mauritius | Mexico | Micronesia (Federated States of) | Monaco | Mongolia | Montenegro | Morocco | Mozambique |
| Myanmar | Namibia | Nauru | Nepal | Netherlands | New Zealand | Nicaragua | Niger | Nigeria |
| Norway | Oman | Pakistan | Palau | Panama | Papua New Guinea | Paraguay | Peru | Philippines |
| Poland | Portugal | Qatar | Republic of Korea | Republic of Moldova | Romania | Russian Federation | Rwanda | Saint Kitts and Nevis |
| Saint Lucia | Saint Vincent and the Grenadines | Samoa | San Marino | Sao Tome and Principe | Saudi Arabia | Senegal | Serbia | Seychelles |
| Sierra Leone | Singapore | Slovakia | Slovenia | Solomon Islands | Somalia | South Africa | South Sudan | Spain |
| Sri Lanka | Sudan | Suriname | Sweden | Switzerland | Syrian Arab Republic | Tajikistan | Thailand | TFYRO Macedonia |
| Timor-Leste | Togo | Tonga | Trinidad and Tobago | Tunisia | Turkey | Turkmenistan | Tuvalu | Uganda |
| Ukraine | United Arab Emirates | United Kingdom of Great Britain and N.I. | United Republic of Tanzania | United States of America | Uruguay | Uzbekistan | Vanuatu | Venezuela (Bolivarian Rep. of) |
| Viet Nam | Yemen | Zambia | Zimbabwe | | | | Holy See Observer State | St of Palestine Observer State |

Name change

 ▶

Swaziland    Eswatini

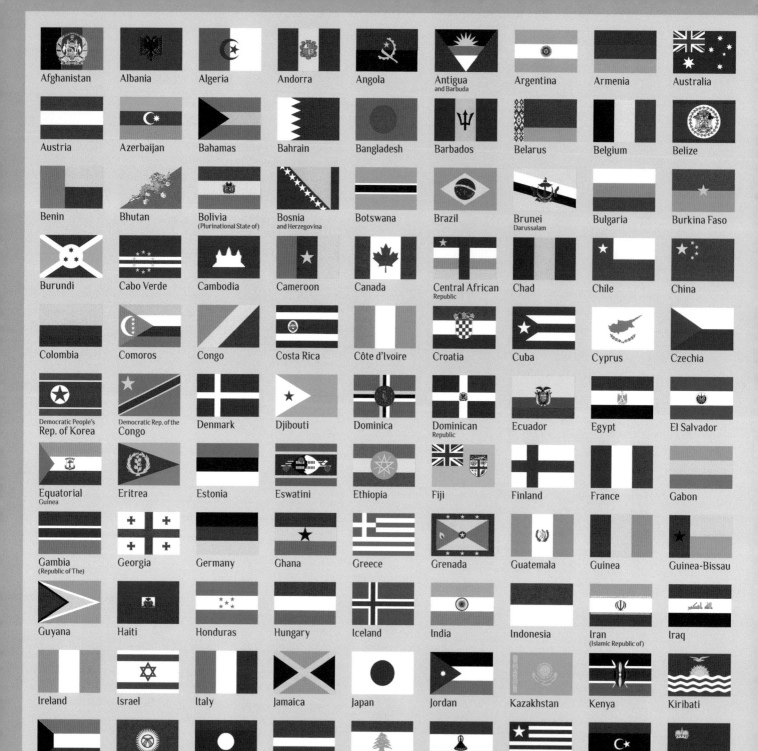

Afghanistan · Albania · Algeria · Andorra · Angola · Antigua and Barbuda · Argentina · Armenia · Australia

Austria · Azerbaijan · Bahamas · Bahrain · Bangladesh · Barbados · Belarus · Belgium · Belize

Benin · Bhutan · Bolivia (Plurinational State of) · Bosnia and Herzegovina · Botswana · Brazil · Brunei Darussalam · Bulgaria · Burkina Faso

Burundi · Cabo Verde · Cambodia · Cameroon · Canada · Central African Republic · Chad · Chile · China

Colombia · Comoros · Congo · Costa Rica · Côte d'Ivoire · Croatia · Cuba · Cyprus · Czechia

Democratic People's Rep. of Korea · Democratic Rep. of the Congo · Denmark · Djibouti · Dominica · Dominican Republic · Ecuador · Egypt · El Salvador

Equatorial Guinea · Eritrea · Estonia · Eswatini · Ethiopia · Fiji · Finland · France · Gabon

Gambia (Republic of The) · Georgia · Germany · Ghana · Greece · Grenada · Guatemala · Guinea · Guinea-Bissau

Guyana · Haiti · Honduras · Hungary · Iceland · India · Indonesia · Iran (Islamic Republic of) · Iraq

Ireland · Israel · Italy · Jamaica · Japan · Jordan · Kazakhstan · Kenya · Kiribati

Kuwait · Kyrgyzstan · Lao People's Dem. Rep. · Latvia · Lebanon · Lesotho · Liberia · Libya · Liechtenstein

| 2019 | | 193 | 2 |
|------|------|------|------|
| Year | United Nations | Member states | Observer states |

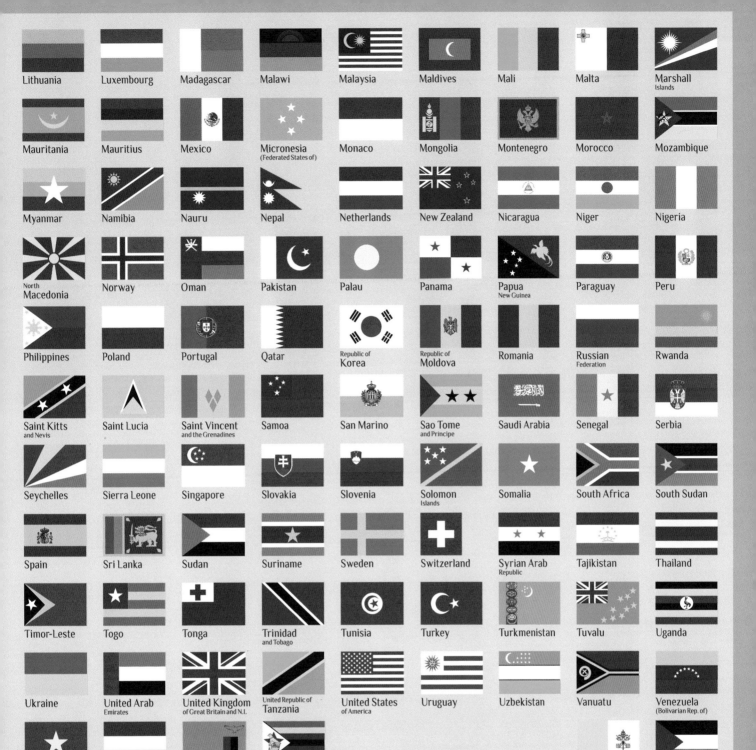

Lithuania    Luxembourg    Madagascar    Malawi    Malaysia    Maldives    Mali    Malta*    Marshall Islands

Mauritania    Mauritius    Mexico    Micronesia (Federated States of)    Monaco    Mongolia    Montenegro    Morocco    Mozambique

Myanmar    Namibia    Nauru    Nepal    Netherlands    New Zealand    Nicaragua    Niger    Nigeria

North Macedonia    Norway    Oman    Pakistan    Palau    Panama    Papua New Guinea    Paraguay    Peru

Philippines    Poland    Portugal    Qatar    Republic of Korea    Republic of Moldova    Romania    Russian Federation    Rwanda

Saint Kitts and Nevis    Saint Lucia    Saint Vincent and the Grenadines    Samoa    San Marino    Sao Tome and Principe    Saudi Arabia    Senegal    Serbia

Seychelles    Sierra Leone    Singapore    Slovakia    Slovenia    Solomon Islands    Somalia    South Africa    South Sudan

Spain    Sri Lanka    Sudan    Suriname    Sweden    Switzerland    Syrian Arab Republic    Tajikistan    Thailand

Timor-Leste    Togo    Tonga    Trinidad and Tobago    Tunisia    Turkey    Turkmenistan    Tuvalu    Uganda

Ukraine    United Arab Emirates    United Kingdom of Great Britain and N.I.    United Republic of Tanzania    United States of America    Uruguay    Uzbekistan    Vanuatu    Venezuela (Bolivarian Rep. of)

Viet Nam    Yemen    Zambia    Zimbabwe    Holy See Observer State    St of Palestine Observer State

*The Former Yugoslav Republic of

Name change (UN listing)

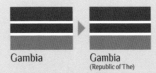

Gambia    ▶    Gambia (Republic of The)

Name change

TFYRO* Macedonia    ▶    North Macedonia

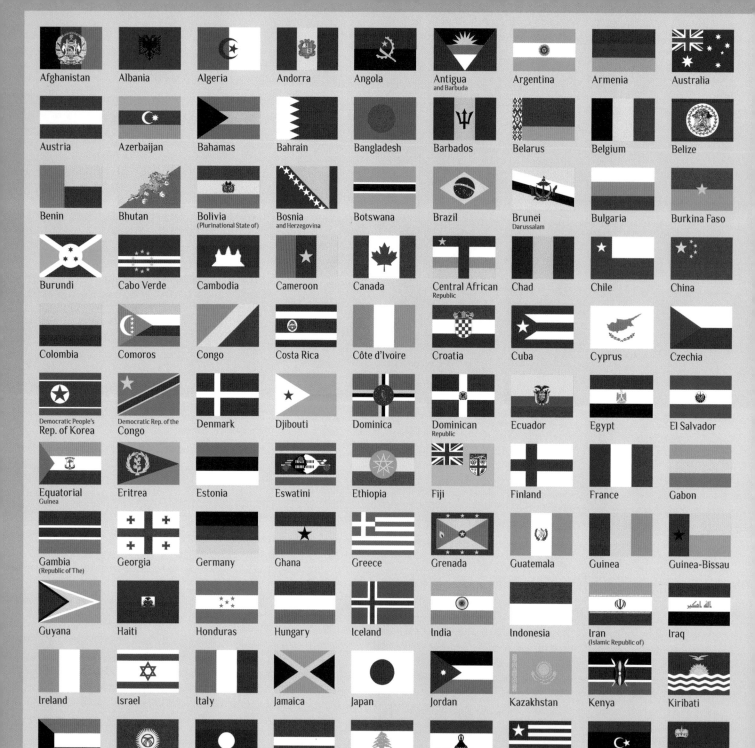

Afghanistan · Albania · Algeria · Andorra · Angola · Antigua and Barbuda · Argentina · Armenia · Australia

Austria · Azerbaijan · Bahamas · Bahrain · Bangladesh · Barbados · Belarus · Belgium · Belize

Benin · Bhutan · Bolivia (Plurinational State of) · Bosnia and Herzegovina · Botswana · Brazil · Brunei Darussalam · Bulgaria · Burkina Faso

Burundi · Cabo Verde · Cambodia · Cameroon · Canada · Central African Republic · Chad · Chile · China

Colombia · Comoros · Congo · Costa Rica · Côte d'Ivoire · Croatia · Cuba · Cyprus · Czechia

Democratic People's Rep. of Korea · Democratic Rep. of the Congo · Denmark · Djibouti · Dominica · Dominican Republic · Ecuador · Egypt · El Salvador

Equatorial Guinea · Eritrea · Estonia · Eswatini · Ethiopia · Fiji · Finland · France · Gabon

Gambia (Republic of The) · Georgia · Germany · Ghana · Greece · Grenada · Guatemala · Guinea · Guinea-Bissau

Guyana · Haiti · Honduras · Hungary · Iceland · India · Indonesia · Iran (Islamic Republic of) · Iraq

Ireland · Israel · Italy · Jamaica · Japan · Jordan · Kazakhstan · Kenya · Kiribati

Kuwait · Kyrgyzstan · Lao People's Dem. Rep. · Latvia · Lebanon · Lesotho · Liberia · Libya · Liechtenstein

No changes in 2020 and 2021

Timeline                                page 148

| 2022 | | 193 | 2 |
|---|---|---|---|
| Year | United Nations | Member states | Observer states |

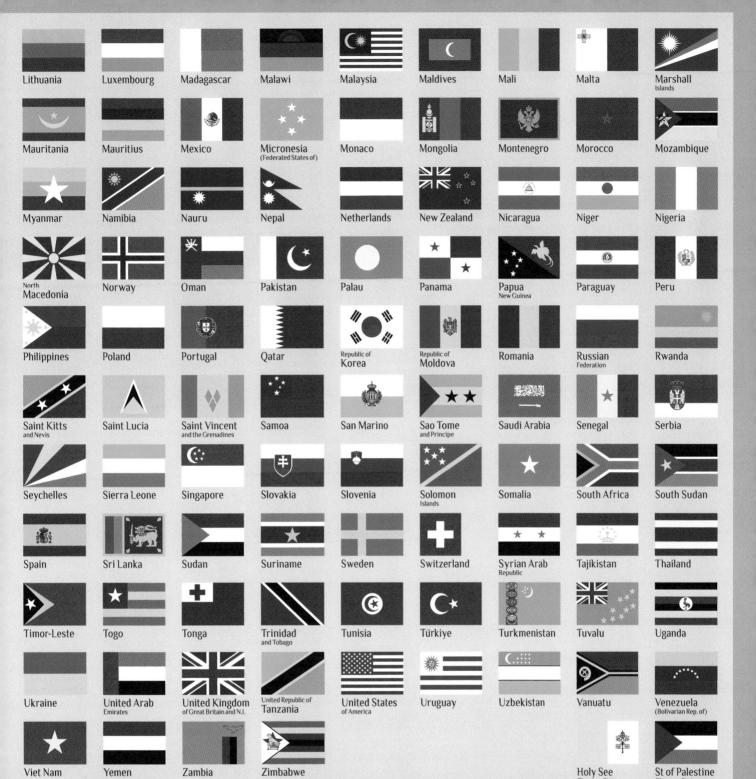

Lithuania · Luxembourg · Madagascar · Malawi · Malaysia · Maldives · Mali · Malta · Marshall Islands

Mauritania · Mauritius · Mexico · Micronesia (Federated States of) · Monaco · Mongolia · Montenegro · Morocco · Mozambique

Myanmar · Namibia · Nauru · Nepal · Netherlands · New Zealand · Nicaragua · Niger · Nigeria

North Macedonia · Norway · Oman · Pakistan · Palau · Panama · Papua New Guinea · Paraguay · Peru

Philippines · Poland · Portugal · Qatar · Republic of Korea · Republic of Moldova · Romania · Russian Federation · Rwanda

Saint Kitts and Nevis · Saint Lucia · Saint Vincent and the Grenadines · Samoa · San Marino · Sao Tome and Principe · Saudi Arabia · Senegal · Serbia

Seychelles · Sierra Leone · Singapore · Slovakia · Slovenia · Solomon Islands · Somalia · South Africa · South Sudan

Spain · Sri Lanka · Sudan · Suriname · Sweden · Switzerland · Syrian Arab Republic · Tajikistan · Thailand

Timor-Leste · Togo · Tonga · Trinidad and Tobago · Tunisia · Türkiye · Turkmenistan · Tuvalu · Uganda

Ukraine · United Arab Emirates · United Kingdom of Great Britain and N.I. · United Republic of Tanzania · United States of America · Uruguay · Uzbekistan · Vanuatu · Venezuela (Bolivarian Rep. of)

Viet Nam · Yemen · Zambia · Zimbabwe · Holy See Observer State · St of Palestine Observer State

Name change (UN listing)

Turkey ▶ Türkiye

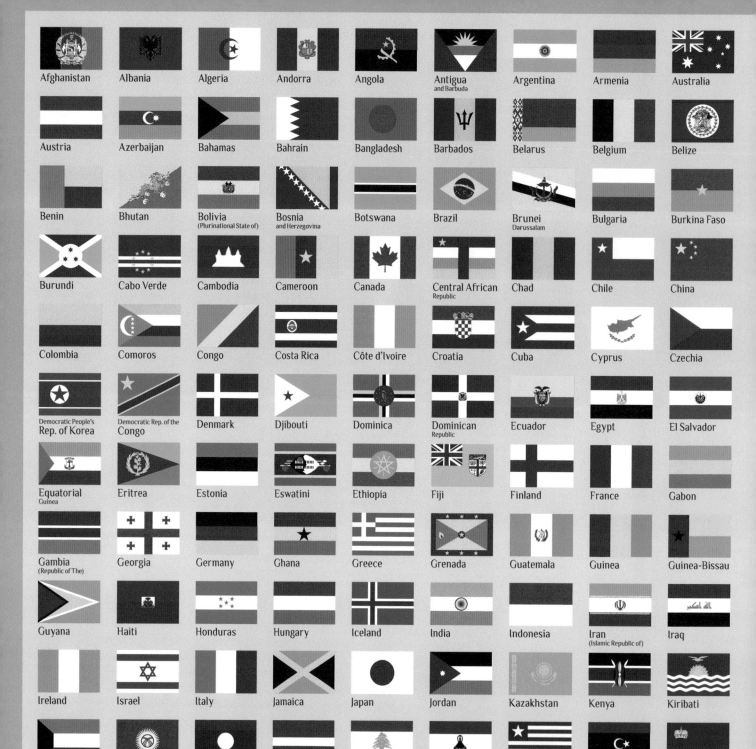

Afghanistan · Albania · Algeria · Andorra · Angola · Antigua and Barbuda · Argentina · Armenia · Australia

Austria · Azerbaijan · Bahamas · Bahrain · Bangladesh · Barbados · Belarus · Belgium · Belize

Benin · Bhutan · Bolivia (Plurinational State of) · Bosnia and Herzegovina · Botswana · Brazil · Brunei Darussalam · Bulgaria · Burkina Faso

Burundi · Cabo Verde · Cambodia · Cameroon · Canada · Central African Republic · Chad · Chile · China

Colombia · Comoros · Congo · Costa Rica · Côte d'Ivoire · Croatia · Cuba · Cyprus · Czechia

Democratic People's Rep. of Korea · Democratic Rep. of the Congo · Denmark · Djibouti · Dominica · Dominican Republic · Ecuador · Egypt · El Salvador

Equatorial Guinea · Eritrea · Estonia · Eswatini · Ethiopia · Fiji · Finland · France · Gabon

Gambia (Republic of The) · Georgia · Germany · Ghana · Greece · Grenada · Guatemala · Guinea · Guinea-Bissau

Guyana · Haiti · Honduras · Hungary · Iceland · India · Indonesia · Iran (Islamic Republic of) · Iraq

Ireland · Israel · Italy · Jamaica · Japan · Jordan · Kazakhstan · Kenya · Kiribati

Kuwait · Kyrgyzstan · Lao People's Dem. Rep. · Latvia · Lebanon · Lesotho · Liberia · Libya · Liechtenstein

| 2023 | | 193 | 2 |
|------|--|-----|---|
| Year | United Nations | Member states | Observer states |

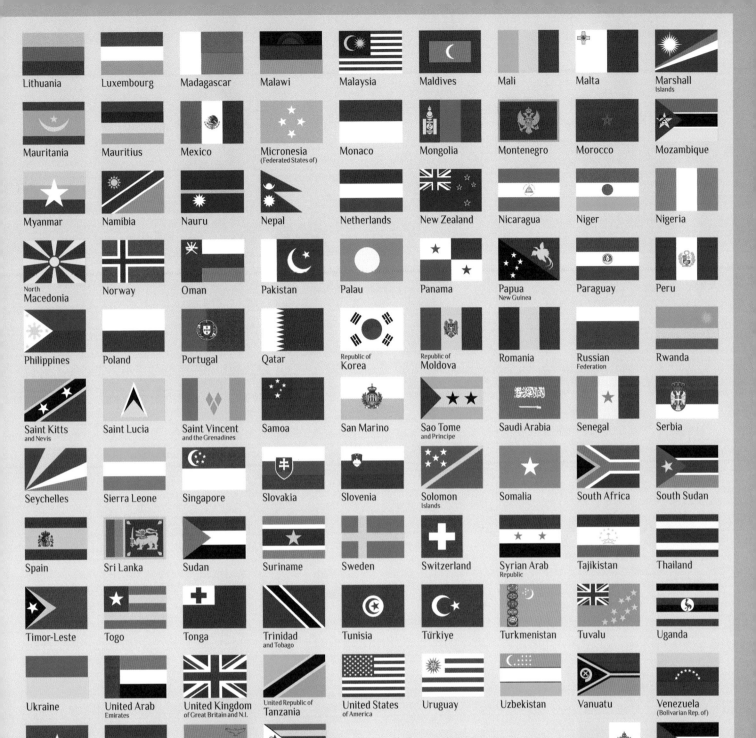

Lithuania   Luxembourg   Madagascar   Malawi   Malaysia   Maldives   Mali   Malta   Marshall Islands

Mauritania   Mauritius   Mexico   Micronesia (Federated States of)   Monaco   Mongolia   Montenegro   Morocco   Mozambique

Myanmar   Namibia   Nauru   Nepal   Netherlands   New Zealand   Nicaragua   Niger   Nigeria

North Macedonia   Norway   Oman   Pakistan   Palau   Panama   Papua New Guinea   Paraguay   Peru

Philippines   Poland   Portugal   Qatar   Republic of Korea   Republic of Moldova   Romania   Russian Federation   Rwanda

Saint Kitts and Nevis   Saint Lucia   Saint Vincent and the Grenadines   Samoa   San Marino   Sao Tome and Principe   Saudi Arabia   Senegal   Serbia

Seychelles   Sierra Leone   Singapore   Slovakia   Slovenia   Solomon Islands   Somalia   South Africa   South Sudan

Spain   Sri Lanka   Sudan   Suriname   Sweden   Switzerland   Syrian Arab Republic   Tajikistan   Thailand

Timor-Leste   Togo   Tonga   Trinidad and Tobago   Tunisia   Türkiye   Turkmenistan   Tuvalu   Uganda

Ukraine   United Arab Emirates   United Kingdom of Great Britain and N.I.   United Republic of Tanzania   United States of America   Uruguay   Uzbekistan   Vanuatu   Venezuela (Bolivarian Rep. of)

Viet Nam   Yemen   Zambia   Zimbabwe   Holy See Observer State   St of Palestine Observer State

# Index

*From 1976 on, United Kingdom includes all references to The United Kingdom of Great Britain and Northern Ireland.

Member flags as seen from inside the United Nations compound, looking south-west toward First Avenue.

Printed in Great Britain
by Amazon

34039213R00089